The Riedesels had proceeded from York, Pennsylvania, to Elizabeth, New Jersey, when negotiations for the General's release hit a snag. The family returned to Bethlehem where they stayed from October 10 to November 22, 1779.

From Berkeley Springs, Baroness von Riedesel and her daughters went to Doughoregan, the Carroll estate near Baltimore, for a short visit before joining her husband at York, Pennsylvania, for the trip to New York.

The Riedesels' Tour of Duty in Revolutionary America
1777-1781

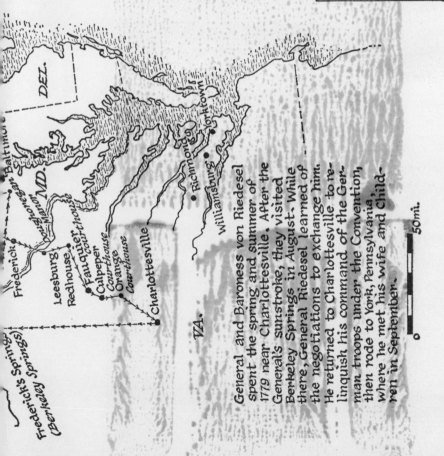

Frederick's Springs
(Berkeley Springs)

Frederick

DEL.

Baltimore

Doughoregan
Manor MD.

Leesburg
Redhouse
Fauquier
Courthouse
Culpeper
Courthouse
Orange
Courthouse

Charlottesville

Richmond

Yorktown

Williamsburg

VA.

General and Baroness von Riedesel spent the spring and summer of 1779 near Charlottesville. After the General's sunstroke, they visited Berkeley Springs in August. While there, General Riedesel learned of the negotiations to exchange him. He returned to Charlottesville to relinquish his command of the German troops under the Convention, then rode to York, Pennsylvania, where he met his wife and children in September.

50mi.

0

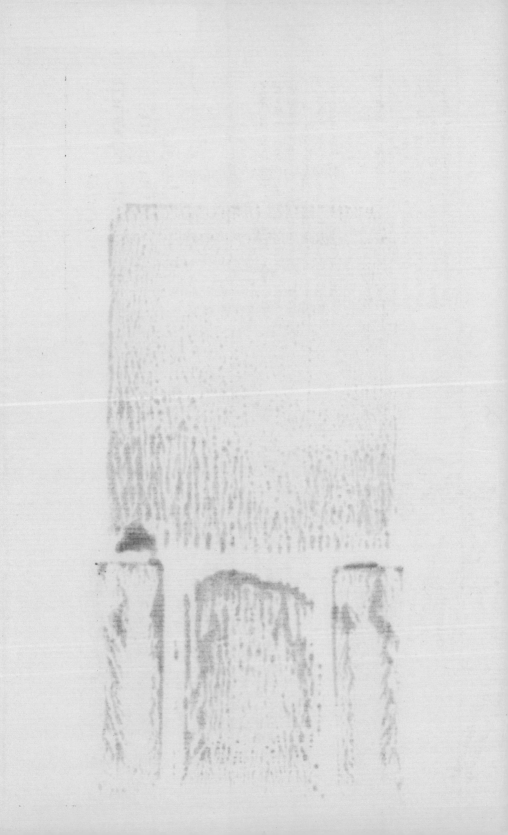

Baroness von Riedesel
and the
American Revolution

JOURNAL AND CORRESPONDENCE
OF A TOUR OF DUTY
1776–1783

Published for the
Institute of Early American History and Culture
at Williamsburg, Virginia
by The University of
North Carolina Press, Chapel Hill

The Institute of Early American History and Culture
is sponsored jointly by the College of William and
Mary and Colonial Williamsburg, Incorporated.

Baroness von Riedesel
and the
American Revolution

<hr/>

JOURNAL AND CORRESPONDENCE
OF A TOUR OF DUTY
1776–1783

<hr/>

*A Revised Translation with Introduction
and Notes by*

MARVIN L. BROWN, JR.

With the Assistance of Marta Huth

To the memory of
Dorothy Clement Dodge
A service wife of the twentieth century

Preface

William L. Stone's translation of Baroness von Riedesel's journal and correspondence, long a standard source for the Revolutionary period, had been out of print for many years when Marta Huth learned in 1937 from Freifrau Till von Lupin, wife of Friedrich Freiherr von Lupin, later German Consul in Chicago, and a collateral relative of the Baroness, that the original manuscript of the journal and many unpublished letters were among the Riedesel Papers owned by Friedrich Freiherr von Rotenhan—now deceased—a descendant of the Baroness' daughter, Frederika.

In 1937 Mrs. Huth visited the Rotenhans at Schloss Neuenhof, their estate near Eisenach, and was given the opportunity to transcribe the Riedesel manuscripts, which had survived the plundering of Burg Lauterbach, the ancestral seat of Baron von Riedesel, in the revolution of 1848. Collating the family papers with the German edition of Baroness von Riedesel's book published in 1800, she copied all letters and journal passages which had been omitted at the time of publication. She also obtained photographs of selected family portraits. The Rotenhan estate now lies in East Germany. It was badly damaged in 1945, and the contents which were not destroyed were scattered and are now presumably lost. Mrs. Huth's transcripts of the German originals, therefore, seem to be the only available copies of the previously unpublished writings of Baroness von Riedesel.

Mrs. Huth's plans for a new edition of Baroness von Riedesel's journal and correspondence were delayed for several years, but in 1960 she turned to the Institute of Early American History and Culture just as its staff was making plans independently for a new translation of the Baroness' fascinating account of Revolutionary America. Mrs. Huth made the new material available to the Institute, and I began my translation at the suggestion of Dr. Lester J. Cappon and Dr. James Morton Smith of the Institute.

The original edition, *Auszüge aus den Briefen und Papieren des*

vii

Generals Freyherrn von Riedesel und seiner Gemalinn, gebornen von Massow. Ihre Beyderseitige Reise nach Amerika und ihren Aufenthalt betreffend. Zusammengetragen und geordnet von ihrem Schwiegersohne Heinrich dem XLIV. Grafen Reuss. Gedruckt als Manuscript für die Familie. [Berlin] [1800], was prepared by Heinrich XLIV, Count of Reuss, son-in-law of the Baroness, during the summer of 1799 and was printed privately in a very limited edition early in 1800. Shortly thereafter Carl Spener, of the publishing house of Haude and Spener, persuaded the Baroness to permit him to publish her journal and letters in a regular edition, and in 1800 and again in 1801 her account was presented to the public under the title, *Die Berufs-Reise nach America. Briefe der Generalin von Riedesel auf dieser Reise und während ihres sechsjährigen Aufenthalts in America zur Zeit des dortigen Krieges in den Jahren 1776 bis 1783 nach Deutschland geschrieben.*

The family edition of 1800 and the editions made that year and the next for the German public differ very little. The choice of insertions and their location in the text of the journal made by Count Heinrich were in no way altered. In the public edition only a few spellings were changed, and some slips were caught. "New Yorck" (family edition, p. 247) becomes "New York," "zwei" (p. 348) becomes "zwey," "ouatiert" (p. 118) becomes "wattirt." The public edition is more compact, having 348 pages instead of 386, but a four-page sketch of the life of the Indian chieftain Brant is appended. Probably the most striking difference is that the family edition appeared in very clear roman letters, whereas the public edition is in gothic letters of poorer quality type.

As early as 1802 the Baroness' book was translated into Dutch. Some fragments of her journal were also translated into English and first appeared in General James Wilkinson's *Memoirs of My Own Times* (3 vols., Philadelphia, 1816), and then in Professor Benjamin Silliman's *A Tour to Quebec in the Autumn of 1819* (London, 1822). In 1827 the New York publishing house of Carvill brought out the first full English edition, rendering the Baroness' words very freely, and often inaccurately, and omitting certain sections, as Stone observed (1867 edition, p. 6), to avoid distressing the "fastidiously inclined." The main interest of this edition for the contemporary reader is the choice of words, which often seem to catch some of the flavor of the late eighteenth century. Not until 1867 did William L. Stone (1835–1908), make his more accurate, though certainly not perfect, translation, but he still preserved the order of material selected by Count Heinrich of Reuss, and, in spite of his remarkable scholarship, he left many things unexplained. Whatever may have been the imperfections in Stone's edition, however, I want to call attention to his real stature and express my debt to and admiration for him. A pioneer in the field of historical editing, his extensive work on the period of the American Revolution is still invaluable, notably his accounts of Burgoyne's campaign and the role of the Germans in the Revolution. Such volumes as his *Letters of Brunswick and Hessian Officers during the American Revolution* (Albany, 1891) were extremely helpful in preparing this edition. Finally, in 1881 and 1893, the publisher Mohr brought out German editions of Baroness von Riedesel's book, which were little more than reprints of the 1800 edition.

Stone's edition is now nearly a hundred years old, and a twentieth-century translation, correcting certain passages, modernizing archaisms, and adding annotation, has long seemed necessary and desirable. I have carefully compared my translation with all previous English editions and a translation made for Mrs. Huth by Miss Elizabeth Back. In addition I also translated from the German and French the new letters of the Baroness, plus passages previously omitted, which Mrs. Huth had copied or photostated, collating my translation with the one prepared by Miss Back. Some parts of the transcript were difficult and occasionally impossible to translate because of obsolete words, eighteenth-century spelling, a peculiar mixture of German and French, or illegible transcription. It might be remarked that the French of the Riedesels was often both phonetic and Teutonic.

The text that follows, therefore, is a new translation of Baroness von Riedesel's journal and correspondence and includes letters never previously published, as well as portions of letters which were omitted from the previous editions. For various reasons, the work of the Count of Reuss was selective. He omitted many of the more personal letters which might have been included, notably those on the Hereditary Prince, who became the Duke of Brunswick in 1780. Moreover, he inserted letters at the appropriate chronological points in the journal, unfortunately interrupting the continuity of the Baroness' account. What really seemed to matter to Count Heinrich was the campaign of General Riedesel, and he therefore inserted the main part of the General's "Military Memoir" dealing with the surrender at Saratoga. This technical piece about the capitulation is clearly tangential to the Baroness' personal story and should scarcely be included any more than many other accounts by General Riedesel, whose writings were edited by Max von Eelking and translated by Stone in 1868, the year after his translation and edition of the Baroness' journal and letters. The "Military Memoir" has accordingly been dropped from this edition, which concentrates instead on the Baroness' tour of duty in America. The present edition also places all the letters, both those which were published in 1800 and the new ones from Mrs. Huth's copybook and photostats, in Part II of this book. I have supplied short introductions to each group of letters; there are also cross references in the journal to the letters at appropriate spots.

Mrs. Huth wishes to thank Freifrau von Lupin for her introduction to Freiherr and Freifrau von Rotenhan and Miss Elizabeth Back for her assistance in translating Baroness von Riedesel's correspondence. I am grateful to Dr. Cappon, Dr. Smith, and Miss Susan Lee Foard of the Institute of Early American History and Culture for advice they have given and for errors they have caught in the translation and notes. I accept, of course, responsibility for any point which might be in error. I also want to acknowledge the aid given by Sofus E. Simonsen of the Department of Modern Languages at North Carolina State of The University of North Carolina at Raleigh in solving some of the knottier problems arising from the supplementary Huth material. Various librarians and the interlibrary loan system in general afforded much help. Finally, I am much indebted to my wife, Elizabeth W. Brown, who assisted me greatly in questions of translation from the French.

Marvin L. Brown, Jr.

North Carolina State
of The University of North Carolina
at Raleigh

Table of Contents

Table of Contents

Table of Contents

xiv

List of Illustrations

⚜

PORTRAIT OF BARONESS VON
RIEDESEL AS "SPRING"   facing page xxi
By Tischbein
This portrait of Frederika Charlotte Louise von Massow (1746–1808), the
sixteen-year-old bride, painted on the eve of her wedding at Wolfenbüttel,
was executed in 1762 by Johann Heinrich Tischbein, who had been com-
missioned to paint the wedding party. Tischbein (1722–1789) was the
court painter of the Elector of Hesse and director of the Academy at Kassel.
Here he portrays the bride as "Spring," draping a garland of gaily colored
flowers over her right shoulder, hanging a basket of flowers on her right arm,
and putting a nosegay of red flowers in her left hand. Her blue satin gown,
cut daringly low, was matched by a blue ribbon and bow around her neck
and by a crown of blue flowers in her fashionable coiffure. But the heavy-
handed symbolism of the romantic trappings fade when compared with the
bright eyes and warm smile of the bride or with General Loos' straight-
forward description of her slender waist, beautiful complexion, and fair
white hands. Permission to reproduce the painting was given to Mrs. Huth
by Freiherr von Rotenhan, Schloss Neuenhof near Eisenach, who owned
the portrait until 1945.

PORTRAIT OF CAPTAIN RIEDESEL
AT 24   between pp. xxxii–xxxiii
By Tischbein
A companion portrait to that of the Baroness, Tischbein's portrait of
Friedrich Adolf Riedesel, Baron of Eisenbach, shows the bridegroom in his
uniform as a Captain in the Hessian Regiment of Blue Hussars at the time
that he was serving on the staff of Duke Ferdinand of Brunswick, brother
of Karl I, the reigning Duke. The white fur on his cape matched his
powdered hair. Gold braid covered him from neck to waistline and orna-
mented his cuffs, cape, and hat, which were blue. The sash and skin-tight
riding trousers were red. As Max von Eelking said: "We see him there in
the elegant and tasty uniform of his regiment, in the freshness of youth
and the vigor of health. He is of medium height, of noble and easy carriage,

and at the same time daring as becomes an officer of cavalry." Permission to reproduce the painting was given to Mrs. Huth by Freiherr von Rotenhan, Schloss Neuenhof near Eisenach, who owned the portrait until 1945.

THE THREE OLDER DAUGHTERS   between pp. xxxii–xxxiii
This romantic sketch of Augusta, Caroline, and Frederika von Riedesel is attributed to Caroline before 1805. Permission to reproduce the painting was given to Mrs. Huth by Freiherr von Rotenhan, Schloss Neuenhof near Eisenach, who owned the portrait until 1945.

THE FIVE RIEDESEL DAUGHTERS   between pp. xxxii–xxxiii
Photographs of the original portraits of the Riedesel daughters—Augusta, Frederika, and Caroline, the three girls who traveled with the Baroness from Wolfenbüttel to the New World; America, born in New York in 1780; and Charlotte, born after the Riedesels returned to their homeland— were made in Germany and are now the property of Mrs. Kenneth Bullard of Schuylerville, New York. When Count Johann Heinrich von Bernstorff, a member of the family of America's husband, was German Ambassador to the United States before World War I, he visited the Schuylerville house where Baroness von Riedesel had taken refuge during the Battle of Saratoga. Later he sent to Mrs. Bullard's father, then owner of the house, photographs of the portraits of the Riedesel daughters. They are reproduced here from *The Baroness and the General* by Louise Hall Tharp, copyright © 1962 by Louise Hall Tharp, by permission of Little, Brown and Company, Publishers, and Mrs. Kenneth Bullard; photographed by George Bolster, Saratoga, New York.

> *AUGUSTA VON RIEDESEL* (1771–1805), afterwards Countess Reuss
> *FREDERIKA VON RIEDESEL* (1774–1854), afterwards Countess Reden
> *CAROLINE VON RIEDESEL* (1776–1861), unmarried
> *AMERICA VON RIEDESEL* (1780–1856), afterwards Countess Ernst von Bernstorff
> *CHARLOTTE VON RIEDESEL* (1784–?), married Major von Schöning

BARONESS VON RIEDESEL
ABOUT 1800   between pp. xxxii–xxxiii
By Schröder
This portrait of the Baroness, done about the time her journal was published, shows the Baroness in her early fifties as a plump matron with a double chin, a pleasant gaze, and an unlined face; it thus gives some support to General Loos' comment nearly twenty years earlier, on her ap-

pearance in New York (p. 102). Johann Heinrich Schröder (1757–1812), court painter at Brunswick, was a student of Tischbein, who had painted the young Baroness as "Spring." The Baroness, who still liked low-cut gowns, is wearing a fashionable high-waisted dress of blue silk with a white lace fichu covering her handsome bosom. She is framed by a black mantilla. Permission to reproduce the painting was given to Mrs. Huth by Freiherr von Rotenhan, Schloss Neuenhof near Eisenach, who owned the portrait until 1945.

Farm on October 7, 1777, died the next morning and was buried at evening time the same day in the Great Redoubt, the retreat of the British army being held up by General Burgoyne long enough to administer the last rites. The English historian Fonblanque has identified the figure at the extreme right as General Riedesel. The others are from left to right: Earl of Harrington; General Burgoyne; General Phillips; Chaplain Brudenel; Captain Green; Lieutenant Colonel Kingston; Major Fraser; Mr. Wood, Surgeon; and Earl of Balcarres. Reproduced from a Library of Congress photograph of an engraving by Bährenstecher and Kessler at the Saratoga National Historical Park.

List of Maps

xix

Frederika Charlotte Louise von Massow, Baroness von Riedesel
(1746–1808)

Portrait of the sixteen-year-old bride as "Spring"
Painted in 1762 by Johann Heinrich Tischbein

(see p. xv)

Introduction

I

One of the most engaging memoirs of the American Revolution published in Europe in the years following the War for Independence is the charming and readable account by the Baroness Frederika Charlotte Louise von Riedesel, wife of the commanding general of the Brunswick troops in the German forces serving with the British army. Written with directness, simplicity, and honesty, her narrative has a ring of genuineness that is as revealing of her own character as it is of conditions in Revolutionary America. Her remarkable account is not, of course, a report on the military events of the war, but rather a journal of her "tour of duty" from the time she left Brunswick in 1776 to join her husband in America until their return in 1783. Her background and training help explain how she adapted herself so completely to the hardships of an army in the field, but only her personality can account for the lengths to which she went in accompanying her husband. Though ever in his shadow in the field, she emerges in the pages that follow as a remarkably agreeable and captivating lady of quality.

Baroness von Riedesel's journal and letters constitute the most detailed account of the Revolutionary era by a woman reporter and the only one by a German wife attached to the so-called Hessian forces. Much of the appeal of her reporting lies in its personal character and in its unstated but pervasive and persuasive demonstration of conjugal fidelity from the moment of the Baroness' decision to follow her husband. But there is also a good deal of significance in this *Berufsreise* as a reflection of the prominence of the women with armies of the eighteenth century. While there were only a very few women like Molly Pitcher who had any hand in actual combat during the American Revolution, thousands were attached formally, or much more commonly, informally, to the armies engaged. Although the armies were superficially formal and disciplined, they actually presented aspects revealing a cross-section of eighteenth-century life. Women played a wide variety of roles and were factors in the general military situation. Some of them were wives of commanders and high-ranking officers; others enjoyed the sobriquet of "officers' wives." Some were regularly enrolled on the regimental lists, and appropriate provisions were made for them; most were not. Of the approximately 2,000 women who at one time or another followed the forces under Burgoyne's command, only 300 appear on the rosters.[1] Many of these women provided useful services. The Anhalt-Zerbst Regiment with 1,164 men had 34 "soldiers' wives, who served as washerwomen."[2] But in spite of their aid, women were something of an impediment. After the Waldeck Regiment sailed, three babies were born on the high seas.[3] The number of women with the British and the German forces grew rapidly, and even before Saratoga they had become a real vexation to the Hessian Colonel Friedrich von Wurmb,[4] a friend of the Riedesels.

When the Brunswickers departed at the beginning of the war, 77 women accompanied them.[5] By June 1781, when the main body of their forces was considerably reduced, about 300 women were in their midst.[6] Although most of the British armies had more women in their following, it would be hard to point to one quite so exemplary as the Baroness von Riedesel. Only Lady Christian Henrietta Caroline Acland (called "Lady Harriet"),[7] a far more cultivated person than her coarse husband, whose wounds she nursed in the American camp (after some prodding by the Baroness to cross the lines to do so) and whose hardships she shared until his death, might be mentioned in the same breath. But the very length of time the Baroness was beside her husband makes her tour of duty in America singular. Daughter of a Prussian general, she knew the ways of military men of her day.

1. Henry Belcher, *The First American Civil War* . . . , 2 vols. (London, 1911), I, 335. See Walter Hart Blumenthal, *Women Camp Followers of the American Revolution* (Philadelphia, 1952), 24–25.

2. Max von Eelking, *The German Allied Troops in the North American War of Independence, 1776–1783*, trans. J. G. Rosengarten (Albany, 1893), 238.

3. Blumenthal, *Women Camp Followers*, 33.

4. *Ibid.*, 16.

5. *Ibid.*, 34.

6. *Ibid.*, 33.

7. W. P. Courtney, "Acland, Lady Christian Henrietta Caroline," *Dictionary of National Biography*.

She knew the situations which her husband would face, and she knew ways in which he could be aided. Louise Hall Tharp suggests some insight into her motivation,[8] but human motivation always remains somewhat elusive. William L. Stone, writing for a nineteenth-century audience, used words in the preface to his 1867 edition of her journal and letters on which it is hard to improve: "Nor can anyone peruse these touching records of a devoted, conjugal love, chastened and sanctified as it was, by unaffected religious experience, without the consciousness of a higher idea of faith and duty."[9] At any rate, the case for lofty and romantic motivation is strong.

Apart from the military aspect, the Baroness' journal has significance for incidental light on social customs of the period. Her relations with her servants illustrate not only the great gap but also the intimacy and devotion that could exist between persons of widely different social classes. Partly because of her caution in money matters, the Baroness left a record of daily life in many of its details. In some respects she seemed always to have the eye of the curious foreign observer. The variety of her observations is equaled by the vividness of her simple portrayals. Although her life was much affected by conditions in her oft-changing environment, nowhere did she blend into the scene. She was ever the noblewoman, and ever the German. In spite of the international aspects of the age, her attire, her speech, her carriage, and many of her ways made her conspicuous against her background.

One thing rather noticeable in Baroness von Riedesel's journal is her keen consciousness of *Deutschland*. Not only had the Seven Years' War and other events made her aware of the community of interests of at least some of the Germanic states; her long sojourns under foreign flags had made Germanic differences much paler in her eyes. Nevertheless, the bonds with her native Prussia remained tight, although she had been a loyal Brunswicker since her marriage and entirely devoted to her husband's allegiance. She could not foresee, of course, the sort of national unification that eventually took place in Germany, but after her return to *Deutschland* this extraordi-

8. Louise Hall Tharp, *The Baroness and the General* (Boston, 1962), 13, 367.

9. William L. Stone, trans. and ed., *Letters and Journals Relating to the War of the American Revolution, and the Capture of the German Troops at Saratoga. By Mrs. General Riedesel* (Albany, 1867), 5, hereafter cited as Stone, trans., *Mrs. General Riedesel.*

nary woman, who might ordinarily have been expected to be pre-occupied with matters of dynasty and class, gives evidence of real national pride.

Although the Baroness revealed tendencies perhaps a bit advanced with regard to German nationalism and demonstrated insight into the ways of many of the people she met, she seems to have had little interest in the political and philosophical currents of the Age of Enlightenment and Revolution. Her simple pietism certainly tended to detach her from some of the ideas and customs of the period. The greater implications of the growing forces of popular sovereignty escaped her. Of course, she could scarcely have been expected to see the interplay between European thought and the American Revolution when even Frederick the Great was largely blind to its ideological significance. The Baroness heartily disliked American republicanism, but apparently had little realization of its possible influence on forces that were to rock Europe after 1789. Even though she lacked interest in the broader meaning of the American Revolution, she nevertheless noted many of the manifestations of the movement.

II

Born at Brandenburg-an-der-Havel on July 11, 1746, the Baroness was the daughter of Hans Jürgen Detloff von Massow, lieutenant general in the Prussian army and commissary in chief for Frederick the Great. [10] Her father, who once had been a captain in the regiment of Potsdam giants, was particularly pleasing to Frederick the Great for his economical ways, a trait the Baroness must have acquired from him. General von Massow was in charge of the military command at Minden on the banks of the Weser when the English and their German allies under Duke Ferdinand of Brunswick

10. There is no full account of the early life of the Baroness de Riedesel. Mrs. Tharp's *The Baroness and the General*, based primarily on the Baroness' journal, deals with the period covered by this source, with only a brief account of her younger days (pp. 3–12). William L. Stone, both in his 1867 edition of her journal especially (pp. 13–14) and in his translation of Max von Eelking's *Memoirs, and Letters and Journals, of Major General Riedesel during his Residence in America*, 2 vols. (Albany, 1868), I, 3–17, hereafter cited as Stone, trans., *General Riedesel*, gives some information. The *Allgemeine deutsche Biographie* (Leipzig, 1875–1912), XVIII, 532–33, contains a solid, if brief, account. In the same source, XX, 572, the sketch of her father is useful for her background.

defeated the French in 1759. It was during these days that the Baroness met her husband, a cavalry officer in the Brunswick service. Although the marriage in 1762 was arranged through the families with the reigning Duke of Brunswick playing a role in the negotiation, it was clearly a love match. The sixteen-year-old bride, painted by the artist Tischbein as "Spring," was a beautiful young lady; the bridegroom, also painted by Tischbein, was a dashing young captain serving as aide-de-camp to the Duke of Brunswick and already a hero in his bride's eyes. [11]

Friedrich Adolf Riedesel, Baron of Eisenbach, was twenty-four when he married the Baroness. He was born at his father's ancestral castle at Lauterbach in Rhine-Hesse in 1738. His mother was the daughter of a Prussian general, the military governor of Stettin, but his father preferred that he study law rather than military science and sent him to Marburg. Instead, Friedrich joined a Hessian regiment stationed there. During the Seven Years' War he served under the Duke of Brunswick, notably at the Battle of Minden, where he received his promotion to the rank of captain at the age of 21. [12] Three years later, after his marriage to Frederika, Riedesel was stationed at Wolfenbüttel, and eventually he bought a home there. At first his wife went home to visit her parents in Berlin while the Captain was on a tour of duty. Here a Prussian chamberlain commented that she was "very young, very good-looking. One would rather think she is an unmarried girl who is just being brought to boarding school, instead of believing that she is a married woman." She was in Berlin when their first child, a son, was born on January 6, 1766. In good European fashion, the Riedesels christened their heir with a string of names—Christian Charles Louis Ferdinand Henry William Herman Valentine—but he lived for hardly more than a year. Not until her ninth and last child was born did she present her husband with another male heir. Her first daughter, Philippina, was born in 1770 but died in 1771, when Frederika was expecting again. Augusta was born on August 3, 1771. Three years later another daughter was born and was named after her mother. [13]

11. Tharp, *The Baroness and the General*, 3–8.

12. Stone, trans., *General Riedesel*, I, 2, 4. This work is the principal source for the General's early life and career.

13. Count Ahasver von Lehndorff, *Dreissig Jahre am Hofe Friedrichs des Grossen* (Gotha, 1907), 448. Stone, trans., *General Riedesel*, I, 8; Tharp, *The Baroness and the General*, 10, 406.

In 1775 George III had begun to look for troops to use against the recalcitrant colonists. Negotiating first with Russia for 20,000 troops, but without success, he then turned to Germany. As early as April 25, the small state of Waldeck had agreed in London to terms of military aid, but substantial support was not definitely agreed upon until the beginning of 1776 when Col. William Faucit of the Guards concluded treaties with the governments of Brunswick, Hesse-Cassel, and Hesse-Hanau. Eventually other treaties, notably those with Ansbach-Bayreuth and Anhalt-Zerbst, brought additional aid, with more than 20,000 men being furnished by German princes. Brunswick specifically was to furnish four infantry regiments, one dragoon regiment, one grenadier battalion, and one light infantry battalion.[14] The price Great Britain paid was considerable, Hesse-Cassel benefiting most. Brunswick, the second-largest ally, was to receive 64,500 reichsthalers as long as the Brunswick troops themselves were being paid, and then 129,000 annually for two years after their return and the discontinuance of their pay.[15] Brunswick eventually sent more than 4,000 men to America, and the units specified were on their way little more than six weeks after the treaty was signed. The German princes had to equip the troops themselves, a small consideration, however, in view of the size of the subsidies. Small wonder that the German princes, including the Duke of Brunswick, readied their forces for service in America with alacrity.

There has long been a stigma attached to the idea of mercenary soldiers in the minds of most Americans, but this stigma did not exist, at least to the same degree, for the Germans of the time. The campaigns of the German mercenaries were followed with interest and pride in their homes, and, to be sure, they were serving their own states by the subsidies paid for them.[16] Other factors besides economic reasons had been driving some of the German states into the British camp for many years. French designs on their territory had long been impelling the Germans in that direction. As Franco-British colonial rivalry in the eighteenth century threw the two powers into war, it is not surprising that the British turned to the

14. Tharp, *The Baroness and the General,* 12; Eelking, *German Allied Troops,* 15–20; Stone, trans., *General Riedesel,* I, 23–24.

15. Eelking, *German Allied Troops,* 17.

16. *Ibid.,* gives a favorable expression to this point of view in the introduction, pp. 15–18.

German princes. With the Seven Years' War and the Diplomatic Revolution that brought Prussia and Great Britain together, the association of Great Britain and other Germanic allies became even closer. Moreover, dynastic bonds were useful in bringing about the treaty of 1776 between Brunswick and Great Britain, which had been ruled by the Hanoverians since 1714. George III's mother was a Saxe-Coburg princess, and one of his sisters, Augusta, married Karl Wilhelm Ferdinand, who became Duke of Brunswick in 1780.[17]

By 1776 Riedesel had risen to the rank of colonel. On January 10, the day after the treaty between Brunswick and Great Britain, he was appointed to command the first contingent headed for America. The command was the thirty-eight-year-old colonel's great opportunity; he and his wife viewed the appointment as though "sent by Providence."[18] Any serious professional soldier would have to expect to leave his home for long periods; opportunity seemed to be knocking. Just as each private soldier was to receive an initial sum of money plus regular British pay, so the commander could expect considerable personal profit, particularly if all went well. Not only was there full British pay; personal benefit from allowances of forage money, which were paid directly to commanders, was an accepted practice of the day. Riedesel, with his "economical turn of mind," was said to have saved 15,000 thalers in this manner.[19]

III

Although she had two small children and was expecting another, the Baroness persuaded her husband that she should accompany him to America. He agreed, with two stipulations: he insisted that she could not travel during her pregnancy and, when she was able to join him, that she must travel with a "lady of quality." When the Brunswick troops marched from Wolfenbüttel in February, therefore, the Baroness remained at home. A few days later, the Colonel reported that he had been promoted to Major General,[20] and he promptly dubbed his wife "Mrs. General." Early in April the troops

17. *Allgemeine deutsche Biographie*, XVIII, 532; Eelking, *German Allied Troops*, 16.
18. Baroness von Riedesel to her mother, Mar. 8, 1776, below, p. 184.
19. Eelking, *German Allied Troops*, 17.
20. General Riedesel to Mrs. Riedesel, Feb. 22, 1776, below, pp. 148–49.

sailed from Portsmouth for Canada to join Burgoyne's campaign
against New York. [21]

Long before General Riedesel landed at Quebec, Mrs. General
had given birth to another daughter; Caroline was born in March
1776. [22] By May 14 mother and child were ready for the long and
frustrating trip to America. Accompanied by the faithful servant
Rockel, she and her three daughters left Wolfenbüttel, passed
through Brussels, Tournay, and St. Omer, reaching Calais on June 1,
the same day her husband landed at Quebec.

At the suggestion of the General, she was to rendezvous in England
with Hannah Foy, the former Hannah Van Horne of New York and
wife of an English army captain. [23] Crossing the Channel, she stopped
in London en route to Bristol. She quickly learned the importance
of feminine fads in London. While walking with her daughters and
the wife of the minister from Hanover, she was acutely embarrassed
when passers-by cried out, "French women. Pretty girls." English
fashion, she discovered, frowned on a lady carrying a fan while wearing a hat; to compound her unstylish felony, moreover, she had put
ribbons on her daughters' hats, which were—perish the thought—
somewhat differently shaped from English hats for children.

But the worst was yet to come. When she went to Bristol to meet
Mrs. Foy, she wore a chintz dress trimmed with green taffeta which
was modeled on French fashion. A group of sailors flocked around,
pointing at her and calling out still worse taunts. From these hectic
and harrowing experiences, she learned "how important it is to conform to the customs of a country in order to live there in peace, for
a crowd is soon gathered together, and any exchange of words with
it only leads to insults." [24]

Mrs. Riedesel also had more serious problems. A series of mis-
adventures and some misinformation delayed her departure from
England until bad weather doomed her to spend a frustrating winter
in England. Despite her strength of character, indecision and desperation seized her and she spilled out her anguished soul in a letter to

21. For General Riedesel's account of his trip, see his letters to Mrs. Riedesel
between Feb. 22 and June 8, 1776, pp. 148–75.

22. Stone, trans., *General Riedesel*, I, 8; General Riedesel to Mrs. Riedesel,
Mar. 4, 1776, below, p. 155.

23. See General Riedesel to Mrs. Riedesel, Mar. 5, 26, 28, 31, Apr. 4, 6,
24, June 1, 28, 1776, pp. 156, 162, 163, 164, 166, 167, 168, 169, 173, 176.

24. For these incidents, see below, pp. 10, 11, 13.

her husband, now published for the first time.[25] Fortunately, she found quarters with the warmhearted Russells, who were ideal landlords and taught the children English. She also became acquainted with the royal family, being presented at court by Lady Germain, wife of the Secretary of the American Department who was directing the war against the rebellious colonies. Mrs. General was flustered when George III kissed her, but pleased when he reported that everybody was satisfied with her husband. Queen Charlotte complimented her on her courage to travel with small children and invited her back for informal visits during the winter.[26]

On April 16, 1777, Madame Riedesel sailed from Portsmouth on a merchant ship in a large convoy and arrived at the Gulf of St. Lawrence on June 3, her husband's birthday. "My heart," she wrote, "was filled with a mixture of joy and sadness and with the longing to be with him again soon, to hold him in my arms, and to bring him our dear children."[27] On June 11 she arrived at Quebec, where "all the ships lying in harbor fired their cannons in welcome."[28] But her husband was not there to welcome her; he was deep in the Canadian woods making preparations for a new attack on the colonial rebels in New York. Madame Riedesel refused to spend the night in Quebec, preferring to push on toward her husband's headquarters. After a dinner party given by Gen. Guy Carleton's wife, Lady Maria, the Baroness and her children boarded a galley and were rowed twenty miles up river to Point de Tremble. By carriage and canoe, the little group moved on to Trois Rivières, Berthier, and Montreal, arriving at Chambly on June 14. Here another disappointment greeted her, for the General had left by another road to meet his family and they had missed connections. But General Riedesel returned the next day, after learning on the road that a German woman and three children had passed that way the day before. "My happiness," the Baroness wrote, "was indescribable." For two happy days the Riedesels tarried, but on the third the General pushed south with the troops. Mrs. General and the children retreated to Trois Rivières, where she made preparations to join the army as soon as she could with safety.[29]

25. Mrs. Riedesel to General Riedesel, Sept. 19, 1776, pp. 187–89.
26. For details of Mrs. Riedesel's stay in London, see below, pp. 20–25.
27. See below, p. 31.
28. See below, pp. 32–33.
29. For Mrs. Riedesel's account of her reunion with her husband, see below, pp. 37–38.

The Brunswickers marched from Chambly and Isle aux Noix into Cumberland Head, River Bouquet, and Crown Point during June.[17] In July the main body of British and German troops took Fort Ticonderoga. Then, cutting their way by the disastrously slow route around Skenesborough, they finally moved through Fort Anne and Fort Edward. The engagement fought at Hubbardton on July 7 brought credit on General Riedesel and his men for their rescue of a British force.[30]

After the fall of Fort Ticonderoga, General Riedesel wrote his wife that she could join him on the advance toward Albany. His aide-de-camp, Capt. Sam Willoe, an Englishman appointed by Lord Germain, guided the family through the wilderness. By boat the group traveled from Trois Rivières up the St. Lawrence, then up the Richelieu River to Lake Champlain, and across the lake to the portage to Lake George. On August 14 the Baroness and her family reached Fort Edward on the east bank of the Hudson. Again she was disappointed; General Riedesel had moved forward to another post, but he returned to Fort Edward for two days before rejoining Burgoyne's troops.

At the same time Burgoyne dispatched troops into Vermont to round up horses, oxen, cattle, and wagons. After "the unfortunate affair at Bennington," as Baroness von Riedesel labeled the American rout of German troops, Burgoyne delayed for four weeks before moving again, and General Riedesel returned to Fort Edward where Mrs. General spent "three happy weeks with him in peace and quiet." When the army finally proceeded toward Albany, the Baroness, by "urgent entreaty," persuaded the General that she and the girls need not return to Canada but might follow the army.[31]

By September the Baroness was in Saratoga not far from Freeman's Farm. During the first Battle of Saratoga on September 19, she was an eyewitness to the whole battle, shivering "whenever a shot was fired." "Knowing that my husband was taking part in it," she wrote, "I was filled with fear and anguish." After the battle, Burgoyne forti-

30. William L. Stone, *The Campaign of Lieut. Gen. John Burgoyne, and the Expedition of Lieut. Col. Barry St. Leger* (Albany, 1877), gives a solid account. For more recent accounts, see Harrison Bird, *March to Saratoga: General Burgoyne and the American Campaign, 1777* (New York, 1963), and Hoffman Nickerson, *The Turning Point of the Revolution, or Burgoyne in America* (Boston and N.Y., 1928).

31. For the account of Mrs. Riedesel's trip to join her husband, see below, pp. 42-44.

fied his position and stayed at Freeman's Farm for three weeks. Each day the Baroness rode up to the General's artillery post. October 7 was no different for her from any other day; after breakfast with the General, she headed back to her children at the farmhouse on the Hudson. Later in the day the second Battle of Saratoga began, and the Baroness and the children could hear the "firing which grew heavier and heavier until the noise was frightful. It was a terrible bombardment," she wrote, "and I was more dead than alive." The next evening she joined the British army in retreat, harassed at times by a "terrifying cannonade." [32]

After retreating a short distance, General Burgoyne spent a merry night with the commissary's wife, shocking the Baroness and sealing the fate of the British forces. [33] When escape became impossible, Burgoyne called a council to discuss capitulation to the Americans. In the negotiations that followed, however, Gen. Horatio Gates, the American commanding general, agreed to call the instrument of surrender a "Convention" rather than a "Capitulation" and to refer to the surrendering army as "troops of the Convention" instead of "prisoners of war." Although the terms of this Convention were not honored subsequently by the Continental Congress, the Brunswick forces, together with the British, were at least allowed to move into Boston on somewhat better conditions than outright surrender would have brought. [34]

When Mrs. General rode through the American camp, the troops bowed to her "and some of them even looked with pity to see a woman with small children there." [35] She was especially pleased with Gen. Philip Schuyler's kindness and accepted his invitation to be a guest at his home in Albany, while the Convention troops marched to Boston. General Riedesel and his family joined the troops after a three-day interlude with the Schuylers.

The troops reached Boston late in October 1777, and the officers were housed in Cambridge for the most part in homes left by fleeing Loyalists. For the Riedesels, Gen. William Heath, the American commandant, located a country farmhouse on Watertown Road, later

32. Mrs. Riedesel's account of Saratoga is below, pp. 48–63.

33. See below, pp. 55–56.

34. William M. Dabney, *After Saratoga: The Story of the Convention Army* (Albuquerque, 1954), 10–21; Alexander J. Wall, *The Story of the Convention Army, 1777–1783* (N. Y., 1927), 1–4.

35. See below, pp. 63–64.

Brattle Street. The Baroness could not have been more pleased with the house; it was "one of the most beautiful houses" in Cambridge, she thought; "I have never seen a lovelier location." [36]

Throughout the winter of 1777 and the spring and summer of 1778 the Riedesels resided in Cambridge on parole, the General visiting his troops daily. Although he and his wife got along agreeably with most of the British officers, their relations with Burgoyne were not so amicable. The difficulties were professional as well as personal, and Riedesel's feelings were given expression at the end of the campaign. In general, he felt that the Brunswickers had not been given proper credit for their role, but he was particularly bitter about Burgoyne's report to Lord Germain in which Burgoyne excused himself for the outcome of the New York campaign on the ground that of the 3,500 men left to him before Saratoga, "scarcely 2,000 were English." [37] Riedesel certainly had good reason to resent any attempt on the part of Burgoyne to deflect the blame for the loss, since with the kind of decisions Burgoyne made at Skenesborough, at Bennington, on crossing the Hudson, and on withdrawing, it mattered little what nationals he commanded. Moreover, Riedesel's rescue of Hamilton's column at Freeman's Farm really had placed the shoe on the other foot.

IV

The Convention troops had gone to Boston originally to await transportation to Great Britain "under Condition of not serving again in North America during the present Contest." [38] Both the Continental Congress and General Washington feared that if these troops returned to England, however, they would be rotated to new posts in Europe and replaced in America with the troops they relieved. Finally, Congress hit upon the scheme of keeping the troops in America until "a distinct and explicit ratification of the convention of Saratoga shall be properly notified by the court of Great Britain to Congress." [39] Since the British government refused to recognize the legality of the Continental Congress, it could not fulfill this stipu-

36. See below, p. 69.
37. Stone, trans., *General Riedesel,* I, 187–88, 203–14.
38. "Articles of Convention," in Dabney, *After Saratoga,* 81.
39. Worthington C. Ford, ed., *Journals of the Continental Congress, 1774–1789,* 34 vols. (Washington, 1904–37), X, 34–35 (Jan. 8, 1778).

Friedrich Adolf von Riedesel, Baron of Eisenbach (1738–1800)

Portrait of the bridegroom at the age of twenty-four
Painted in 1762 by Johann Heinrich Tischbein

(see pp. xv-xvi)

Augusta, Caroline, and Frederika von Riedesel
Attributed to Caroline von Riedesel before 1805

(see p. xvi)

Augusta von Riedesel (1771–1805)

Oldest daughter of General and Baroness von Riedesel, afterwards Countess Reuss

(*see p. xvi*)

Frederika von Riedesel (1774–1854)
Second daughter of General and Baroness von Riedesel, afterwards Countess Reden
(see p. xvi)

Caroline von Riedesel (1776–1861)
Third daughter of General and Baroness von Riedesel, unmarried
(see p. xvi)

America von Riedesel (1780–1856)

Fourth daughter of General and Baroness von Riedesel, afterwards Countess Bernstorff

(see p. xvi)

Charlotte von Riedesel (1784– ?)

Youngest daughter of General and Baroness von Riedesel, married Major von Schöning

(see p. xvi)

General Riedesel about 1800
By Johann Heinrich Schröder
(see p. xvii)

Baroness von Riedesel about 1800
By Johann Heinrich Schröder
(see pp. xvi-xvii)

A Letter by Baroness von Riedesel

(see p. xvii)

Rockel, the Riedesel Servant in America
(*see p. xvii*)

The Burial of General Fraser

An engraving of the painting by John Graham

(see pp. xvii-xviii)

lation, and the troops were forced to remain in America until the war ended.

But supplies were scarce in Massachusetts, and costs high. When it became clear that the Convention troops were being treated as prisoners, General Clinton refused to provide supplies for them and shifted the cost for subsistence to the Americans. When French troops landed in New England, the shortage of food and fuel in the area became critical. Congress resolved to transfer the Convention troops to Charlottesville, Virginia, where supplies were more plentiful. After a year in Massachusetts, therefore, the Riedesels departed in November 1778. [40]

Through Connecticut, New York, New Jersey, Pennsylvania, and Maryland, the Riedesels traveled by carriage in December and January. Snow clogged the rutted roads, slowing their progress; at times four men had to ride ahead of the Baroness' carriage to make a path for it. From his hilltop near Charlottesville, Thomas Jefferson watched the arrival of the Convention troops, lamenting that "there could not have been a more unlucky concurrence of circumstances than when these troops first came. The barracks unfinished for want of labourers, the worst spell of weather ever known within the memory of man, no stores of bread laid in, the roads by the weather and number of waggons soon rendered impassable." [41]

General Riedesel moved on ahead of his family to hunt for accommodations in Charlottesville. After a frantic search he persuaded four young officers with the Convention troops to let him have a plantation house they had just rented from Jefferson. Colle, the Riedesels' new residence, belonged to Philip Mazzei, a former Italian physician and scientist and now an ardent patriot who was in Williamsburg making preparations for a voyage to Europe as Virginia's financial agent. [42] According to Jefferson, Riedesel advanced the rent for two years and built "additional buildings for the accommodation of part of his family for which there was not room in the

40. Dabney, *After Saratoga*, 47–49.

41. Thomas Jefferson to Patrick Henry, Mar. 27, 1779, in Julian P. Boyd *et al.,* eds., *The Papers of Thomas Jefferson* (Princeton, 1950———), II, 243.

42. Mazzei says that Riedesel, "aside from his advanced age [the General was then forty-one] and his duty to remain with his troops, which were quartered in the neighborhood, was expecting his wife the same evening, with their two [three] children, and he had no place in which to shelter them." Howard R. Marraro, trans., *Memoirs of the Life and Peregrinations of the Florentine, Philip Mazzei, 1730–1816* (N. Y., 1942), 225.

house rented. Independent of the brick work, for the carpentry of these additional buildings I know he is to pay 1500 dollars. The same gentleman to my knolege also has paid to one person 3670 dollars for different articles to fix himself commodiously." [43]

Life in Virginia was pleasant for the Riedesels. They became friends of the Jeffersons, who sold their piano to the General for the delighted Baroness. When Jefferson was in Williamsburg, he made small purchases for her, having eight silver spoons made on one occasion and buying a calfskin on another. [44] After Jefferson's election as governor took him to Williamsburg, he wrote Riedesel that he regretted "the loss of the agreeable society I have left, of which Madme. de Riedesel and yourself were an important part. Mrs. Jefferson in this particular sympathizes with me, and especially on her separation from Madme. de Riedesel." [45]

It seems clear that the treatment of the Convention troops as prisoners of war was mild. Jefferson pointed out that "General Riedesel alone laid out upwards of 200£ in garden seeds for the German troops only. . . . Their poultry, pigeons and other preparations of that kind present to the mind an idea of a company of farmers rather than of a camp of soldiers. In addition to the barracks built for them by the publick and now very comfortable they have built great numbers for themselves in such messes as fancied each other: and the whole corps both officers and men seem now happy and satisfied with their situation." [46]

The presence of more than 4,000 British and German troops, guarded by only 600 American soldiers, created some uneasiness in the Charlottesville area, and rumors circulated that the additional demand for food might lead to such scarcity that starvation might result. Governor Patrick Henry and the Virginia Council discussed the possibility of redistributing the troops, an option which the Continental Congress left to the state executive. [47] When the troops protested against another move only three months after getting situated,

43. Thomas Jefferson to Patrick Henry, Mar. 27, 1779, Boyd, ed., *Jefferson Papers*, II, 242.

44. Marie Kimball, *Jefferson: War and Peace, 1776 to 1784* (N. Y., 1947), 36.

45. Thomas Jefferson to Riedesel, July 4, 1779, Boyd, ed., *Jefferson Papers*, III, 24.

46. Thomas Jefferson to Patrick Henry, Mar. 27, 1779, *ibid.*, II, 242–43.

47. Dabney, *After Saratoga*, 59–60, 62.

Jefferson wrote Governor Henry, pleading that humanitarianism and self-interest argued against uprooting the troops again. "Is an enemy so execrable," he asked, "that tho in captivity his wishes and comforts are to be disregarded and even crossed? I think not. It is for the benefit of mankind to mitigate the horrors of war as much as possible. The practice therefore of modern nations of treating captive enemies with politeness and generosity is not only delightful in contemplation but really interesting to all the world, friends foes and neutrals. Let us apply this." After outlining the accommodations that had been built for the troops—"the expence of building barracks [is] said to have been £25,000"—and the improvements made since their arrival, Jefferson argued that "every sentiment of humanity revolt[s] against the proposition of stripping them of all this and removing them into new situations where from the advanced season of the year no preparations can be made for carrying themselves comfortably through the heats of summer, and when it is known that the necessary advances for the conveniencies already provided have exhausted their funds and left them unable to make like exertions anew."[48]

The troops and the Riedesels were not removed. The only real difficulty which befell the Riedesels in Virginia came when the General suffered a "sunstroke"—or perhaps a heart attack—while working in his garden. To facilitate the General's recovery, Governor Jefferson lifted the travel restrictions clamped on the Convention troops and officers, granting a passport to allow the Riedesels to visit medicinal springs in Virginia. While recuperating at Berkeley Springs, General Riedesel learned that he and Gen. William Phillips, the ranking British officer, were to be exchanged on parole in New York for captured American officers. The General returned to Charlottesville to terminate his connection with the Convention troops and to dispose of his furnishings and provisions; the Baroness accepted an invitation to visit the Carroll family in Maryland until the General arrived in York, Pennsylvania, where she and the girls would join him for the journey to New York.[49]

When the Riedesels left Virginia, the General sent Jefferson a farewell note of "heartiest thanks for every mark of Friendship which

48. Thomas Jefferson to Patrick Henry, Mar. 27, 1779, Boyd, ed., *Jefferson Papers,* II, 238, 242, 243.

49. For the Riedesels' stay in Virginia, see below, pp. 80–87. Tharp, *The Baroness and the General,* 434–35, identifies the Carroll family, whom Mrs. Riedesel called "Garel."

you have so kindly testified to me from the first moments of our acquaintance; and for the Assistance and hospitality which you have shewn the Troops under my Command since you have assumed the Government of Virginia: I beg you will be assured I shall ever retain a grateful rememberance of them and deem myself singularly happy, after this unnatural War is ended, to render you any Service in my power as a token of my personal regard for you and your Family . . . . Madame de Riedesels best Compliments to Mrs. Jefferson, whose very amiable Character and the many proofs which we have experienced of Her Friendship can never be effaced from out of our Memory." [50]

The Riedesels regrouped at York in August, stopped at Bethlehem, pushed through New Jersey to Elizabeth, and then were ordered back into Pennsylvania by General Washington, at the direction of the Continental Congress; until the British had settled debts incurred for the maintenance of the Convention troops, the paroles of the officers headed for New York were withdrawn. Retreating to Bethlehem, the family spent six weeks among the German Moravians.

When the Continental Congress finally released Riedesel to go to New York on parole in November, he left his family in Bethlehem while he sought a place to live in New York. Eventually, General Pattison, the commandant of the city, commandeered a house for them and furnished it luxuriously with furniture and carpets confiscated from wealthy rebels. Although Mrs. Riedesel was "far advanced in pregnancy," she was chosen Queen of the Ball given by British officers in honor of Queen Charlotte's birthday; she danced several dances and stayed until two o'clock in the morning. In March 1780 the Riedesel's fourth daughter was born, and the Baroness named her "America." She lived to be a symbol of the expedition, and a member of her husband's family, Count Johann Heinrich von Bernstorff, became Ambassador of the German Empire to the United States on the eve of the First World War. [51]

On October 13, 1780, after nearly a year in New York on parole, General Riedesel and General Phillips, second in command to Burgoyne at Saratoga, were restored to active duty in exchange for General Benjamin Lincoln, captured by the British at Charleston

50. Riedesel to Thomas Jefferson, Dec. 4, 1779, Boyd, ed., *Jefferson Papers,* III, 212.

51. For the trip to New York and Mrs. Riedesel's activities there, see below, pp. 88–110. See also Stone, trans., *General Riedesel,* I, 8.

during the summer. Riedesel was given a command on Long Island, and the next spring he and the family moved to his Brooklyn headquarters, a farmhouse across the East River from New York. By early summer, the General requested a transfer to Canada, and he was relieved of his Long Island assignment in July. After a trip of eight weeks by ship and land, the Riedesels reached Quebec in September 1781, happy to be back from the land of rebels. Gen. Sir Frederick Haldimand, governor of Canada, appointed Riedesel to command all German troops in Canada and assigned him the Richelieu River approach to New York, with headquarters at Sorel, where the Richelieu joins the St. Lawrence River. There General Haldimand had a new house built for the Riedesels, who moved in on Christmas Eve. The Baroness quickly discovered the convenience of frozen foods; using her attic as a gigantic freezer, she stored several hundred frozen fish, fowls, beef, and lamb. The meat, she said, was "just as juicy, even more tender than that we have at home." From the Indians she purchased a new delicacy, the "ottocas"; a tasty red fruit, she called it, "the size of a small cherry, but without the stone"; it was, of course, the cranberry. In the spring the General planted his usual garden and 1,200 fruit trees, and the Riedesels lived a bucolic life. It was, said Mrs. Riedesel, "a magnificent farm. I had my cows, many fowl, and Virginia hogs, which are black and smaller than ours and are especially short-legged. I also made my own butter." [52]

Although Cornwallis' surrender at Yorktown in October 1781 had dealt a mortal blow to the ministry's hope for victory in America, the British still had large troop concentrations in America, particularly in Canada and New York. In the spring of 1782, when Germain ordered Haldimand to try to detach Vermont from the rebellious colonies and annex it to Canada, Riedesel spent much of the summer at Isle aux Noix and Pointe au Fer. Mrs. Riedesel remained at Sorel, awaiting her next accouchement. On November 1 a daughter named Louisa Augusta Elizabeth Canada was born. But little "Canada," as she was called, lived only five months. [53]

By March 1783 the Riedesels knew that the seven-year war with America would soon end, and on April 9 General Carleton, now governor of New York, notified them that a preliminary peace treaty had been signed. While the General rounded up the troops and pre-

52. Mrs. Riedesel recounts her experiences in Canada below, pp. 111–13.
53. Stone, trans., *General Riedesel*, I, 8, II, 147, 213, 230. Also see below, pp. 126–27.

pared for the voyage to Germany, the Baroness supervised family arrangements. From Governor Haldimand she received a sable cape and muff, and the officers of the garrison at Quebec presented a play in her honor, concluding with a song wishing them a safe voyage.[54]

V

The Riedesels sailed in August on a voyage that was alternately frustrating and exciting. Becalmed in the St. Lawrence for eleven days, they moved out with a slow convoy, but were finally given permission to sail alone. Quickly outdistancing the slower ships, they promptly ran into a fierce storm which lasted three weeks. As they entered Spithead en route to Portsmouth, their ship struck the uncharted sunken hulk of the *Royal George* and stuck fast for two terrifying days. They reached Portsmouth in mid-September, hastened on to London, where the style-conscious Baroness, years behind the latest trends, immediately sent for a dressmaker. Before she could get her court dress designed, however, she received an invitation from Queen Charlotte to come to St. James' Palace. Since she did not have a thing to wear—familiar feminine lament—she first sent her apologies and then repeated them upon arrival, but the Queen assured her that the royal family did "not look at clothes when we are happy to see the people." She and the General were entertained at the palace *en famille* with so much informality, the Baroness noted, "that one would think he were in a happy family circle of his own station."

The Riedesels received visits from Lord North, General Tryon, Charles James Fox, and others, but not all of their social life moved at such high levels. Mrs. Riedesel had fond memories of the Russells, her landlord and landlady who had taught her daughters to speak English in 1776–77 during her first stay in England. She therefore hastened "to call upon that good family, the Russells, who during my first stay in London, before my voyage to America, had been so good and considerate to me." It was a tearful reunion. "My tears of joy betrayed me," she said, and "these kind people wept very much when I left them." [55]

From London the Riedesels went to Deal to embark for the homeward voyage. They landed in Stade after a hectic trip, where the

54. See below, p. 31.
55. For activities in London, see below, pp. 139–41.

General remained with the Brunswick troops while Mrs. General and the children went to her home in Wolfenbüttel. The Duchess of Brunswick, Princess Augusta, hurried over to greet the Baroness the day after she arrived. A week later, the General and his troops marched home and were quickly surrounded by a "partly happy, partly pathetic bustle of fathers, mothers, wives, children, brothers and sisters, and friends, who all pressed about to see their loved ones again." A few days later, on October 8, 1783, General Riedesel marched his troops from Wolfenbüttel to Brunswick where the Duke of Brunswick gave them a royal welcome.[56]

VI

The postwar years were good to the Riedesels. In 1785 the Baroness produced the male heir which she and the General had so fervently prayed for—five years earlier, when she had borne little America, Jefferson had sent his "condolences" in lieu of congratulations![57] The General had also inherited the castle of Lauterbach in 1782 when his father died, but he did not retire to his estate. When the Duke of Brunswick appointed him Lieutenant General, the Riedesels moved to Brunswick where she furnished her new home "entirely in the English style."[58]

In 1788 the Duke of Brunswick sent General Riedesel to the Netherlands to command the Brunswick troops supporting the Stadholder. Although this tour of duty lasted five years, the Baroness remained with her family, since the General could come home periodically. In 1793 he returned and retired to Lauterbach. But after the "reign of terror" began in France the Duke of Brunswick recalled him to Brunswick in 1794 as commandant of the city. For five years he served with honor and distinction in that post, visiting Lauterbach and occasionally Berlin, after the marriage of Augusta to Count von Reuss. In the castle at Lauterbach in October 1799, the General made his last will and testament.[59] When the family returned to Brunswick, they made plans for a New Year's Eve party to welcome the new

56. The return to Germany is recounted below, pp. 141–44.

57. Thomas Jefferson to Riedesel, May 3, 1780, Boyd, ed., *Jefferson Papers*, III, 368–69.

58. Tharp, *The Baroness and the General*, 403–4; Stone, trans., *General Riedesel*, I, 11, II, 169.

59. Tharp, *The Baroness and the General*, 406–7, 411–13.

century. It was a lively party, and even the General, now sixty-one, "danced a few rounds." The next day he came down with a cold but insisted on visiting the Duke's court to pay the traditional homage on New Year's Day. When he returned from the palace, he became ill and "was obliged to lie down." But he recovered rapidly and on January 6 felt well enough to play a game of whist. It was his last game. During the night he died in his sleep. The bereaved Baroness buried him in the family vault at Lauterbach, sold the Brunswick house and furnishings, and retired to Lauterbach.[60]

Before the General's death, the Baroness and her son-in-law, Count von Reuss, had discussed the publication of her letters and the journal of her journey to America "as a manuscript for the family." From internal evidence, it is clear that the final draft of the journal was written near the end of the eighteenth century; the latest dateable reference is to the death of Gen. Henry Clinton, who died in 1795. During the summer of 1799, Count Reuss arranged the letters and journal while visiting his wife's parents at Lauterbach. The General had urged them on, but he did not live to see the printed volume. It was issued in a limited edition for the family early in 1800 and aroused so much interest that a public edition was printed in Berlin by Carl Spener, who dated his preface May 8, 1800.[61]

During her eight years as a widow, the Baroness could turn to her book to reminiscence about the six-year tour of duty she had shared with her husband in America. There she could see, self-revealed, a word portrait of herself and an account of the exciting and almost exotic times which constituted one of the highlights of her thirty-seven-year marriage.

At one level, Baroness von Riedesel's letters and journal form a fascinating autobiography of a remarkable woman—"the worthiest woman," as her husband's superior officer, General Phillips, observed in a congratulatory note, "best wife and most amiable companion and Friend." "It was the peculiar order of Providence," the British general told the German commander, "to give her to the world for your happiness."[62] And her journal and letters are her peculiar gift to posterity. Although they contain an engaging self-portrait, they are even more important for their general observations, for they are now, as they

60. Stone, trans., *General Riedesel*, I, 11–12.
61. See Spener's preface, below, pp. xlv–vii.
62. General William Phillips to General Riedesel, June 18, 1778, cited by Tharp, *The Baroness and the General*, 280.

were when Francis Parkman reviewed an earlier translation in 1868, an excellent example of "good historical memoirs—the very life of historical literature." [63]

63. *Atlantic Monthly,* 21 (1868), 127–28.

Die
Berufs-Reise nach America

*

Briefe
der
Generalin von Riedesel
auf dieser Reise
und
während ihres sechsjährigen Aufenthalts
in America
zur Zeit des dortigen Krieges
in den Jahren 1776 bis 1783
nach Deutschland geschrieben

Berlin
bei Haude und Spener
1800

PUBLISHER'S PREFACE

TO THE FIRST AND SECOND TRADE EDITIONS,

1800 AND 1801

Of the German troops which England hired for the subduing of her rebellious colonies, the Brunswickers were commanded by General Riedesel. In the year 1776 he went at their head to America, leaving his wife with the wish that she, together with their children, should follow him to that part of the world. This she did, furnishing the occasion for the letters which the reader will find in this little volume. The authoress wrote them to her mother, who lived here in Berlin, the widow of the former minister of state, His Excellency, Herr von Massow, and also to other trusted friends, while on that dangerous journey and during her stay in America.

A few years ago these letters came into the hands of her son-in-law, Royal Prussian Court Marshal and Chamberlain Heinrich XLIV, Count Reuss of Berlin. He took advantage of the leisure of a summer which he spent in the country with his parents-in-law to put the letters in order, and because of the great interest they aroused in all the relatives, he had them printed the following winter as a manuscript for the family, but only in a very small number of copies.

General Riedesel did not live to see them in print. He died the sixth of January this year [1800] as Lieutenant General and Commandant of Brunswick.

Even without this history of the appearance of these letters, one would see from the letters themselves that they were definitely not for the public. But just as surely as not everything intended for publication is, for this very reason, deserving of publication, so there surely is much which is withheld from the public that is worthy of being shared with it. So much so did this seem to me to be the case with these letters that when my eyes fell on a copy which the honorable editor presented to me, I entreated him to prepare an edition for the public. The Count granted me this request with the remark, "Yes, if you think any use could be served thereby." I am most assuredly of this opinion. If examples such as fervid constantcy in marriage, stead-fast resignation in unavoidable circumstances, and religious observance of a mother's duties really make more impression than mere precepts, if the principle that in all circumstances and relationships in life noth-ing gives such peace as the consciousness of having done one's duty, if sacrifices and denials of many kinds do not weaken this striving toward the fulfillment of duty, if all this is worthy of imitation and so much the more to be prized as it is seldom found, perhaps especially among the upper classes, then a book which presents the practice of all those virtues cannot be without use. In so far as truth is of more value than fiction, so much the greater must be the interest with which one reads these letters, because they rest on facts, while in even the best fiction the conviction that all was invented for the purpose of instruction will disturb heartfelt sympathy and weaken the moral effect intended.

With the approval of the honorable editor, I have altered the title of this little work for the present edition. In the one intended only for the family it runs thus: *Extracts from the Letters and Papers of General Baron von Riedesel and his Wife (née Massow) Concerning their Common Voyage to America and their Sojourn in that Country, Compiled and Arranged by their Son-in-Law, Heinrich XLIV, Count Reuss (Printed as a Manuscript for the Family).*

The great abundance of books make it particularly desirable, if not for the general reader, at least for the trade, that books of related contents be distinguished from each other by title, and under the wide heading, travel, this necessity is doubly felt. If then a title is so much the better for being characteristic, then I need make no apology for calling this *The Voyage of Duty to America,* especially as Mrs. General von Riedesel does not come under any of the categories Yorick classified as "travelers." Proofs of the appropriateness of this discriminating title the reader will find on almost every page of the book, even if it is not literally justified on pages [3, 4, 73, and 184]. That the title does not mention the letters of General Riedesel and the fragment from his diary about the military operations of the English General Burgoyne must be excused by the fact that these letters are, in this connection, nothing other than the exposition in the drame, and the military report merely an episode.

The vignette on the title page presents the Diamond Point, a prominent cape in the gentle Saint Lawrence, which rises a thousand feet over the water and can be distinguished as the highest of several fortified points before Quebec, and which may be regarded as the citadel of the city. In addition to the fact that this promontory presents a picturesque view, it is extremely appropriate to be portrayed here, because it was the oft-longed-for goal of the long voyage of the authoress as well as the signal of its end. I have borrowed this suitable little decoration from Weld's *Journey to North America*, which came out of my publishing house at the same time as the letters of Mrs. General von Riedesel, and the reading of which I can recommend to those who wish to have a true and comprehensive idea of the most recent condition of the free states of North America and of Canada.

Berlin, 8 May 1800   CARL SPENER

POSTSCRIPT TO THE SECOND EDITION

If after the course of but one year a new edition of a book like the present one is demanded, the taste of the great reading public must not be so badly out of tune as the host of knightly romances and adventurous ghost stories has indicated so abundantly. The quick sale which the *Voyage of Mrs. General von Riedesel* has had shows very surely that realization of what is good is still sufficiently dominant and taste is not so degenerate that every book in which, as in the letters of Mrs. Riedesel, instruction is united with conversation, cannot be assured of the most favorable reception.

Berlin, 25 April 1801   CARL SPENER

Part I

Baroness von Riedesel's Journal

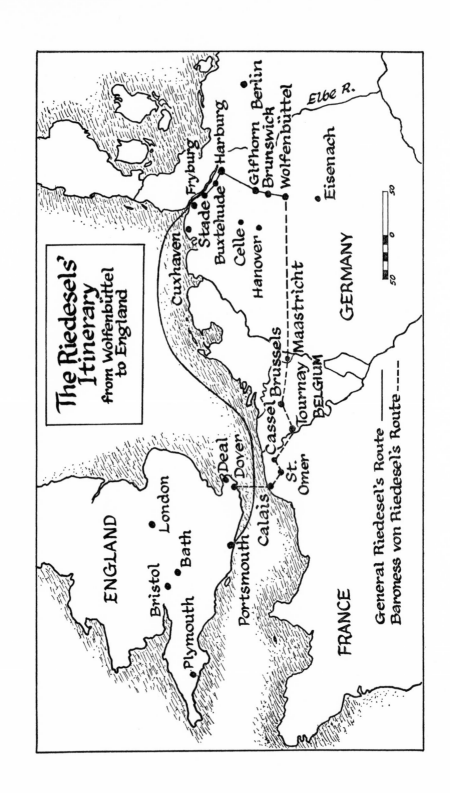

I

From Brunswick to Bristol

꒐————◀◖◔◈◙▷━━━ᴸᵒ

I left Wolfenbüttel[1] on the 14th of May, 1776, at five o'clock in the morning, and in spite of my ardent longing to see my husband again I could only have a heavy heart from the full realization of the magnitude of my undertaking, especially as I had been told repeatedly about the dangers connected with such a voyage.[2] Little Augusta, my eldest daughter, was four years and nine months old; little Frederika, my second, was two years, and Caroline, my youngest child, was only ten weeks old.[3] It took all my courage and tenderness, therefore, not to renounce my only wish, my resolution to follow him. I was told not only of the dangers of the sea, but that we might be eaten by the

1. Wolfenbüttel, seven miles south of Brunswick in Lower Saxony, came into the hands of the Wolfenbüttel-Lüneburg Dukes in 1671, although the castle had been their residence since 1267. The town, on the Oker River, is notable for its Renaissance architecture. Both Leibniz and Lessing played roles in the development of the Herzog-August Archiv. Even after Duke Karl I moved his capital to Brunswick in 1753, Wolfenbüttel remained a cultural center in spite of its small size, the theater being of particular note. In 1772 Lessing's *Emilia Galotti* was first performed in Wolfenbüttel. *Der grosse Brockhaus* (Wiesbaden, 1952–58), XII, 581; *Allgemeine deutsche Biographie* (Leipzig, 1875–1912), XV, 269.

2. Dangers and problems incidental to a voyage by a private person in the 18th century can be gleaned from such accounts as: *The Life and Adventures of John Nichol, Mariner* (New York, 1936); William E. Mead, *The Grand Tour in the Eighteenth Century* (Boston, 1914); Seymour Dunbar, *A History of Travel in America . . .* , 4 vols. (Indianapolis, 1915).

3. The Riedesels had nine children, born between the years 1766 and 1785, six of whom reached adulthood. They were Christian Herman (1766–67); Philippina (1770–71); Augusta (1771–1805), who married Count Heinrich XLIV of Reuss, the original editor of the Baroness' journal; Frederika (1774–1854), who married Count Reden; Caroline (1776–1861), unmarried; America (1780–1856), who was born in New York and married Count Ernst von

3

savages; that people in America ate horsemeat and cats;[4] but all of this was less frightening than the thought of going into a strange country where I did not understand the language. However, in the meantime I was prepared for everything, and the thought of following my husband and fulfilling my duty sustained me throughout the entire journey.

At my first halt, my good old Rockel[5] said, with a confident expression on his face, as he lifted the children from the carriage, "Just see how God blesses our journey! Our children look healthier than ever!" Rockel had been with us eight years when my father appointed him forester. When he heard of my husband's departure, and of my intention to follow him, he forsook everything to go with me as footman, and throughout the entire journey he made it his duty to show us all his utmost devotion and attention, especially the children, waiting on us hand and foot. The very first noon I came to an inn where the innkeeper was a very rude fellow. While the horses were being fed I ordered a beer-soup[6] for which he charged me ten groschen.[7] When

---

Bernstorff, and one of whose collateral descendants was German ambassador to the United States on the eve of the First World War; Canada (1782–83); Charlotte (1784–?), who married a Major von Schöning in the service of Saxony; Georg (1785–1854), whose death at Bachwald, Silesia, ended the direct Riedesel line. Max von Eelking, ed., *Memoirs, and Letters and Journals, of Major General Riedesel during his Residence in America*, trans. William L. Stone (Albany, 1868), I, 8; hereafter cited as Stone, trans., *General Riedesel*.

4. For various kinds of false stories about the New World told by early travelers see Percy G. Adams, *Travelers and Travel Liars, 1660–1880* (Berkeley, 1962), *passim*. See below, for General Riedesel's reassurances to his wife, p. 167.

5. The earliest edition and all following have spelled the name of this good and faithful servant without an umlaut. The Huth transcripts, however, show it spelled "Röckel." For the life of an English footman, whose position and experiences were similar to those of Rockel, see John Macdonald, *Memoirs of an Eighteenth-Century Footman, John Macdonald (1745–1779)* (London, 1927).

6. Perhaps this was "Brunswick Mumme," a peculiar type of brew prepared from malt and wheat, and sometimes with oats and bran meal added, which is said to have been first made by one Christian Mumme in the year 1492. The term "beer-soup" was commonly used in the 18th century and undoubtedly covered a wide number of products, often including eggs. See *Meyer's Lexikon* (Leipzig, 1939), VII, 1655; *Der grosse Brockhaus*, VIII, 188; *The New International Encyclopedia* (1914), III, 57.

7. For the evolution of the groschen, see *Der grosse Brockhaus*, V, 77–78. The groschen was worth perhaps a shade more than three cents after American currency was begun, and it was 1/24 of the Prussian thaler. Since the value of currencies fluctuated so much, I have not attempted to translate 18th-century terms into 20th-century values.

I complained that this was an exorbitant price, he replied snappishly that I would have to pay him this, and that I had not been obliged to stop at his inn if I had not chosen to. He allowed he was rude, to be sure, but added I would find still ruder innkeepers who would charge me six times as much. Fine comfort this was, since I had resolved to live very carefully.

At Maastricht[8] I was warned to be on my guard, the roads being infested with highwaymen, 130 having been either hanged or executed some other way during the past two weeks, that that was less than one-quarter of the entire band, and that they were being hanged right on the spot without trial when caught. These tales were very frightening, and I decided to do no traveling by night; but since the horses I had obtained were poor ones, I was obliged to pass through a forest at dusk. While doing so something hanging from a tree crashed through the open window of the carriage. I reached out, and when I felt something rough, I asked what it might be. It was the corpse of a man, with woolen stockings, who had been hanged! My terror became still greater when we stopped in front of a lonely house in the same forest, beyond which the postilions would go no farther. The name of the place was Hune—I shall never forget it! A rather suspicious-looking man received us and led us to a quite remote room where I found only a bed. It was cold, so I ordered a fire to be made in the huge fireplace. Our whole supper consisted of tea and very coarse bread. My faithful Rockel came to me with a very anxious face and said, "Things are not quite right in this place. There is a room full of weapons. I believe the other people are all out. They are surely rogues! But I will sit in front of your door all night with my gun, and they shall enter over my dead body. The other servant will sit up all night in the carriage with his gun too." All this naturally kept me from sleeping peacefully; I seated myself on a chair with my head resting on the bed. However, I finally fell asleep, and you can imagine how happy I was when I was awakened at four o'clock and told everything was ready for our departure, and when I looked out of the window I discovered a host of nightingales in the forest whose sweet singing drove away all fear.

The rest of my trip was very happy. I passed through Brussels, Tournay, and St. Omer, where I arrived at one o'clock in the afternoon of May 31. Between Tournay and St. Omer I passed through a town called Cassel, where there is a mountain which I climbed.

8. See route followed by Madame de Riedesel, p. 2.

From this point one can see thirty-two towns, not counting villages between. It is one of the most beautiful views a person can have!

As soon as I arrived in Calais I sent for the captain of a ship and made all arrangements with him for my crossing to England. I hired, in accordance with advice I received here, a packet boat for us alone, to get along better, but I left the carriage behind because I was told that in Dover I would have to pay thirty and perhaps even sixty guineas duty for bringing into England a carriage built in a foreign country. Contrary winds detained me two days in Calais.[9] Finally I was called to the ship. I must confess my heart pounded a bit. My two older children were delighted, for in order to encourage them I had told them that after making the crossing they would see their father. I pretended that I was not afraid myself so that they would have no fear. We drove to the shore. The boatmen took the two older children and carried them aboard. I carried the little one myself. The servants followed. I looked around to see where the children were and, to my astonishment, found them already aboard, playing around among the sailors. I had the little one lifted up also, and now I had magnets enough to lift me and give me courage to go on board myself, and I found that it was not so bad as I had feared. A plank was laid from the shore to the ship, and I walked across it with a firm step. The ship was so nice and clean that all my fears vanished. The sailors seemed so jolly. I had the very best of cabins, in which there were eight beds. All the furniture was of mahogany and brass, polished like a mirror.

It was suggested that my children and I should lie down; but we had no desire to retire so early, and we walked around on deck instead, and we had something to eat and drink, for we were really hungry. My daughter Frederika became so well acquainted with the sailors that when she wanted to go up or down she had only to say: "My good man, take my arm!" These people love children very much and look after them well. One of them always took Caroline around,

9. Although General Riedesel and his troops sailed from the German port of Stade for England, Madame de Riedesel sailed from France, which was already aiding England's rebellious colonies and shortly was to be a belligerent. Packet-boat connections with the continent continued through the war. While Frederick the Great was watching the peace negotiations, he concluded that the more frequent service that set in toward the end of the war was an indication that peace might be concluded. Marvin L. Brown, Jr., ed., *American Independence through Prussian Eyes* (Durham, 1959), 151.

carried her, and waited on her. It was amusing to see him, a large, swarthy man with a little child who was always laughing at him. None of us got seasick. The captain assured us he had not had such a favorable wind for a long while. It was quite a strong wind, but a good one. In five hours we were across. Because of the tide we could not have gone ashore until eight or nine o'clock, so we got into a ship's boat, and in six minutes we were on land. My heart was deeply moved with gratitude to God for having let us cross safely, and full of the thought: "You will bring your children safely to your husband." But the children wanted their father now, and this made me very sad. I comforted them by saying that we would have to get aboard another ship [and then we would be with him]. But now they nagged me steadily, and jumped about whenever they saw a ship.

On our landing at Dover we were greeted by a crowd of well-wishers and congratulated on having withstood so long a voyage. This cost us money. I was accosted by more than thirty innkeepers, who all begged me to take lodgings at their houses. I chose a French inn, and was much pleased by it. It was a splendid establishment and noteworthy for its cleanliness. The customs officials came to inspect my luggage, which is such a bother, but I had a letter to the chief inspector, and when he heard I had determined to follow my husband to America, he replied very courteously that it would be cruel to trouble the wife of a general who had undertaken to go to that land in the service of the King. Thus I came out all right.

Since I was obliged to leave my carriage behind (in Calais) I had to take the post chaise to London, which was very expensive for me, because the charge for luggage was by weight.

I arrived in London on the evening of the first of June and met many acquaintances there, among whom were General Schlieffen,[10] Herr von Kutzleben, Count Taube,[11] and others. My husband had

10. Gen. Martin Ernst von Schlieffen (1732–1825) was Hessian ambassador to London. He had been adjutant to Duke Ferdinand of Brunswick and had negotiated with Col. William Faucit the Anglo-Hessian treaty of Jan. 13, 1776. A man of real diplomatic as well as military skill, he recovered £40,000 of hospital-money from England following the Seven Years' War. *Allgemeine deutsche Biographie*, XXXI, 516–17; Max von Eelking, *The German Allied Troops in the North American War of Independence, 1776–1783*, trans. J. G. Rosengarten (Albany, 1893), 19; hereafter cited as Eelking, *German Allied Troops*.

11. Captain (later Major) Karl August (or Christian Moritz) von Kutzleben was the Hessian resident minister in London. Bernhard A. Uhlendorf, trans.,

written to the last named and had asked him to rent private quarters for me, but, fearing I would not come, he forbore doing so; otherwise I would have been better and more inexpensively accommodated. Nevertheless I was happy to see how much concerned about my journey my husband was and how little he doubted that I would carry out my plan. I was gladder than ever that nothing had frightened me into abandoning it.

I must mention yet another incident which initially had an unpleasant influence on my stay in London.

In Calais I relied entirely on the innkeeper, who had been recommended to me, but I think that he betrayed my confidence and misused it by bringing a lot of things into England at my expense. Also he advised me to take a trustworthy man with me for protection, for without such I would be exposed to great danger. He pretended as though he had gone to a lot of trouble to find a suitable person, and finally he brought me a well-dressed man whom he introduced as an aristocrat who was his good friend, who was willing to accompany me to London. I received him with great civility and did not know how to repay him for so much kindness. I put the children opposite me so that he would have a better seat and did everything I could to prevent their causing him any annoyance. He had the appearance of a man of importance and dined with me on the trip. I noticed, to be sure, that the servants in the inns treated him with unusual familiarity, but I thought nothing of it because the gratitude which I thought I owed him prevented me from seeing clearly. When we arrived in London and I asked for good quarters I was astonished when I was led to a very poor room on the fifth floor. I thought, however, that this was because all the other rooms were taken, since in Brunswick Herr von Feronce [12] had assured me that I would be lodged magnifi-

---

Revolution in America; Confidential Letters and Journals, 1776–1784, of Adjutant General Major Baurmeister of the Hessian Forces (New Brunswick, N. J., 1957), 85, 603. Friedrich Wilhelm von Taube (1728–79) had been Austrian ambassador to London since 1763. He was born in London, where his father served as physician to the Queen, had been in America, and was the author of various works about trade and the colonies. *Allgemeine deutsche Biographie,* XXXVII, 420-22.

12. Jean Baptiste Feronce von Notenkreuz (1723–99) was appointed Brunswick finance minister in 1773. It was he who signed the Brunswick treaty with the English negotiator, Colonel Faucit, on Jan. 9, 1776, which certainly reflected the mercenary aspect of the negotiations. *Allgemeine deutsche Biographie,* VI, 717–18; Stone, trans., *General Riedesel,* I, 24.

cently. General Schlieffen and many others who came to visit me, especially the ladies to whom the Hereditary Princess, now Duchess, of Brunswick [13] had given me letters of introduction, were surprised to find me in such bad quarters.

The following day the landlord came to me with a thoroughly ashamed air and inquired very humbly whether I knew the man with whom I had arrived and whom I had had put up well (for I had not thought it proper to let him dine with me in London). I told him that he was an aristocrat who, at the request of my innkeeper in Calais, Mr. Guilhaudin, had been kind enough to accompany me on my journey. "Ha!" he replied, "this is one of his tricks! This man is a hired servant, an arch-rogue, whom he uses to promote his own interests, and when I saw you sitting in the carriage with this man, I could not believe, I must confess, you were the lady you claimed to be, and thought therefore that these rooms would be good enough for you. But now I can judge by the persons who visit you that I made a mistake. So I beg you very much to forgive me, and I beseech you to come to other rooms, for which you will not have to pay any more than for these, for I really wish to atone for my mistake." I thanked my host and requested him to get rid of this person as soon as possible, who, nevertheless, demanded four or six guineas (I no longer remember exactly how much it was) for his company. For this trick I could never forgive Mr. Guilhaudin, who also made use of my carriage. It was he who told me I would have to leave it behind, because I would not be allowed to take it into England. I later heard that most probably he intended to rent it to travelers going to Germany, a trick he had played several times before. But this I prevented, because when I was in London I wrote to the Prime Minister, Lord North, [14] who immediately gave me permission to bring the carriage

13. The Duchess Augusta of Brunswick was the sister of George III of England. She married the Hereditary Prince of Brunswick, Karl Wilhelm Ferdinand in 1764, and played a role in the cultural development of Brunswick, becoming the Duchess in 1780 upon the death of her father-in-law. *Allgemeine deutsche Biographie,* XV, 273.

14. For biographies of Lord North, second Earl of Guilford (1732–92), who headed the King's ministry from 1770 to 1782, see Reginald Lucas, *Lord North* . . . , 2 vols. (London, 1913), and William B. Pemberton, *Lord North* (N. Y., 1938). Lord North's ways are revealed in Sir John W. Fortescue, *The Correspondence of King George the Third from 1760 to December, 1783* . . . , 6 vols. (London, 1927–28), and William B. Donne, *Correspondence with Lord North, 1768 to 1783,* 2 vols. (London, 1867).

duty-free into England. While all this held me up some time, it nevertheless saved me money and added to my comfort.

When I arrived in London my eyes had suffered so much from the heat that one of them was quite irritated, and even badly inflamed. General Schlieffen insisted upon my consulting an oculist and took me to the one who attended the Queen. He was alarmed over the condition of my eye, but he also encouraged me about curing it. He put some sort of powder into a quill, had me open my eye wide, which I did without hesitation, little knowing what pain I was to suffer; thereupon he blew all the powder into my eye to cure the proud flesh. The pain was indescribable, and never again have I been able to take this treatment. Even when I tried to do so my eye closed involuntarily. However, the treatment did me much good. The doctor gave me yet another prescription, and I had to pay him three guineas, which did not seem right to me, but General Schlieffen told me I could not pay less since he was the oculist to the Queen.

While in London I lodged in Suffolk Street, where I found everything very dear. As I intended to remain only two days, I made no agreement; but after the first week I called for my bill.

I drove around in the city a bit, but on account of little Caroline, whom I nursed myself, I did not see all that I might have. I saved all this for my return trip. However, I went to St. James Park twice, and there I had a close view of the King and the Queen in their sedans. The walk through the Park is lovely, and more than five or six thousand people daily stroll around in it.

One day I had an unpleasant adventure in London. I had been advised to buy a light cape and hat, as it was not proper to go about without them. I was invited to dinner at the home of the Hanoverian minister, Herr von Hinüber. His wife suggested that we walk through St. James Park, but she neglected to point out to me that we were not dressed in the English style. Little Augusta was dressed in French style, with a little panier and a pretty little round hat. I noticed that people almost pointed fingers at us, and I asked what it meant. She told me that I was carrying a fan, which was not to be carried while wearing a hat and that my little girl was too finely dressed, and that people therefore took us for French women, who were looked on askance here. I came back the following day to the same place, and we were dressed completely in the English fashion, and so I thought no one would notice us. But I was wrong, for again I heard the cry: "French women! Pretty girls!" I asked the servant who accompanied us why we were taken for French women and learned it was because I had put ribbons on my children. I tore these off and put them in my pocket, but people only stared more, and I heard that it was on account of the hats which were of a different shape from those of English children. I was thus led to know how important it is to conform to the customs of a country in order to live there in peace, for a crowd is soon gathered together, and any exchange of words with it only leads to insults.

My plan was to go to Bristol and there to await an opportunity to embark for America. To be sure, everyone in London to whom I had been recommended tried to dissuade me from it on the ground I would not get such good information on the sailing of ships, but my husband had strongly recommended that I go there, and therefore I did not want to give up the plan. So I left London on the 10th and arrived in Bristol on the 11th. When I drove up to the inn a crowd gathered and stared at my carriage because the German steps struck them funny, as did the two guns which my servants had fastened to the driver's seat. They felt of them, and lifted up the oilcloth cover of my carriage to see how it was painted. Instead of keeping quiet, my servant, who could speak a few words of English, began to call them names in English, to which they responded in kind. At this he lost control of himself and laid one of them low. Now they all fell on him, and the story might have had a sad ending had not the local chief magistrate, the uncle of Mrs. Foy [15] (to whom I had written asking her to engage rooms for us, and whose same uncle I had sent for so that he might lead me to them) arrived in the nick of time. This worthy old gentleman went in all haste and fetched his niece, with whom I could speak some French and ride to my lodgings, which were large and handsome, but also very dear.

15. Harriet Van Horne Foy was the wife of Capt. Edward Foy, a commissary who became adjutant-general in Canada in 1777. She was the daughter of John Van Horne of New York. Captain Foy's uncle, Nathaniel Foy, was a Bristol merchant who had been mayor in 1772–73, and became alderman in 1776. After Captain Foy's death in 1779, she married Lt. Col. Thomas Carleton, a younger brother of Guy Carleton, in 1783. See Louise Hall Tharp, *The Baroness and the General* (Boston, 1962), 34–35, 421; James M. Hadden, *A Journal Kept on Canada and upon Burgoyne's Campaign in 1776 and 1777*, ed. Horatio Rogers (Albany, 1884), 20, 381–86; William L. Stone, trans., *Letters of Brunswick and Hessian Officers during the American Revolution* (Albany, 1891), 74.

II

Frustration in England

⟡————⟡

Soon after my arrival in Bristol I realized how unpleasant it is to be in a city and not understand the language spoken there. My servants had lost all their courage, and therefore I had to conceal from them what I myself felt. I often wept for hours on end in my room. Finally I found the courage to overcome everything. I spared no pains to learn the English language, and at the end of six weeks I had at least gone far enough to be able to ask for all necessities and to understand the newspapers, which were then most interesting to me, especially the articles about Quebec, where my husband was.

I was soon obliged to change my lodgings. My landlady did not allow me to have the least thing washed for the children. Therefore I looked for another place. In my new lodgings I had a very beautiful view. I looked out over the whole "College Green,"[1] a beautiful place to stroll, where under the trees are lawns and paths, and many grownups and children go promenading. My own children often played there. Bristol would be a very agreeable place to stay if the people were of a better sort, but the large number of sailors there makes this city unpleasant. On the day after my arrival my hostess called me to see a delightful spectacle (as she called it). When I reached the window I saw two naked men boxing with the greatest fury. I saw the blood running from them, and how rage was painted in their eyes. Little accustomed to such a hateful sight, I quickly retired to the remotest corner of the house to avoid hearing the shouts of joy of the spectators when one of the men received a blow.

During my stay in Bristol I had an unpleasant adventure. I was

1. The College Green is a park immediately opposite to and north of the Cathedral. See *Blue Guide: England* (London, 1957), 140–42.

wearing a chintz gown trimmed with green taffeta. This probably seemed outlandish to the people of Bristol, for as I walked one day with Mrs. Foy over a hundred sailors gathered around us, pointed their fingers at me, and cried, "French whore!" I retreated as quickly as possible into a shop under the pretense of buying something, and in the meantime the crowd dispersed. This adventure, however, made me dislike my gown, and when I returned home I gave it to my cook, although it was still quite new.

About three English miles from Bristol is a bathing place called Hot Wells,[2] which is very similar to Wendefurth,[3] near Blankenburg in the Harz, except that in Hot Wells there are nice houses and a casino. Hot Wells has many visitors, but most are sick, especially those suffering from lung trouble. Almost all the ladies ride horseback because of the mountains and rocky valleys, and those who cannot manage a horse are seated behind a guide in a kind of saddle which is made like a small armchair. Hot Wells is frequented in the summer and Bath, eight miles away, in the winter. There are all kinds of amusements in Bath, the place is delightful, and it is full of beautiful buildings. But since I saw it in summer when no one was there, I found it very lonely.

In the house in which I lived in Bristol there was a Captain Fenton[4] whose wife had remained in Boston with her fourteen-year-old daughter. He loved them both very dearly and begged me to take some letters to them when I left for America. On my arrival I learned that since he had not returned they had been arrested and treated very badly; but of this I shall speak in its place.[5]

I made still another acquaintance in Bristol, which I shall ever

2. At Hot Wells today there is little more than "remains" of a resort that was a very thriving place in the 18th century. Hot Wells, or Hotwells, figured in Tobias Smollett's novel *Humphrey Clinker* (1771) and Fanny Burney's *Evelina* (1778). See *Blue Guide: England*, 143.

3. Wendefurth is mentioned, without description, in Karl Baedeker's *Deutschland* (Leipzig, 1932), 205. Nearby Blankenburg was also a health resort at the foot of the lower Harz. The county of Blankenburg passed to the duchy of Brunswick-Wolfenbüttel in 1599.

4. There are two Fentons mentioned in Worthington C. Ford, *British Officers Serving in the American Revolution, 1774–1783* (Brooklyn, 1897), 69. The second one (who is not listed with a Christian name) was appointed an ensign in the 44th Regiment on Aug. 15, 1775. It is possible, though questionable, that this is the same man.

5. See below, p. 70.

prize dearly. When I left Wolfenbüttel a young Mr. Lee, nephew of the American General Lee,[6] a student at Caroline College in Brunswick,[7] had given me a letter of introduction to an English banker named Ireland, whom he recommended to me highly, assuring me that I would be well satisfied with him. Although I had little confidence in the recommendation of this young man, I nevertheless sent the letter to the above-mentioned banker, who lived six English miles from the city. One day shortly afterwards a gentleman, already elderly but with a very pretty wife, came to call on me. I had the fortune to win their friendship right away, and they urged me very much to visit them. I therefore drove over to their place to dine. They resided on a magnificient estate, which had a delightful situation and garden. I found there two of the most charming little girls, their daughters, their whole joy, although they still wanted a son very much. They were rich, and everything they had was magnificent.

These good people showed me much friendship, and when I set out to embark at Portsmouth, I had to promise them that if the ship were delayed, as often is the case, I would not sail after the middle of October. Afterwards, having just missed sailing, I came back to London, from which I wrote them in the spring that I was then about to sail. Hereupon these good people came all the way to London, which, I believe, is eighty-six English miles from their estate, to offer me their services. Since there was nothing I needed, they gave me letters of introduction for all the ports at which I might possibly be detained by unfavorable winds, so that I should lack for nothing. When I arrived safely in Quebec, and no longer needed the letters, I opened them, and was deeply moved when I found that they had asked all their friends to give me as much money as I might wish,

6. Gen. Charles Lee had traveled in Germany in 1765, visiting Brunswick and Berlin, where he had met the Hereditary Prince of Brunswick and Frederick the Great, who "was sufficiently impressed by Lee to remember him more than a decade later." Lee was appointed second-ranking major general of the American army in June 1775. Lee, however, had only an unmarried sister; therefore, the "young Mr. Lee" could not have been his nephew. John R. Alden, *General Charles Lee, Traitor or Patriot?* (Baton Rouge, 1951), 2–3, 26–27, 75. See also H. Manners Chichester, "Lee, Charles," *Dictionary of National Biography,* and Randolph G. Adams, "Lee, Charles," *Dictionary of American Biography.*

7. This establishment for higher learning was founded by Duke Karl I (1713–80). See article on Karl I in *Allgemeine deutsche Biographie,* XV, 266–72.

however much that might be. When the lady finally gave birth to a son, they asked me to be a godparent, which among the English is a great mark of friendship. I have often wished that this son might someday come to Brunswick, so that I might repay his parents for all the friendship they expressed to me, which I have never forgotten.

I spent three or four months in Bristol, and I longed for nothing more ardently than to follow my husband soon, especially since I knew that Quebec was in English hands. But I could never persuade Mrs. Foy to leave. She told me that first she would have to await letters from her husband in America. In the meantime it became ever later in the year. Therefore I wrote to the minister, Lord George Germain,[8] seeking his advice. He answered me very courteously, that it was quite true the latter part of the year was at hand, which must make me long all the more to sail, since my husband had written me to come. But since he had at the same time imposed the condition that I was to travel with Mrs. Foy, and since he realized I was determined to carry out his wishes in every particular, he [Germain] knew not exactly what to advise me. In any case he would offer me passage in a packet-ship. All that I had to do was to induce Mrs. Foy to join me. But with her, every persuasion was fruitless. At last came the long-expected letter from her husband in America, which brought my patience, and also her determination, to an end. At length I succeeded in persuading her to consent to our departure. Therefore I wrote again to Lord Germain, who very obligingly wrote me right away that he had a packet-ship which was to leave without delay, and that he was offering me all the cabins for myself and those with me, and that I could let Mrs. Foy share them. He added that I would find

8. George Sackville Germain, first Viscount Sackville (1716–85), a follower of Lord North, became secretary of state for the colonies in 1775. His military career was badly blemished. At Minden (1759) he was thoroughly inept and was found guilty by a court martial of not obeying Prince Ferdinand of Brunswick. Nevertheless, he was given this high post by Lord North. He was no more successful in bringing Madame de Riedesel and her husband together than he was in effecting a union between Burgoyne and Howe. Gerald S. Brown, "The Court Martial of Lord George Sackville, Whipping Boy of the Revolutionary War," *William and Mary Quarterly*, 3d Ser., 9 (1952), 317–24. Recent studies of Germain include G. S. Brown, *The American Secretary: The Colonial Policy of Lord George Germain, 1775–1778* (Ann Arbor, 1963), and Alan Valentine, *Lord George Germain* (Oxford, 1962). General Riedesel had instructed his wife to write Germain when she got to England. See below, p. 162.

everything aboard set in suitable order, and that it was a boundless satisfaction to him to be of service to me. I later learned also that he had actually given orders for all necessary provisions to be brought aboard for us, even a cow, so that the children might have milk. Yet the captain of the packet-ship made my husband pay for all this at his arrival in Quebec.

The nearer the moment of our departure approached, the more irresolute became Mrs. Foy, who loved her comforts and who was loath to leave her pretty and well-furnished house. Finally we left for Portsmouth, where we were to embark. Here Mrs. Foy and her sister found many old acquaintances among the officers, with whom they spent a very gay evening, while I busied myself putting the children to bed. These officers told them that it was already too late in the year, that they would have an unpleasant voyage, that it would be a great pity for such pretty ladies to expose themselves to such danger, and many other things which I did not understand because I did not have enough command of the language. Suffice it to say, the result was that she assured me the very same evening she would return to Bristol. I urgently entreated her not to make a hasty decision, and went to bed while she remained with her company.

The following morning at eight o'clock I was told I must report immediately. I begged and I wept, but all in vain, for she knew all too well that my husband had recommended that I not travel without her. She had already sent our cartman back to Bristol with our baggage. I knew, therefore, that there was nothing I could do; our carriage was in front of the door, and I must go. As we were driving out of the city I saw a large wagon, escorted by a mounted guard. I asked what it meant. My English girl (I had engaged an English maid here for my trip) told me it was money, which was being brought onto the ship. My heart sank at this, and I remarked to Mrs. Foy that if they yet dared to ship so much money on this vessel it could hardly be so late in the year.[9]

"Very well," she answered me, "if you think that, why do you not set out?"

"Because you have prevented me," I replied, "by sending our luggage back to Bristol without consulting me."

She answered me in a mocking tone that, if I were so stouthearted,

---

9. Compare with the previously unpublished letter of Madame de Riedesel on pp. 187–89.

I could go ahead on my journey with the few clothes I had with me, and she would send my baggage after me on another ship. This woman was generally very gentle, but allowed herself to be misled by her sister, who was disagreeable, and who was in dread of the trip. The tone in which she said this gave me the courage and resolution to leave her and to turn back to Portsmouth to await ship there, for another was yet to arrive. It was expected at any minute, and I had all the less reason for doubting its speedy arrival, for I had no conception of the dilatory nature of seafaring people and how often they are delayed. Accordingly I sent my trusty footman, Rockel, with all dispatch after the cartman, who fortunately understood a little German, and was easily persuaded, therefore, to unload my baggage. Then I left Mrs. Foy and returned to the place from which I had come, where I resolved to wait for the ship as long as the time of the year would permit, promised by my friends, the Irelands, and especially assured by the family of Admiral Douglas,[10] whose acquaintance I had made there, and by other good people, that I could probably count on two weeks yet of good weather. Even the officers whom I had seen with Mrs. Foy could not deny this, excusing themselves, when I reproached them for having ever spoken to the contrary, on the score that they had found those ladies so timid that they thought they would make themselves much more pleasing to them by advising against the trip.

I often dined at the Douglas house. Since I was not yet sufficiently acquainted with the customs of the country, I was always afraid of appearing like Ninette at court,[11] in the comedy. For example, I could never bring myself to eat vegetables simply boiled in water, as the English do, until I noticed that others poured an excellent butter sauce over them. Hereupon I did likewise, and found them even better than the way we eat them. However, vegetables in England are so good that one can even eat them simply boiled in water with salt.

10. Sir James Douglas (1703–87) had captured Dominica in 1761 and helped take Martinique in 1762, but he saw little service after the start of the American Revolution. J. K. Laughton, "Douglas, Sir James (1703–1787)," *DNB*. General Riedesel also visited Admiral Douglas. See below, p. 165.

11. *Ninette à la Cour*, a comedy in two acts by the composer Charles Favart (for whom the Salle Favart in Paris is named), was first performed in 1755. It is the story of a peasant maid who found herself in the thick of affairs at court. La Harpe judged the piece to be very superior. Larousse, *Grand Dictionnaire Universel*, XI, 1009.

Yet another embarrassment I encountered was in the matter of drinking. People did me the honor of offering in turn to drink a glass of wine with me. I had already heard something about this custom, and that a person would be offended if someone refused such an offer. Since I was nursing my youngest daughter, Caroline, and therefore could not drink any wine at all, I had much embarrassment. The first day I did not have the heart to decline, but since I feared I would do eventual harm to my little one, I finally asked, in all frankness, whether they would be offended if I returned the compliment in water rather than in wine. They smiled and assured me that ill-natured or poorly bred persons perhaps might take this ill, but proper people would excuse it, and thus I was relieved of hesitation about this.

In the English Church prayers, the Lord's Prayer, and the Ten Commandments are said aloud. I was astounded at first hearing everyone praying aloud, which made such a great noise that I was on the point of running out of the church. Finally, however, I did as the others.

The women in England must always wear a bonnet in church, and fingers would be pointed at them if they entered without them. When I returned to Germany and my daughters and I appeared in church in bonnets, people stared at me. Now many wear hats in church. So it goes with every strange fashion.

I stayed in Portsmouth, constantly expecting the arrival of the ship. Finally, everyone assured me that I would be risking too much, especially on account of the children, by going to sea this late in the year, and that there were a hundred chances to one against any more ships reaching Quebec this year, on account of the ice with which the St. Lawrence River would be covered at this season.[12] This was a dreadful state of affairs, since I had waited so long, but to have remained aboard ship that length of time would have been still worse, and I resolved to give up the voyage entirely, particularly because of the children, for whom I felt anxious. Had I been alone, I would have risked it.

Portsmouth is an agreeable seaport, and what makes it an all the more interesting place in which to reside is that one sees ships arriving there every day, announcing themselves by their cannon. Then people run to the shore and await their arrival with impatience. Ships

12. For freezing of the St. Lawrence, see Hadden, *Journal,* 39–42.

are built there, and the dockyard is magnificent, as is also the academy in which the young people who are destined for the merchant marine service are trained. Never before have I seen such order and cleanliness in a public school. Since my visit all this has burned to the ground. The admiral's house is beautiful, and has a magnificent view. The city is surrounded by a wall, on which are beautiful promenades. There are a number of beautiful houses in Portsmouth, and the people, although sailors for the most part, are more courteous than in Bristol. The admiral saw to all this, and strictly punished all disorder, though otherwise he was a kind and pleasing man.

My money was running short, for I had only sent for what I needed for my passage and for equipment during the trip. The voyage and my stay in Portsmouth, which cost me so much, had completely exhausted my purse. I was, therefore, no little pleased to find friends in the same inn where I was staying, to whom I might turn in case of some possible embarrassment. These were Captain Young and his wife, who came from Tobago. The Captain had served in the Seven Years' War as adjutant under our Duke,[13] then Hereditary Prince, to whom he was very much devoted, and since he also knew my husband well, he offered to have me go with them to London and reside there with them, with me sharing my part of the expenses. He was a man of middle age, and his wife about thirty years old, very sallow and not pretty, but with a friendly face. I thanked Heaven for this discovery, and since I saw that all my hopes of going to Quebec this year had been denied, I promised to follow them, which I did in a few days.

On the way I stopped at a small but nice town, whose name escapes me. Since I was afraid I would have to pay as much as I did in Portsmouth, I asked only for a small room, a leg of mutton, and potatoes. The hotel itself was magnificent, and all its interiors were of the greatest elegance. The halls and the gallery, in a word the whole house, were decorated from the outside in with potted flowers and trees that intertwined, between which hung glass globes with goldfish and birds. I was alarmed at this elegance and feared for my guineas, especially when I saw myself led into the most handsome

13. Karl Wilhelm Ferdinand (1735–1806) was the eldest son of Karl I and Philippine Charlotte, sister of Frederick the Great. He fought at Minden, and became the reigning Duke in 1780. *Allgemeine deutsche Biographie*, XV, 272–81. The Riedesels felt more affectionate towards Karl I, and Madame de Riedesel spoke indiscreetly about the Hereditary Prince. See below, p. 155.

rooms and my table bounteously supplied with five or six of the most choice dishes. When the proprietor himself served me at the table, I said to myself: "This will cost yet another guinea!" The next morning I found my servants drinking chocolate and coffee and eating tarts and other tidbits, and I could not restrain myself from giving them a small reproof for having ordered such treats when they knew how little money I had. They assured me that they had ordered nothing more than tea, but that the proprietor had said to them that such good people, who wanted to follow their master and mistress to America, must be well provided for. In short, there was no attention or courtesy that was not heaped on me. At last, with fear and trembling, I asked for my bill, and lo and behold, I had to pay only ten shillings! I said to my host that surely he had made a mistake. "No," he answered me, "I have charged you more than my expenses, and I consider myself fortunate to be able to show you that there are honest people in England. I admire your courage, and I want to express to you my admiration."

When I climbed into my carriage, I found it decorated with garlands and wreaths, and when I accidently put my hand into one of the pockets I found that our host had had the kindness to fill it with cakes and oranges for the children.

I arrived in London at the end of September, and shortly learned, to my great chagrin, that the ship, for which I had so ardently waited, had reached Portsmouth and had straightway departed again for America. Meanwhile, people assured me that I would have been taking too great a risk by having left so late in the year. However, I later learned that the ship reached its destination safely, but another, which left only a few days later, had been shattered by the ice, although its crew was rescued.

I was now in London with the Youngs, where my board and lodging were the very best, and whenever I spoke of paying, I would receive the answer, that they were only too fortunate to have found me to live with them. This really placed me in a very embarrassing position, for I supposed they were immeasurably wealthy, and that for this reason they did not want to take money from me. Therefore it occurred to me to have my portrait painted on a bracelet set with diamonds which I still had, and to present this to the lady at my departure, since in this way I could discharge my obligations without expense to my husband.

I spent my time with Mrs. Young, who was at the same time both very sickly and something of a hypochondriac, and with our housekeeper, Mrs. Bohlen, a worthy and lovely lady, and I considered myself quite fortunate. Meanwhile, Mrs. Young renewed her old acquaintances, spent a good deal of money, bought gowns and hats by the dozens, and filled the house with dressmakers and milliners, and, when she was finished with all this preparation, asked me to go with her to public resorts and to parties. I excused myself on the score that I was nursing my child, whom I therefore could not leave; moreover, that I was too sad and ill-at-ease with my husband away to want to have any part in such things. Finally, I added that I also dreaded the great expense, and that she knew I was expecting money from Germany and wanted not to misuse the confidence of my husband who had provided for my expenses with a completely free hand. She took my refusal very badly, for it was her intention to go out, and she thought it would be more becoming if she were accompanied. Therefore, instead of acting in her hitherto friendly way, she became almost rude to me, and what made matters even worse was that her husband praised me for having such love for my children that I did not go out. Therefore, she came to me one day and asked me whether I had found lodgings. Since they had so often repeated their invitation for me to stay still longer with them, I had, to be sure, given the matter no further thought; nevertheless, I now answered that I was already seeing to it. She replied that she knew of a place for me, and that she would go with me to look at it. Thereupon she led me to a wretched little place, which was on a bad and out-of-the-way street. I told her I thought this was too poor a place, and that I would rather economize in other ways than on my dwelling, which would have to be good since I had letters of introduction to various ladies of quality and would be in the position of having to receive them in a fitting way. She answered me sarcastically that, since I was such a good housekeeper and lived so quietly, she would have thought that this would have sufficed for me.

As we were driving away from there, I noticed an advertisement on a corner house in a good neighborhood. I went in and found that, although the dwelling was indeed small, it was clean and respectable. Four pounds a week was being asked. I said that this was more than I was in a position to give, but that I could give assurance that if they would let me have it at a lower rate, I would always be home at an early hour, and my doors would be closed by ten o'clock. The landlady looked at my children, and, when she heard my story and my predicament, said to her husband: "Just hear! We have no children, and these will take the place of children of our own. That is better than a few more guineas!" And at this she let us have the lodgings for three pounds a week, with furniture, kitchen utensils, and linen.

I immediately took leave of my former hosts and moved to my new dwelling, where I was very happy, for not only was I well lodged, but also my host and hostess became my warmest friends. I said to them in all sincerity that it was my intention not to spend too much, that my husband, to be sure, had given me a free hand, but that for just this very reason I wanted to limit my expenditures. Furthermore, I told them that my total capital at that time consisted of ten guineas, and I might receive nothing more for six weeks. "Well," replied Mrs. Russell, my new landlady, "I shall be your housekeeper, and buy your bread and meat, and the rest you can have from us, and as for your rent, you can pay at your convenience."

Both of them taught my children English, and when I had to go out I confidently left them in their charge. When I was about to leave the following spring, I could see that the husband was very sad and worried. I inquired as to the cause. "Ah," said the wife, "It is your leaving which saddens him so, and especially little Caroline, and he has charged me to beg you to leave her with us." "What would you do with her were I perchance to die?" I answered. "Oh," she replied, "the moment you left her with us, we should take her as our own, and give her all we have." Whenever I wanted to buy trifles for my children the good woman asked me every time whether the expediture did not exceed the sum which I had allowed for myself. I felt myself very fortunate to be with such upright people, and I had all the more reason to thank Providence for having been delivered from the Youngs, for she had subsequently contracted so many debts that she was nearly arrested, and after the husband fled their belongings were attached. In the end the woman lived on the charity of her friends. I would, therefore, have had a thousand vexations had I kept my connection with these people.

I cannot praise too highly the conduct of the English nation towards me. Even persons whom I did not know came and offered me as much money as I might need, and, when I expressed my amazement at this to them, saying that they could not really know whether I were not an imposter, they would answer that, if this were the case, I would not live in such a retiring way and would not devote all care to my children as I did.

I was advised that I should be presented at court, since the Queen had expressed the desire to see me. Therefore, I had a court-dress made, and Lady George Germain presented me. It was on New Year's Day, 1777. I found the palace very ugly and furnished in an old-fashioned style.[14] The ladies and gentlemen all placed themselves in the audience room. Hereupon the King, preceded by three courtiers, entered the room. He was followed by the Queen, accompanied by a lady who carried her train, and a chamberlain. The King went around to the right, and the Queen to the left. Neither passed anyone without saying something to him. At the end of the hall they met, exchanged low obeisances, and each went where the other had been. I asked Lady Germain what I was supposed to do, and whether the King, as I had heard, kissed all the ladies. "No," she replied, "only English women and marchionesses, and the only thing to do is to stand quietly in place." When the King reached me, then, I was much amazed that he kissed me, and turned fiery red as a result, since it came to me quite unexpectedly. He asked me right away whether I had letters from my husband. "Yes," I said, "of the 22nd of November." "He is well," he replied. "I have made special inquiries about him. Everyone is well satisfied with him, and I hope the cold will not do him harm." I answered I believed and hoped that, since he was born in a cold climate, the cold would not trouble him. "I hope so also," said he, "but of this I can assure you, the air there is very healthful and clear." At this he gave me a very friendly salutation and went on. After he had moved along, I said to Lady Germain that now, through the King's kiss, I was naturalized. Then came the Queen, who was also very friendly towards me, and asked me whether I had been long in London. "Two months," I said. "I thought it was longer," she replied. I answered that I had been in London only that long, but that I had been in England already seven months.[15] She asked me whether I liked it here. "Yes," I said, "but I nevertheless badly want to be in Canada." "Are you not," she further queried, "afraid of the sea? I do not care for it at all." "Neither do I," I replied, "but there is no other way to see my husband again, and, therefore, I shall joyfully make the voyage." "I admire your courage,"

14. This was St. James' Palace, built by Henry VIII. Tharp, *The Baroness and the General*, 67–68.

15. Perhaps the Baroness was being polite in insisting she had been in London only two months. Above she says she arrived at the end of September.

said she, "for that is a great undertaking, and especially difficult with three children."

From this conversation I saw that she had already heard more of me, and for this reason I was very pleased to have been presented at court. After this levée I saw all the royal children, with the exception of one, who was sick. There were ten, all of whom were pretty as a picture. Since I had been so well received, I returned a number of times. In the spring, just before my departure to Portsmouth to embark, when I was taking my leave of the Queen, she asked me again several times whether I was not afraid of such a dreadful voyage. And, when I replied that since my husband wanted me to follow him I found courage and satisfaction in doing so, because I believed I was fulfilling my duty, and that I was assured that were she in my place she would do the same thing, she said to me: "Yes, but people have written to me that you are undertaking this voyage without the knowledge of your husband." I responded that since she was a German princess, she would know full well that I could not undertake this without the consent of my husband, because otherwise the money for it would have been lacking. "You are right," said she, "I approve of your resolution, and wish you every imaginable success. What is the name of your ship? I will often inquire after you, and when you return I hope you will visit me." She kept her word and often inquired after me and often sent me her greetings.

General Burgoyne [16] had promised my husband that I could travel with him, and for this reason I asked Lord George Germain for advice. He told me that a man-of-war would indeed be safer, but since on such a ship the captain was completely independent, taking no pay for the cost and the passage, this would be unpleasant for me,

16. John Burgoyne (1722–92) became a member of Parliament in 1761, and such claim as he had to military success was largely based on his actions the following year in Portugal. At the outbreak of the American Revolution he had already served in America during 1774–75. While most of his career as a dramatist was after the American Revolution, his *Maid of the Oaks* appeared in 1774 and was a success. It is significant that H. M. Stephens, "Burgoyne, John," *DNB*, called him "dramatist and general" in that order. Burgoyne returned to England in the winter of 1776–77, presumably carrying General Riedesel's letter of Oct. 26 to the Baroness, and subsequently overseeing the Baroness' sailing arrangements; see General Riedesel's letter of June 5, 1777, below, p. 193; and see also Edward B. De Fonblanque, *Political and Military Episodes in . . . the Life and Correspondence of . . . John Burgoyne . . .* (London, 1876); Hadden, *Journal*, 387–429.

especially since I had children. Therefore he advised me rather to take a merchantman. Mr. Watson,[17] a rich London banker, a worthy man who had already been lord mayor three times (the same whose foot once had been bitten off by a shark while he was bathing in the West Indies), had seen my husband in Canada and had promised him his ship for me. General Howe, an old friend of my late father and also my friend, strongly advised me to accept it,[18] and he promised me, in order to give more importance and safety to the ship, a letter of marque and sixty men and two officers. Mr. Watson was well pleased with this arrangement, for it was very advantageous for the ship's owner; but, on the other hand, a ship is thus exposed to danger if it encounters the enemy. Mr. Watson showed me the ship and introduced me to the captain and the entire crew, declaring to them that whoever might give me offense might expect the same punishment as though he had done the same to himself, and that should I complain of any one of them that man would be discharged immediately.

The ship was large and spacious, and right away all was arranged just as I wanted.

Since I knew that it would please my husband, I wrote to Mrs. Foy and invited her to sail with me. She accepted, and all that was past was forgiven and forgotten. We met in Portsmouth and on the 15th of April, 1777, at about five in the afternoon we boarded ship, where the entire evening we were much busied with putting our things in order, and at nine o'clock we retired.

17. Sir Brook Watson (1735–1807), merchant, was a member of Parliament for London, 1784–93. He was Lord Mayor in 1796, and baronet in 1803. In 1782 he became commissary under Carleton in Canada. Col. E. M. Lloyd, "Watson, Sir Brook," *DNB*. Lt. August Wilhelm Du Roi also records Watson's mishap with the sharks. Charlotte S. J. Epping, trans., *Journal of Du Roi the Elder* . . . (N. Y., 1911), 29.

18. Madame Riedesel and her father could have known Gen. William Howe (1729–1814) through Howe's mother, Sophie Charlotte Marie, sister of the General Kielmansegg mentioned in General Riedesel's letter of Mar. 21, 1776. However, it is doubtful that General Howe advised the Baroness on transportation at this time, for he was busily engaged in America as commander in chief of the British army. He was relieved by Clinton in May 1778. H. Manners Chichester, "Howe, William," *DNB*. See also Hadden, *Journal*, 373–80.

III

Voyage to Quebec

On April 16, 1777, when the warship *Blonde*[1] had given the signal, our fleet, consisting of thirty-one ships, sailed from Spithead to St. Helen's,[2] where we waited for the warship *Porpoise* which was to accompany us. Almost all of us were seasick that day, particularly as we had dropped anchor; for then I feel the motion of the ship is much more unpleasant.

On the 17th the wind came up and on the 18th at six o'clock in the morning the second signal was given, and, much to the satisfaction of all, we sailed off.

On the 19th we passed Plymouth with a good wind. Almost all of us were well, and my three children and I felt entirely at home. The weather was so fine that we danced on deck to the music of an excellent fifer and two drummers.

On the 20th, 21st, 22nd, and 23rd we had contrary winds, storms, high waves, and rain. All the passengers were ill except myself, and I had no time to be sick, as my servants were sicker than all the rest, and I had to take care of my three children alone. I believe there is no better preventative against seasickness than to keep busy, for on the first day out I was as ill as the others; however, when I saw that the children were also ill, with nobody to care for them, all my thoughts were concentrated on them, and I immediately felt better myself, and my appetite returned. In fact, one has nothing else to

1. The *Blonde* was a 32-gun, fifth-rate ship. *Royal Kalendar* (1778), 144. This ship, which escorted the Brunswickers to Canada the previous year (see below, chap. 4, n. 1), was now commanded by the obviously inexperienced Capt. Milligen. Lord Howe to Admiralty, Aug. 28, 1777, Admiralty Papers 1/487, Public Record Office, London.

2. St. Helen's is on the east of the Isle of Wight, just south of Portsmouth.

do aboard ship but to eat and drink. We had four and sometimes five or six dishes daily, all excellently cooked. On rising in the morning I had breakfast in our cabin, washed and dressed the children, then dressed myself and went up on deck. When I could, I sewed or embroidered.[3] At two o'clock we had dinner, at six o'clock tea, and at eight o'clock I went below and undressed the children. Then I had my supper, and at ten o'clock I went to bed. My eldest daughter, Augusta, was very ill for two days, but after that she felt better than ever; the other two children were scarcely sick. All three had excellent appetites.

On the 24th we had clear but rather cool weather, and the wind was very low.

On the 25th day we were becalmed and hardly moved from the spot. The rudder broke, but the captain, who understood such things well, repaired it immediately. Since our departure we had sailed only 250 nautical miles.

I do not know whether it was because the joy of seeing my husband soon again had given me courage, but I did not find the sea so frightful as I had thought, and did not regret in the least having undertaken the voyage. I was conscious of doing my duty and was calm, because I had absolute faith that God would guide me safely to my husband. I would gladly have sent my servants back home, because they were much more nervous and afraid than I and were, therefore, almost useless to me. I felt sorry for them, for they really had not the same interest in the trip as I, since I constantly looked forward to seeing my beloved husband again. With the children it was an entirely different matter, for even when they were very seasick, if I asked them whether they would rather go back home than continue with the trip, they replied, "Oh, we will cheerfully be sick if we can only go to Papa!"

On the 26th the wind picked up again and we made good headway.

On the 27th we had divine services on the ship. It was a very edifying sight to behold the entire crew kneeling in fervent prayer. In the evening the wind changed, and the ship rocked so terribly that many of the passengers got sick again, but not so badly as the first time. I fell several times, and one of my daughters got her finger pinched in a door that slammed shut, and the other hurt her chin.

On the 2nd of May we had gone 650 nautical miles.

3. Madame de Riedesel's words: "so arbeitete ich."

From the 3rd to the 6th we had a bad wind and storm, so that on account of the bad weather no services were held on the 4th. In the night, from the 5th to the 6th, the storm rocked the ship about so terribly that we could not sleep a wink, and I was constantly in fear of crushing one of the children, as all three of them slept with me. Little Frederika never went to bed without praying for her father, and one night after her prayers she said, "I wish that I could soon see my dear Papa." I asked her what she would pray for when she was with her father again, to which she replied, "Then I shall pray to God every day that He will never separate us from him again." I was so touched that I could not help weeping.

Towards noon on the 6th the wind finally changed and was very good on the 7th, so that we were able to sail 130 miles in 24 hours. Everyone on board was delighted, and visits were exchanged between the ships. The ship *Henry* which had 134 men of our troops on board, was so polite as to hoist its flag, and the men aboard shouted "Long live our good General and his lady!" I called back, "Long live the whole ship!" and pointed to my three children as my most precious possession. Thereupon they shouted again, "Hurrah! Hurrah!" Immediately following they held their hour of prayer and sang hymns. My heart was very much touched. The battleship *Porpoise* came up beside us almost every day in order to inquire how I was feeling and to ask whether they could help us out with anything we might need. The captain of the ship had been a lieutenant on the ship on which my husband had sailed for Canada and through my husband's intervention had been made captain. Colonel Skin, Governor of Georgia,[4] and his son were also on board this ship. I had made his

4. This was no doubt Col. Philip Skene of Skenesborough, appointed lieutenant governor of Ticonderoga and Crown Point, and the townships in New York and New Hampshire which bordered on Lake George, Lake Champlain, and the Hudson in 1774. In England, with his son Andrew Philip Skene, during the winter of 1776–77, "he volunteered to join the proposed expedition under Burgoyne, became an intimate friend and companion of that General, returned to Canada in the spring of 1777, accompanied and took a prominent part in the expedition and surrendered with it at Saratoga." Thomas Jones, *History of New York during the Revolutionary War . . .* , ed. Edward F. de Lancey, 2 vols. (N. Y., 1879), I, 692–95. See also Doris Morton, *Philip Skene of Skenesborough* (Granville, N. Y., 1959), 52; Hadden, *Journal*, 505–17; Stone, trans., *General Riedesel*, I, 120. Du Roi laid the blame for Burgoyne's defeat on Skene. Epping, trans., *Journal of Du Roi*, 100–101, 113–15.

acquaintance in Portsmouth, where they were so kind as to offer to lend me two hundred guineas, if I should need money. Although I did not need the money, I will never forget their kindness.

On the 8th we met another ship which at first we took for an American. Although we had nothing to fear, I was a bit frightened anyhow, for I had no desire to witness a battle at sea. On the warship *Blonde* one of the ropes tore and four sailors fell into the water. One of them was saved, but the other three were drowned.

On the 9th we had sailed one thousand nautical miles, or about one-third of the voyage.

The wind was good on the 10th and 11th, so that on the latter day we coiled up one knot an hour (that is, a nautical mile, thus called because of the knots in the log line which is used for measuring the number of nautical miles).[5] On that day services were held and all the soldiers attended in dress uniform.

On the 12th the weather was fair, but the wind was not very favorable.

On the 13th it was better, and on the 14th it was variable and so foggy that during the night we were obliged to blow trumpets in order to warn the other ships not to come too close to us.

On the 15th it rained all day and was very cold, but the wind was favorable until noon, when it changed again, and from the 16th to the 21st we had an unfavorable wind, and the weather was mostly rainy and very cold. Another difficulty was that the captain of the *Blonde,* one of the ships convoying us, who had never made this voyage before, had sailed too far northward, which brought us back five hundred miles, so that we had to wait for a north wind to bring us to the Banks of Newfoundland.

On the 22nd we had a full moon and with it came a good wind, which brightened up all faces.

On the 23rd the wind was variable. While we could see the Banks, we could not reach them. I was reminded of the fox with the grapes in the fable and could have wept. We had been at sea five weeks already and had only gone 1660 miles. Moreover, it was so foggy that the warships fired off cannons every hour to prevent the other ships from getting lost.

5. Nautical terminology is confused here. Knotted ropes were uncoiled to indicate the number of nautical miles per hour, or knots, a ship was making. The number of knots reeled off on a log line in 28 seconds would indicate the number of nautical miles a ship would make in an hour.

One of the ships, the *Silver Eel,* lost her main mast, and during the night this ship and the *Porpoise* lost contact with us, which made me very unhappy because all my luggage, my husband's wine, and his uniforms were on board that ship. Not until the 30th did both ships catch up with us again.

On the 24th the weather was good, but the wind was contrary. Likewise on the 25th.

On the 26th we had a better wind and safely reached the Banks of Newfoundland. The cook caught a big codfish and brought it to me. Our captain, who was an old intimate friend of Madame Foy and took offense that the cook had not given the fish to her, tore it out of his hands, and threw it back into the water. However, I gave the good man a guinea for his kindness. We caught no more fish the whole day, and I had my triumph when the captain of the *Porpoise* sent me four codfish by tying them onto a board that was fastened to a rope and thrown into the water again. I treated all people on board with this fish as though nothing had happened, which apparently embarrassed the captain very much and made him regret his rudeness to me.

This incident was not the only unpleasantness which Madame Foy had caused me; indeed, I frequently had reason to regret having taken her along, because her sister, who also accompanied us, was not of the best demeanor, and was also capricious; and Madame Foy's old friendship with the captain prevented her from refusing him liberties which he had enjoyed in the past. Her maid, a beautiful creature, only made the trip in order to escape from a country in which she was too well known and in order to find the dissolute sort of friends she liked among the sailors. One day some of the captain's wine had been stolen, and my poor Rockel was accused of the theft. I felt deeply for the poor, honest fellow. Fortunately, however, another night when Mademoiselle Nancy (that was the maid's name) was about to pilfer some more wine, the ship suddenly gave such a lurch that she fell with the two bottles in her hands; she uttered such a cry that people came running to her, and thus the theft was discovered. She tried to explain that the sergeant in charge of the troops had told her to get the wine for him. This man was an old sot, who often spent the night with her in my antechamber, particularly on Saturday nights, when it was the custom on board to drink toasts to the wives and sweethearts. Fortunately I had made friends with the lieutenant, the old petty officers, and the pilot by often sharing my meals with them and their wives and children. They all came to me one night when these two had been carrying on the worst and said that they had felt sorry for me and had watched carefully, and if these wretches had troubled me, they would have immediately come to my assistance; they promised that they would thus keep watch over me every Saturday. I was touched by such kindness, which made me feel much relieved.

On the 27th, 28th, and 29th the wind was good and the weather fine. The *Blonde* had caught a hundred fish. They were big codfish, some of them weighing fifty pounds, and they were very good. They were hung about the ship, mouth upwards, cleaned and salted so that they would keep well.

On the 30th we had the finest weather in the world, but we were becalmed. It was a marvelous sight to behold each of the thirty ships on the open sea, which was as clear that day as a mirror. We had now passed the Great Bank and had gone 2112 miles altogether, or more than two-thirds of the voyage. We saw a number of whales quite close to our ship, and some of the young ones among them were from thirty-five to forty feet long.

On the 31st we had the joy of getting our first glimpse of land, called Chapeau Rouge. My heart beat faster with happiness. In the afternoon we passed the Isle of St. Pierre.

On June 1st it was rather rainy, but the wind was good.

On the 2nd it was calm at first, but a good wind came up later, and we passed the Isle of St. Paul and Cape Breton.

On the 3rd we reached St. Lawrence Bay and saw the Port Islands, which are great rocks. It was my husband's birthday, and my heart was filled with a mixture of joy and sadness and with the longing to be with him again soon, to hold him in my arms, and to bring him our dear children.

On the 4th we reached the St. Lawrence River and saw the mountains to our left. We met a multitude of ships making their way back to Europe, but the wind was so brisk that we could not converse with them. Many of our passengers said they had seen soldiers on board. This caused me inexpressible grief until our arrival, for it would have been dreadful to arrive in the strange country just as my husband was leaving it to return to Europe!

In the night of the 5th we passed Anticosti Island.

On the 6th we could see land and mountains on both sides of us and had gone 2760 nautical miles. I grew more restless from day to day and tried to calm myself by keeping as busy as possible. I had already finished a knitted nightcap for my husband, two purses, and seven caps for myself and the children, and a number of other small articles.

On the 7th the wind was very bad.

On the 8th, however, it was good again, and we only had 160 miles farther to go to Quebec.

On the 9th there was no wind at all, and we anchored near the island, Pot de Brandi.

On the 10th at four o'clock in the morning we weighed anchor and fortunately had now passed all the dangerous places. It was a wonderful sight to behold the shore on both sides, the houses, the big Montmorency Falls and then Quebec, which we reached on the 11th at ten o'clock in the morning. The heartfelt joy of seeing at last the so eagerly desired journey's end made me tremble from head to foot. Quebec presents a fine view from the water, and as I gazed upon it I thought of Emily Montague's letters,[6] in which she gives a lovely description of it with which I fully agree. However, the city, itself, is as ugly as can be and very inconvenient to walk about in, for one has to climb mountains when walking its streets. Few of the houses are good-looking either, but the inhabitants are polite. When we anchored I had a great satisfaction. The captain of our ship, who is otherwise a good man, but who, through his intimacy with Madame Foy, had not treated me very well, came to me and begged my pardon and asked for my intervention that none of his sailors be impressed. It happened that all ships were examined upon arrival to see how many sailors were on board, and if the number was considered larger than necessary, then some of them were taken away and put on the King's ships. I made this petition for him and was fortunate enough to have it granted.

When the news of my arrival reached Quebec all the ships lying in harbor fired their cannons in welcome, and at twelve o'clock noon we saw a boat approaching with twelve sailors dressed in white with silver helmets and green sashes. They had been sent to fetch me and brought me letters from my husband, in which he wrote me that he

6. Madame de Riedesel is referring to Mrs. Frances Brooke's *Emily Montague* (London, 1784), which gave a description of the natural setting of Quebec. See William L. Stone, trans. and ed., *Letters and Journals Relating to the War of the American Revolution, and the Capture of the German Troops at Saratoga. By Mrs. General Riedesel* (Albany, 1807), 75; hereafter cited as Stone, trans. *Mrs. General Riedesel*. This description is referred to by Thomas Anburey in his *Travels through the Interior Parts of America*, 2 vols. (London, 1789), I, 150.

had left to join the army. This news frightened and saddened me very much; but I immediately decided to follow him, even if only to be with him a few days. I got into the boat with my children and the servants and also asked for permission to take Madame Foy and her sister along, thus having the pleasure of making them ashamed of the troubles they had caused me. After our voyage of eight weeks filled with longing to reach our destination, we finally landed safely toward one o'clock. When we set foot on land I found a small carryall with one horse to meet me. This was Lady Carleton's[7] equipage, which she had sent with an invitation to come to dinner and to stay at her home. I accepted only the former invitation, because I wanted to join my husband immediately. I was very heartily welcomed by all at General Carleton's, and they could not do enough to express their joy over my safe arrival and assured me how very happy it would make my husband. Lady Carleton had been kind enough to send a messenger to her husband as soon as she learned that the fleet was expected and that I was on board, so that he could pass the good news on to my husband. Everyone was surprised to see me dressed like an Englishwoman, because the wives of our soldiers[8] had all arrived dressed in waistcoats, short wraps, and round caps with a *flebbe*,[9] and this was thought to be the German fashion. The general Canadian fashion for women is a very long coat of scarlet cloth; the wealthy ladies wear such a coat of silk; they never go out without it.

7. Lady Maria Carleton was the wife of Gen. Guy Carleton, first Lord Dorchester (1724–1808), who had a remarkable record at Louisbourg, Quebec (at which he was wounded), Belle Isle, and Havana, and became lieutenant governor of Quebec and finally governor after the departure of Gen. James Murray. After the resignation of Gage, command of British forces was divided between Carleton and Howe. Carleton withstood the siege of Quebec and retook Crown Point, only to be superseded by Burgoyne following a disagreement with Lord George Germain. Carleton left Canada in 1778, returning in 1782, when he replaced Clinton in command of North American forces in New York City. He was again governor of Quebec for the period 1786–96. G. F. Russell Barker, "Carleton, Guy," *DNB*. See also, Hadden, *Journal*, 429–38. For German praise of Carleton's efficiency and character, see Eelking, *German Allied Troops*, 90. For General Riedesel's opinion of Lady Maria Carleton, see his letter of April 16, 1777, below, p. 192.

8. Seventy-seven wives had accompanied the Brunswick soldiers. Eelking, *German Allied Troops*, 88. In England Madame de Riedesel dressed like a Frenchwoman, but in Quebec she dressed like an Englishwoman!

9. The *flebbe* came down from the sides of the cap to cover the ears. See Stone, trans., *Mrs. General Riedesel*, 77.

They wear a sort of *dormeuse* trimmed with large colored bows of ribbon, which distinguishes the aristocrats from the ordinary people, and of which the aristocrats are so proud that if one of the common women should dare to wear one, they would be apt to tear this decoration off her head. The long coats are often worn over very old and dirty dresses. In addition, they wear petticoats and jackets with long sleeves, and when they go out they wear big hoods which cover the whole head and face, and which in the winter are lined with down.

At two o'clock we sat down to dinner at Lady Carleton's table.

IV

An Interrupted Reunion

Captain Pownall,[1] with whom, as I have said before, my husband had made the voyage to Canada, offered to take me to Point de Tremble by water, and a Mrs. Johnson offered to accompany me. We embarked at six o'clock in the evening on the 11th of June, the day of my arrival in Quebec, in one of the boats of the warship, and with beautiful moonlight and splendid music we arrived at midnight at a place seven miles from Quebec. I put the children to bed, and the rest of us stayed up and drank tea.

On the 12th at half-past two in the morning we drove away in three calèches (a sort of light carriage or carryall, very small and uncomfortable, but in which one can drive very fast).[2] I had not the heart to leave a single one of my children with the maids but as the calèches were open and very small, I fastened my second daughter, little Frederika, in the corner, took the baby Caroline on my lap, and

1. Philemon Pownall was captain of the *Blonde* in 1776, carrying Burgoyne to Canada and escorting the first division of Brunswickers, with General Riedesel. He also was captain of the *Apollo,* which brought Burgoyne back to Canada on May 6, 1777. Admiralty's orders to Lord Howe, May 4, 1776, PRO Adm 2/1332; Lord Howe to Admiralty, Aug. 28, 1777, *ibid.,* 1/487. The Baroness, however, has not mentioned him before.

2. Throughout her journal Madame de Riedesel speaks of *Kalechen* (sing., *Kaleche*). She was probably using the word in two senses. Elsewhere this word has been translated "calash." A calash, properly speaking, was a conveyance with four low wheels, two seats intended for four people together, a separate seat for the driver, a removable front permitting the conveyance to be either open or closed, and a folding hood. A calèche, on the other hand, had two high wheels and a single seat, being built for speed. The calèche was something distinctive of Quebec. I have attempted to distinguish between the two sorts of conveyances. Besides the various better dictionaries, see Eelking, *German Allied Troops,* 95.

my eldest, little Augusta, most sensible, sat between my legs on my bag. I knew that if I wanted to see my husband I had no time to lose, as he was constantly marching farther away. I offered the servants a reward if they would drive me rapidly, and so they did. The Canadians always talk to their horses and give them all sorts of names. Whisking the whip they kept saying or singing, "Allons, mon prince!" "Pour mon général!" or sometimes, "Fi, donc, madame!" I thought they meant me and said "Plaît-il?" "Oh!" they replied, "ce n'est que mon cheval, la petite coquine!" Wherever I passed, the farmers greeted me and called "Voilà la femme de notre cher général!" and almost carried me on their shoulders. I was very happy to see how much everyone loved my husband and to hear them say to me, "Oh, qu'il sera content! Combien il a parlé de vous! Oh, qu'il vous aime!" That afternoon I arrived in Berthieux,[3] where I was told that I could get no calèche and would have to proceed in a boat, or rather a light canoe made of bark. I pleaded with the people and offered to pay any price whatever, as the weather was dreadful, and I would have to cross the three rivers which join and lead to the town of Trois Rivières. But it was all in vain, because the price for crossing by this ferry was the same as the mail-coach rate, and, since I was a stranger, they wanted to get out of me what they could. There was nothing left for me to do but to climb into the canoe. Sitting on the bottom in the corner of the canoe I held my three children in my lap, and my three servants sat on the opposite side. We had to keep absolutely balanced, but our boatman did not tell me this until suddenly a heavy hailstorm came up, which frightened my little Frederika so that she cried out and wanted to jump up from my lap. Then he told me that the slightest move we made could overturn the boat. I, therefore, had to hold her tight and not mind her crying; thus we finally arrived safe at Trois Rivières that evening, where our officers threw up their hands in horror, and I learned only then in what danger we had been. Two gentlemen had gone fishing, and when the storm came up their canoe had upset, and they were both drowned. I thanked God for having protected us, but I would rather have been left ignorant of the danger we had been in, because this made me afraid hereafter to cross the tiniest stream even in the finest weather.

3. Mrs. Tharp speculates that "Berthieux" was Batiscan. It certainly was some town on the right bank of the St. Maurice River, and not Berthier, which was up the St. Lawrence beyond Trois Rivières. Tharp, *The Baroness and the General*, 93.

The grand vicar called on me immediately. My husband, who had spent the whole winter at Trois Rivières,[4] had grown very dear to him, and he further increased my longing to join my husband by telling me about his devoted love and his anxiety about us during the voyage. He also told me that my husband had been ill, and that he was certain that it was due to the sorrow of having to leave without seeing us, particularly as all sorts of reports—fortunately false ones—had frightened him terribly. For instance, among others, that a lady with three children had been on board a ship that sank; and, another, that I had gone on board the first ship, but had suddenly become frightened and had insisted upon being taken back ashore. All this made me determined to hasten my journey as much as possible, and I had already sent a messenger to my husband to advise him of our coming. As the horrid weather continued, the grand vicar was so kind as to offer me a covered calèche, which I accepted, and at six o'clock the next morning we departed in it. This carriage rode so fast that we got all out of breath, and I was shaken about so, that I had to keep hold of the children constantly. I was bruised all over, and at every post station I had to get out in order to move my arms and legs and get the stiffness out of them. I had to choose between two roads to get to Chambly, where my husband was supposed to be. I took the road through Montreal, where I arrived in the evening of the 13th, spent the night there, and proceeded early the next morning in order to be with my husband as soon as possible. I arrived in Chambly[5] on the 14th, and the first thing I saw was a group of officers and our coachman, whom my husband had left behind. I ran up to him and asked him where my husband was. "He has gone to Berthier (which was a distance of fifteen English miles) to meet you," he said. I realized then that I had taken the wrong road and had therefore missed him. General Carleton, who was among the above-mentioned officers, came up to me and assured me that my husband would be back by the next day at the latest. He bade me goodbye and went back to Quebec, having turned over the command of the troops to General Burgoyne. An aide of my husband kept me company, and I waited with impatience for the next day to come, the 15th of June.

4. Trois Rivières was the center of the winter quarters for the German troops. The General recommended the grand vicar, M. Saint-Onge, to the Baroness in his letter of Apr. 16, 1777, below, p. 192. See also below, n. 8.

5. The winter quarters extended as far up the Richelieu River as Chambly, while the artillery of Hesse-Hanau was at Montreal.

My children and my faithful Rockel constantly stood in the road, watching so that they could bring me the news immediately when they saw my husband coming. At last a calèche, in which a Canadian sat, came into view. I saw the calèche halt, the Canadian step out, come nearer, and clasp the children in his arms. It was my husband! Since he still had a fever, although it was summer, he was dressed in Canadian fashion in a sort of cassock made of woolen blankets, from which the red and blue borders had not been removed, and which were heavily trimmed with ribbons. With the infant Caroline in my arms I ran as fast as I could to join this darling group. My happiness was indescribable, but my husband looked so ill and weak that I was very much frightened and my joy was somewhat dimmed. My two elder daughters were in tears, little Augusta because of the joy of seeing her father again, and little Frederika because he was dressed so oddly. She did not want to go to him at all and said "No, no! This is a nasty Papa; my Papa is pretty!" This outburst came because I had often showed her the picture of her father and pointed out to her that he had such pretty clothes. Accordingly, she did not recognize him in his present costume. However, when he took off the Canadian coat she embraced him affectionately.

My husband told me that when he had driven to meet me he had stopped for a rest with Colonel Anstruther[6] and had dinner there and learned that a woman had arrived from Berthier. They had asked her to come in and inquired whether there was any news from Berthier. She said there was none, except that a German lady had arrived with her children, who, it was said, was the wife of the German General. "How many children were there?" my husband asked immediately. "Three," she replied. He knew all he wanted to know then and was happy to learn that all three children were alive and well, because he had heard nothing from us all winter, and our ships were the first to arrive this year.[7]

We spent two happy days together. I wanted very much to accompany my husband, but he would not allow me to do so. To my great

6. Lt. Col. John Anstruther commanded the 62nd English regiment at Saratoga. He became full colonel in November, 1780. Anstruther was stationed at Sorel with his regiment to protect the transports and magazines, and presumably this is where the Baron dined with him. Stone, trans., *General Riedesel*, I, 102, 104, 120, 138. Ford, *British Officers*, lists him correctly on p. 18, but fails to show on p. 8 that he commanded this regiment.

7. General Riedesel had received direct news of his wife from Burgoyne, who had arrived in Quebec May 6, 1777. See below, p. 193.

sorrow, therefore, I was obliged to return to Trois Rivières. My sadness was intensified because the troops were marching toward the enemy, and my children and I were left to return alone and to live in a strange country among strangers. Sad and depressed I started on my journey. What a difference between this journey and the previous one! I was in no hurry this time, because my heart ached anew each time we reached another post station that increased the distance between my husband and me.

As we drove through the woods I suddenly saw something rise in front of our carriage like a cloud, which frightened us, until we discovered that it was a flock of wild pigeons, called *tourtes,* which are so plentiful there that the Canadian lives on them entirely more than six weeks in the year. He sets out on his pigeon hunt with a gun loaded with the smallest size shot. When he discovers a flock he makes a noise so as to startle them, whereupon they fly up and he fires at them at random, thus wounding as many as two to three hundred at a time, which he kills with sticks when they have dropped to the ground. The Canadian sells part of them and eats the rest himself, either in the form of delicious fricassee with cream and chives, or cooked as soup. At this time of the year everyone eats them.

The countryfolk are friendly and for the most part live in nice houses with large rooms, comfortably furnished, with good, curtained beds. Each house has a large entrance hall and at least three or four rooms. When the daughter of a Canadian marries, her father asks the son-in-law whether he wants to live with them; in that case the father builds the young couple a house and barn near his own house, and the surrounding land is made productive, thus increasing its cultivation and the population. The houses are all painted white, making a very pretty picture when one sails on the St. Lawrence River, because distance lends enchantment to everything. Each house has a little garden with fruit trees, and in the evening it is a charming sight to see the cows coming home. The cattle (together with the swine) are driven into the woods here, and the cows are brought back at a certain hour to be milked. Farmers do not fail to offer them some good food then, for otherwise they would not come back so readily. Sometimes a big sow, which is about to have young ones, stays away for a long time and then comes back with her litter. If they were kept locked up in a pen, like the pigs in our country, they would all die. They are very vicious and seem to be a cross between wild and domestic pigs.

I returned to Trois Rivières feeling very sad and uneasy. My constant companions were the grand vicar and his so-called "cousin."[8] At least my husband had presented her to me as such. She was very cheerful and conversed pleasantly. The grand vicar had these same qualities and was a man of intelligence. I learned later on that each of these gentlemen had a similar "cousin" as housekeeper and that almost every year these "cousins" were obliged, for certain reasons, to leave town for a while in order to avoid causing scandal.

In addition to these acquaintances I had the convent of the Ursuline Nuns,[9] or Sisters of Charity, who devoted their entire time to nursing the sick in a hospital there. On my first visit there, as I passed the door of the ward, one of the male patients saw me, ran to me and threw himself down before me crying, "Be my rescuer! Help me to die so that I may return to Germany!" I was told that the man was insane. I gave him something and hastened away.

Some of the nuns were very charming, and I spent many a pleasant day with them. They liked my husband very much, and I learned that he had often sent them wine and meat. I did likewise, and, what was more, I had my own food brought to the convent and ate with them. The pleasant company and, yes, perhaps also the wine and, finally, the desire to divert my thoughts often put the nuns into such good humor that they dressed up and danced a Cossack dance, or dressed me up as a nun. One of the novices who had taken a particular liking to me said that I looked very much like the Virgin Mary when I wore a nun's habit and pleaded with me to become a nun too. I said, "I should be glad to, if you will make my husband a prior and let him live with us." She was so innocent that she thought this could be done. She left me, and later on we found her kneeling before the crucifix, thanking God for my conversion. Then I sent for the children. Little Augusta started to cry when she saw me in the nun's

8. See the Baron's letter of Apr. 16, 1777, below, p. 192, for his comments on the grand vicar and his "cousin," Miss Cabenac. Abbé Pierre Maugue-Garaut de Saint-Onge (1721–95), a native of Montreal, was grand vicar and ecclesiastical superior of the Ursuline Convent at Trois Rivières from 1764 to 1788. Information provided by Bernard Weil Brenner and J. Antoine Pelletier, Archives, Ministère des Affaires Culturelles du Québec.

9. For the Ursuline Convent and nursing of the sick Brunswickers, see Stone, trans., *Letters of Hessian and Brunswick Officers*, 46; Eelking, *German Allied Troops*. Gérard Morisset, *Les arts au Canada Français: peintres et tableaux*, 2 vols. (Quebec, 1936–37), discusses the school of artists at the Ursuline Convent.

habit and said "Mama! do not become a nun, I beg of you!" In order to quiet the child I had to take off the clothes immediately. There was also a school for girls in the convent, where they were taught all sorts of handicraft. The nuns sang beautifully, and as the choir is always hidden by a curtain, one imagines that angels are singing.

My time at home was devoted mainly to caring for the children, doing needlework, and a little reading. The officers who had stayed behind were not a bit pleasant. Among them was a very disagreeable paymaster-general, who enraged me by his rude behavior and increased my uneasiness. When I wanted to give the money for my passage to Captain Arbuthnot,[10] whom I daily expected back from Montreal,[11] I presented the paymaster[12] an order from my husband to pay me one hundred and fifty pounds sterling. He refused to give me the money. I asked him whether my husband owed him anything. "No," he said, "on the contrary, he still has money to his credit," but as my husband was in danger and might be killed any day, he thought it wiser to be careful and not pay out any money to me. I was furious at this and told him that he made it very hard for me to ask him for money again, but I knew that even if I should have the misfortune of losing my husband, I would still be entitled to receive his pay for another quarter, which would amount to more than the sum for which I had asked. "That is true," he said, "but what about your return passage?" "Heaven will take care of that too," I rejoined. Without another word to him on the matter I turned from him to one of the English paymasters, who not only gave me the sum I asked for, but even offered to give me as much money as I might need. I reported this incident to my husband, who was very angry and wrote a very curt letter to the paymaster, giving him explicit orders to give me as much money as I might ask for. After this he grew more polite, and I even advanced so far in his favor that after his death letters

10. This reference is probably to Marriot Arbuthnot (1711–94), who was at this time lieutenant governor of Nova Scotia and commissioner of the navy at Halifax. He was promoted to flag rank in 1778 and in 1779 replaced Admiral Lord Richard Howe as commander in American waters. Beamish Murdoch, *A History of Nova-Scotia or Acadie,* 3 vols. (Halifax, 1866), II, 569, 593. J. K. Laughton, "Arbuthnot, Marriot," *DNB.*

11. The Baroness includes this footnote: "There furs can be bought very cheaply and are sold in England at a good price—many people make a lot of money in this way."

12. Johann Conrad Gödecke, who held the title of "Keeper of the Military Chest." He died Dec. 25, 1782 in America. Stone, trans., *General Riedesel,* II, 265.

from his wife were found in which she wrote, "You write me so many fine things about the general's wife that I am quite uneasy." Four years later, during his last illness I had the pleasure of sending him all sorts of things for his comfort, and he sent me word, begging my forgiveness for his uncivil behavior.

This man's remarks and the various disquieting reports received daily depressed me very much and embittered my days, particularly as I was often without mail from my husband, although he wrote me constantly. When letters did arrive, they were old. It is certain that one suffers a great deal more in anxiety for an absent loved one who is in danger than when one can share the danger with him. Therefore I wrote my husband and urgently begged him to let me join him, saying that I was well enough and had sufficient courage and would never complain regardless of what hardships I might have to endure. On the contrary, I hoped in many cases to be of help to him. He replied that as soon as it were possible for women to join the army, I should be among the first to come. He wrote later that my wish would soon be granted, and while I was eagerly waiting and had my things ready, Captain Willoe [13] came at last to fetch me. One can readily imagine what a welcome I gave him!

Two days later we started on our journey. Two boats, one belonging to my husband, took us to Trois Rivières. The crew on the former was under the good Sergeant Burich, who did everything he possibly could for me and looked after our luggage. When night came we were obliged to land on an island. The other boat, which was more heavily loaded and not so well manned, had not been able to keep up with us. We therefore had neither bedding nor light and, worst of all, no more food, for we had only taken on board what we required for the day, and we could find nothing on the island except the four bare walls of a deserted, half-built house, which was covered with bushes, in which to spend the night. I put our coats on the ground and got the cushions from the boat, and thus we slept quite well.

I could not persuade Captain Willoe to come into the cabin and noticed that he was very uneasy, but could not understand why. In the meantime I noticed that one of the soldiers had put a kettle on the fire. I asked him what was in it. "Potatoes, which I brought with

13. Capt. Samuel Willoe, who had been with the 8th English regiment, was attached to General Riedesel as an aide on Nov. 7, 1776. He remained long with the General in this capacity, and was regarded as "faithful and competent." Stone, trans., *General Riedesel*, I, 82; Ford, *British Officers*, 183.

me," he replied. I cast a longing glance at them. He had only such a few that I thought it would be cruel to deprive him of any, particularly as he seemed so happy to have them. In the end, however, my inordinate desire to give the children something to eat got the better of my modesty, so I begged him for some of the potatoes, and he gave me half of all he had, which was a dozen at the most. In addition, he took two or three bits of candle from his pocket and gave them to me, which made me very happy, as the children were afraid to stay in the dark. I gave him a plump thaler for everything, which made him just as happy as I was. In the meantime I heard Captain Willoe give the command that fires be made all around the cabin, and that his men make the rounds all night. I heard noises all night, which prevented my sleeping soundly. The next morning at breakfast, which was set out on a big flat rock, serving as a table, when I asked Captain Willoe, who had slept in the boat, what the noise in the night was, he told me that we had been in great danger, as this island is called *L'Isle aux Sonnettes* (Rattlesnake Island), so called because there are so many rattlesnakes on it; that he had not known this before and was very frightened when he learned it, but on the other hand, because of the currents, he could not risk going farther by water at night. There was nothing left but to build big fires and make as much noise as possible, in order to frighten the snakes and thus keep them away. He, himself, in his anxiety for our safety, had not slept a wink all night. I was horrified when I heard this tale, and remarked that we had increased our danger by lying on the grass, in which the snakes conceal themselves. He admitted this and said, had he known it sooner, he would have had all the grass removed, or would have told us to sleep in the boat. But he had only learned it from one of the men in the other boat, which had joined us later. In the morning we found the skins and slime of these horrible reptiles all over and hurried with our breakfast so as to get away as quickly as possible.

We crossed Lake Champlain and arrived in Fort John [?] at noon, where we were met with great friendliness and ceremony by the commander. This happened wherever we went, for my husband was very well liked by the natives, as well as by the English. We got into another boat, which took us out to a cutter by which we sailed to Wolf's Island, where we anchored and spent the night on board. There was a terrific thunderstorm during the night, which was particularly bad there, because, surrounded by hills and big trees, it was as though we were in a caldron. On the following day we passed

Ticonderoga, and toward noon we arrived at Fort George, where we had dinner with Colonel Anstruther, a very kind, pleasant man, in command of the 62nd Regiment. In the afternoon we got into a calash and arrived that same day (August 14) at Fort Edward, which place my husband had left with a farther advance of the army the day previous, but where he returned on the 15th when he learned of our arrival. He stayed with us there until the 16th. Then, to my great sorrow, he had to leave and join the army again. However, after the unfortunate affair at Bennington,[14] I had the pleasure of having him with us again on the 18th, and thereafter spent three happy weeks with him in peace and quiet.

A few days after my arrival the news came that we were cut off from Canada. Had I not availed myself of the fortunate opportunity when I did, I would have had to spend three years in Canada without my husband. The sole circumstance that led to this decision, so lucky for us, was the arrival of Lady Acland in camp,[15] on which occasion General Burgoyne said to my husband, "General, you ought to let your wife come too," whereupon my husband immediately sent Captain Willoe to fetch me. We were very happy during these three weeks! The country there was lovely, and we were in the midst of the camps of the English and the German troops. The place where we lived was called the Red House.[16] I had only one room for my husband, myself, and my children, in which all of us slept, and a tiny study. My maids slept in a sort of hall. When the weather was good we had our meals out under the trees, otherwise we had them in the barn, laying boards across barrels for tables. It was here that I

14. Well might she call the affair "unfortunate." After British victories at Castleton and Hubbardton, the Americans reversed the tide at Bennington. Riedesel had not agreed with Burgoyne's scheme; nevertheless, it was the battalion of Brunswick Dragoons which, with all their awkward equipment, fell victims of Stark's militiamen. This continental success encouraged a rapid swelling of the American forces, a major factor in Burgoyne's defeat. For good accounts, see Stone, trans., *General Riedesel,* I, 127–33; Eelking, *German Allied Troops,* 130; John R. Alden, *The American Revolution, 1775–1783* (N.Y., 1954), 141–42.

15. Lady Harriet Acland (1750–1815), had a fate quite different from Madame de Riedesel. See W. P. Courtney, "Acland, Lady Christian Henrietta Caroline," *DNB.* For her husband, see references below in Chap. 5, n. 15.

16. The Red House was at John's Farm between Fort Edward and Fort George. See Stone, trans., *Mrs. General Riedesel,* 92, 97; Stone, trans., *General Riedesel,* I, 133–34, 295.

ate bear meat for the first time, and it tasted very good to me. Sometimes we had nothing at all; but in spite of everything, I was very happy and satisfied, for I was with my children and was beloved by all about me. If I remember correctly, there were four or five aides with us. The evenings were spent at cards, while I busied myself putting the children to bed.

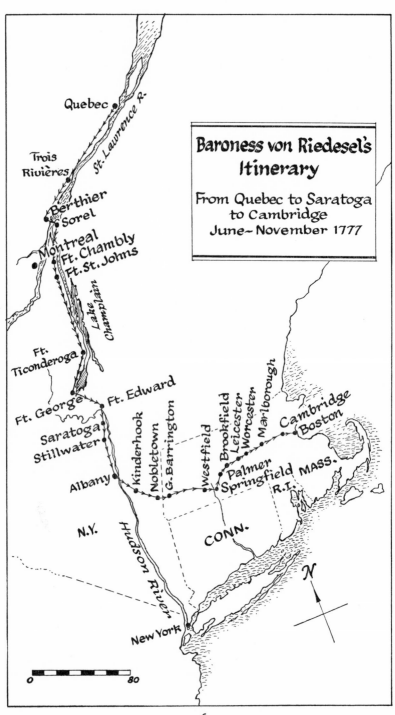

Baroness von Riedesel's
Itinerary

From Quebec to Saratoga
to Cambridge
June-November 1777

V

Saratoga

When the army marched again (September 11, 1777), it was at first decided that I was to stay behind, but upon my urgent entreaty, as some of the other ladies had followed the army, I was likewise finally allowed to do so.[1] We traveled only a short distance each day and were very often sorely tried, but nevertheless we were happy to be allowed to follow at all. I had the joy of seeing my husband every day. I had sent back the greater part of my luggage and had kept only a few of my summer clothes. Everything went well at first. We had high hopes of victory and of reaching the "promised land," and when we had crossed the Hudson and General Burgoyne said, "Britons never retreat,"[2] we were all in very high spirits. It displeased me, however, that the officers' wives were familiar with all of the army's plans and seemed all the more strange to me, as during the Seven Years' War I had noticed that in Duke Ferdinand's[3] army everything

1. For a criticism of Burgoyne for having allowed Madame de Riedesel to accompany the army, see Hadden, *Journal,* lxxxi. For a copy of Burgoyne's letter of Sept. 5, 1777, authorizing Madame de Riedesel to follow the army, see Hoffman Nickerson, *The Turning Point of the Revolution, or Burgoyne in America* (Boston and N. Y., 1928), facing 296–97.

2. For the recklessness of this move, which really committed the British completely after they broke up their bridge over the Hudson, see Alden, *The American Revolution,* 143, and Bruce Lancaster, *From Lexington to Liberty; The Story of the American Revolution* (N. Y., 1955), 286.

3. The Duke Ferdinand of Brunswick and Lüneburg (1721–92) was the brother of the reigning Duke Karl I and lieutenant field marshal in the Prussian army, the hero of the Battle of Minden (1759). *Allgemeine deutsche Biographie,* VI, 682–90. For General Riedesel's service under him during the Seven Years' War, see Stone, trans., *General Riedesel,* I, 3–8. General Riedesel himself was a stickler for secrecy. See below, p. 159, for his instructions to his wife not to reveal anything he wrote her "about American affairs."

was kept absolutely secret. Here, on the contrary, even the Americans were acquainted with all our plans in advance, with the result that wherever we came they were ready for us, which cost us dearly. On September 19 there was a battle, which, although it resulted in our favor, forced us to halt at a place called Freeman's Farm.[4] I saw the whole battle myself, and, knowing that my husband was taking part in it, I was filled with fear and anguish and shivered whenever a shot was fired, as nothing escaped my ear. I saw a number of wounded men, and, what was even worse, three of them were brought to the house where I was. One of them was Major Harnage,[5] the husband of one of the ladies of our party, the second a lieutenant, whose wife was also an acquaintance of ours, and the third was a young English officer named Young.[6] Major Harnage and his wife had the room next to mine. He had been shot in the abdomen and suffered much. A few days after our arrival I heard moaning in the other room next to mine and learned that it was the young English officer, Young, who was suffering great pain from his wound.

I was all the more interested in him as a family named Young had

4. This is something of an overstatement in view of the fact that Burgoyne's casualties were double those of the Americans. Although the British held their ground, they did not find it possible to advance, and their position now required nothing short of clear-cut victory. However, from Madame de Riedesel's point of view the engagement was a moral victory, since Burgoyne's forces, largely out of touch with Fraser's off to the right, were about to be broken, when Riedesel arrived from the left and prevented defeat. Stone, trans., *General Riedesel*, I, 149–50; Alden, *The American Revolution*, 144, 146.

5. Maj. Henry Harnage served on Colonel Anstruther's staff. He survived this ordeal and was promoted in 1780 to colonel. William L. Stone, *Visits to the Saratoga Battle Grounds, 1780–1880* (Albany, 1895), 194; Ford, *British Officers*, 90; Lt. Col. George Stanley, ed., *For Want of a Horse* (Sackville, N. B., 1961), 179.

6. The unidentified lieutenant was probably Lt. Thomas Reynell of the 62nd English Regiment, who died Sept. 19. Mrs. Reynell, who is mentioned also below, p. 59, by the Baroness, was left with three small children all under six years of age. Stanley, ed., *For Want of a Horse*, 179; James Phinney Baxter, ed., *The British Invasion from the North. The Campaign of Generals Carleton and Burgoyne from Canada, 1776–1777, with the Journal of Lieut. William Digby . . .* (Albany, 1887), 336, 339–40, where Baxter confuses the Baroness' account of another officer's death with that of Reynell's. Ens. Henry Young of the 62nd Regiment also died as a result of the Sept. 19 action. Ford, *British Officers*, 187; Stanley, ed., *For Want of a Horse*, 179; Baxter, ed., *Digby's Journal*, 336, 346.

been very kind to me while I was in England. I sent word to him
that I would be glad to do whatever I could for him and sent some
food and refreshment. He expressed a great desire to see his "bene-
factress," as he called me. I went to him and found him lying on
some straw, as he had lost all his baggage. He was a young man of
about 18 or 19 years old, actually a nephew of the Mr. Young whom
I had met in England, and an only son. His parents were his only
concern; he uttered no complaint about his pain. He had lost a great
deal of blood, and the doctors wanted to amputate his leg, but he
would not let them, and now gangrene had set in. I sent him some
pillows and blankets, and my maids sent a mattress. I redoubled my
efforts to help him and visited him every day, for which he called
down a thousand blessings upon me. In the end the amputation was
attempted, but it was too late, and he died a few days later. As he
lay in the room next to mine, the walls being very thin, I could hear
his groaning until the end came.

The house where I was staying was fairly well built, and I had a
large room.[7] The doors and wainscot were of solid cedar, which is
quite common here. It is often used for firewood, particularly when
there are many insects, because they cannot bear the smell of it. It is
said, though, that the smoke is bad for the nerves, and that it can
even cause pregnant women to give birth prematurely. When we
marched on I had a large calash readied, with room for myself and
the three children and my two maids; thus I followed the army right
in the midst of the soldiers, who sang and were jolly, burning with
the desire for victory. We passed through endless woods, and the
country was magnificent, but completely deserted, as all the people
had fled before and had gone to strengthen the American army under
General Gates.[8] This was a great disadvantage for us, because every

7. This was the Taylor, later Smith, House, 3½ miles south of Fish Creek.
This may be the house in which Gen. Simon Fraser died on Oct. 8, although
Stone expresses doubts in *General Riedesel*, I, 145, 164. See also, Stone, trans.,
Mrs. General Riedesel, 119.

8. Gen. Horatio Gates (1727–1806) had recently replaced Gen. Philip
Schuyler, to whom, along with certain of Gates's subordinates, some of the
credit for the American victory at Saratoga must be given. Though Gates was
the victor at Saratoga, his military shortcomings contributed to the loss at
Camden, S. C. (1780), and resulted in his retirement. For a discerning sketch
of Gates, see George A. Billias, "Horatio Gates: Professional Soldier," in Billias,
ed., *George Washington's Generals* (N. Y., 1964), 79–108. The only biography is Samuel W. Patterson, *Horatio Gates, Defender of American Liberties*
(N. Y., 1941).

inhabitant is a born soldier and a good marksman;[9] in addition, the thought of fighting for their country and for freedom made them braver than ever.

All this time my husband, like the rest of the army, had to stay in camp. I followed at about an hour's distance and visited my husband in camp every morning. Sometimes I had dinner with him in camp, but mostly he came to my place for dinner. The army made brief attacks every day, but none of them amounted to much. My poor husband, however, was unable to go to bed, or even undress a single night. As the weather was beginning to grow cool, Colonel Williams of the artillery,[10] observing that our mutual visits were very fatiguing, offered to have a house with a chimney built for me for five to six guineas, where I could make my home. I accepted his offer, and the house, which was about twenty feet square and had a good fireplace, was begun. These houses are called log cabins.[11] They are made by fitting together thick logs all of about the same size, which makes a sturdy building, and one that is quite warm, particularly when the roof is covered with clay. The house was ready for me to move into the next day, and I was all the more happy, because the nights were getting damp and cold, and my husband could have lived there with me, as the house was near his camp; but suddenly on October 7 my husband, with his whole staff, had to break camp. This moment was the beginning of our unhappiness! I was just taking breakfast with my husband when I noticed that something was going on. General

---

9. The Germans were impressed with American marksmanship from the start, and there was an attempt to emulate it and to learn the American loose order of skirmishing. Eelking, *German Allied Troops,* p. 93.

10. This must be Maj. Griffith Williams, an artillery officer who supported Brigadier General Hamilton at Saratoga, and who made a reconnaissance with General Phillips through the dense woods before the first engagement at Freeman's Farm. Stone, trans., *Letters of Hessian and Brunswick Officers,* 121; Hadden, *Journal,* lvi; Stone, trans., *General Riedesel,* I, 195.

11. This is the house known as the "Block House." It was built from a plan for such block houses, and it had an overhanging second story. The fire set by the Americans was extinguished and this particular structure stood until the middle of the 19th century. Benson Lossing mistakenly immortalized "the Blockhouse" as the location of Gen. Fraser's death. See Stone, trans., *General Riedesel,* I, 167. For a further description and a plan of blockhouses, see Anburey, *Travels,* I, 123–25.

Fraser[12] and, I think, General Burgoyne and General Phillips[13] also were to have had dinner that same day with me. I noticed a great deal of commotion among the soldiers. My husband told me that they were to go out on a reconnaissance, of which I thought nothing, as this often happened. On my way back to the house I met a number of savages in war dress, carrying guns.[14] When I asked them whither they were bound, they replied, "War! War!"—which meant that they were going into battle. I was completely overwhelmed and had hardly returned to the house, when I heard firing which grew heavier and heavier until the noise was frightful. It was a terrible bombardment, and I was more dead than alive!

Toward three o'clock in the afternoon, instead of my dinner guests arriving as expected, poor General Fraser, who was to have been one of them, was brought to me on a stretcher, mortally wounded. The table, which had already been set for dinner, was removed and a bed for the General was put in its place. I sat in a corner of the room, shivering and trembling. The noise of the firing grew constantly louder. The thought that perhaps my husband would also be brought home wounded was terrifying and worried me incessantly. The General said to the doctor, "Don't conceal anything from me! Must I die?" The bullet had gone through his abdomen precisely as in Major Harnage's case; unfortunately the General had eaten a heavy breakfast, so that the intestines were expanded, and, as the doctor explained, the bullet had gone through them, not between them, as in Major Harnage's case.[15] I heard him often exclaim, between moans, "Oh,

12. Gen. Simon Fraser, who died after the engagement of Oct. 7, 1777, had been in the Dutch service, and later at Louisbourg and Quebec. He fought in Germany during the Seven Years' War, and defeated the Americans at Hubbardton (July 7, 1777). H. Manners Chichester, "Fraser, Simon (d. 1777)," *DNB*. See also, Hadden, *Journal*, 454–63.

13. Maj. Gen. William Phillips was distinguished in the Battle of Minden for his artillery work. Captured at Saratoga, he was exchanged in early 1781 for General Lincoln. Col. R. H. Vetch, "Phillips, William," *DNB*; Hadden, *Journal*, 343–61.

14. The Indians who were aiding the British included Iroquois, Abenakis, Hurons, Nepissings, and Ottawas. Burgoyne himself had a dim view of these auxiliaries. The forward elements of Phillips' wing were Canadians, but Riedesel had Indians. Stone, trans., *General Riedesel*, I, 51; Eelking, *German Allied Troops*, 91; Hadden, *Journal*, 14–15.

15. See W. L. Stone, *Visits to the Saratoga Battle Grounds*, 39. It has long been a German practice to avoid eating before going into battle.

fatal ambition! Poor General Burgoyne! Poor Mrs. Fraser." Prayers were said, then he asked that General Burgoyne have him buried the next day at six o'clock in the evening, on a hill, which was a sort of redoubt. I no longer knew where to go; the whole hall and the other rooms were full of sick men, suffering from camp sickness. Finally toward evening I saw my husband coming; then I forgot all my sorrow and had no other thought but to thank God for sparing him! He ate in great haste with me and his aides behind the house. We had been told that we had gained an advantage over the enemy, but the sad, disheartened faces I saw indicated quite the contrary, and before his departure again my husband took me aside and told me that things were going badly and that I must be ready to leave at any moment, but not to let anyone notice this. On the pretext, therefore, of wanting to move into my new house I had all my things packed. Lady Acland had a tent not far from our house;[16] she slept there at night and spent the day in camp. Suddenly a messenger came to tell her that her husband had been mortally wounded and taken prisoner. She was deeply saddened. We tried to comfort her by telling her that the wound was only a light one, and urged her to go to him, as she would surely be permitted to do, in order that he be better nursed. She loved him dearly, although he was a rough fellow who was drunk almost every day, but, nevertheless, a brave officer. She was the loveliest of women. I spent the whole night trying to comfort her and then went back to my children, whom I had put to

16. Lady Christian Henrietta Caroline Acland, called Lady Harriet (1750–1815), was the daughter of the first Earl of Ilchester. She married John Dyke Acland, who was elected to Parliament in 1774. W. P. Courtney, "Acland, John Dyke," *DNB*. They had already had some hair-raising experiences in the New York campaign, including the burning of their tent when their Newfoundland dog overturned a lantern (Anburey, *Travels*, I, 359–60); when the Americans overran the position of his grenadiers during the second Battle of Saratoga, he was captured. She received permission to go into the American camp and nurse him back to health. A bas-relief in bronze commemorates this episode at the Saratoga memorial. Unfortunately, he died not long after this as a result of a duel with a fellow officer. Stone, *The Campaign of Lieut. Gen. John Burgoyne, and the Expedition of Lieut. Col. Barry St. Leger* (Albany, 1877), 331, says he fell and struck his head on a "pebble." Courtney, in the *DNB*, says he died of exposure. At any rate the tragic fate of the Aclands is to be contrasted with the better fortune of the Riedesels. The story that she subsequently married Chaplain Brudenel is apparently incorrect. See Hadden, *Journal*, lv-lvi. For Acland, see Stone, trans., *General Riedesel*, I, 163–64*n*, 205; Anburey, *Travels*, I, 332.

bed. I, myself, could not sleep, as I had General Fraser and all the other gentlemen in my room, and I was constantly afraid that my children might wake up and cry, thus disturbing the poor dying man, who kept apologizing to me for causing me so much trouble. Toward three o'clock in the morning I was told that the end was near. I had asked to be told of the approach of this moment; I wrapped the children in blankets and went into the hall with them. At eight o'clock in the morning he died. His body was washed, wrapped in a sheet, and put back into the bed. Then we returned to the room and had to see this sad sight throughout the day. Moreover, wounded officers of our acquaintance kept arriving, and the bombardment was renewed again and again. There was talk of making a retreat, but no steps were taken in this direction. Toward four o'clock in the afternoon I saw flames rising from the new house which had been built for me, so I knew that the enemy was not far away.

We learned that General Burgoyne wanted to carry out General Fraser's last wish and intended having him buried in the place designated at six o'clock. This caused an unnecessary delay and served to increase the army's misfortune. At precisely six o'clock the body was actually carried away, and we saw all the generals and their staffs take part in the funeral services on the hilltop. The English chaplain, Mr. Brudenel,[17] held the services. Cannon balls constantly flew around and over the heads of the mourners. The American General Gates said later on that, had he known that a funeral was being held, he would have allowed no firing in that direction. A number of cannon balls also flew about where I stood, but I had no thought for my own safety, my eyes being constantly directed toward the hill, where I could see my husband distinctly, standing in the midst of the enemy's fire.

The command had been given for the army to withdraw immediately after the funeral, and our calashes were ready and waiting. I did not want to leave before the troops did. Major Harnage, miserably ill as he was, crept out of bed so that he would not be left behind in the hospital, over which a flag of truce had been raised. When he saw me standing in the midst of danger, he ordered my children and the maidservants to be brought to the calashes and told me I would have to leave immediately. When I repeated my plea to be allowed to stay,

17. See Hadden, *Journal*, lv-lvi, for a denial of the story that he married Lady Acland. For her trip to Albany with the Chaplain to care for her husband, see Anburey, *Travels*, II, 56.

he said, "All right, then your children must go without you, so that I can at least save them from danger." He knew the weakest spot in my armor and thus persuaded me to get into the calash, and we drove away on the evening of the 8th.

We had been warned to keep extremely quiet, fires were left burning everywhere, and many tents were left standing, so that the enemy would think the camp was still there. Thus we drove on all through the night. Little Frederika, was very much frightened, often starting to cry, and I had to hold my handkerchief over her mouth to prevent our being discovered.

At six o'clock in the morning we stopped, to the amazement of all. General Burgoyne ordered the cannons to be lined up and counted, which vexed everyone because only a few more good marches and we would have been in safety.[18] My husband was completely exhausted and during this halt sat in my calash, where my maids had to make room for him and where he slept about three hours with his head on my shoulder. In the meantime Captain Willoe brought me his wallet with banknotes, and Captain Geismar [19] brought me his beautiful watch, a ring, and a well-filled purse and asked me to take care of these things for them. I promised to do my utmost. Finally the order was given to march on, but we had hardly gone an hour when we stopped again, because we caught sight of the enemy. There were about two hundred men who had come out to reconnoiter and could easily have been taken prisoners by our troops, if General Burgoyne had not lost his head. It was pouring; Lady Acland had had her tent put up. I urged her again to go to her husband, to whom she could have been of so much help in his present condition. She finally listened to my reasoning and, through General Burgoyne's adjutant, Lord Petersham,[20] requested permission to go. I told her she had only

18. This was not really the case. The British force could not have escaped, and Gates knew it as well as Burgoyne. Alden, *The American Revolution,* 147–48. With regard to this particular halt Burgoyne defended himself on the ground that the troops needed time to refresh themselves, and that time was needed for the boats paralleling them on the Hudson to catch up. John Burgoyne, *A State of the Expedition from Canada . . .* (London, 1780), 170.

19. Captain von Geismar was a Hessian adjutant on Riedesel's staff, particularly concerned with the Hesse-Hanau troops. Stone, trans., *General Riedesel,* II, 87–88.

20. Although Madame de Riedesel speaks of "Lord Patterson," she is undoubtedly referring to Captain Stanhope, Viscount Petersham, later the third Earl of Harrington, and aide to Burgoyne. He was praised by Riedesel.

to insist upon being allowed to go, and, in the end, the General finally did give her permission. The English chaplain, Mr. Brudenel, accompanied her, and the two got into a boat with a flag of truce and sailed across to the enemy (there is a handsome and well-known etching of this incident). Later on I saw her again in Albany, where her husband was fully recovered, and they both thanked me for my advice. We spent the whole of the 9th in a terrible rainstorm, ready to march on at a moment's notice. The savages had lost courage, and everywhere they were seen retreating. The slightest setback makes cowards of them, especially if they see no chance of plundering. My maid did nothing but bemoan her plight and tear her hair. I begged her to quiet herself, as otherwise she would be taken for a savage. Hereupon she became still more frantic, and she asked me whether I minded her behavior, and when I answered, "Yes," she tore off her hat, let her hair hang down over her face, and said, "It is easy for you to talk! You have your husband, but we have nothing except the prospect of being killed or of losing all we have." With regard to the latter I consoled her by promising that I would compensate her and the others for anything they might lose. The other maid, my good Lena, although very much afraid, nevertheless said nothing.

Toward evening we finally reached Saratoga which is only half an hour on the way from the place where we had spent the whole day. I was wet to the skin from the rain and had to remain so throughout the night as there was no place to change into dry clothes. So I sat down before a good fire, took off the children's clothes, and then we lay down together on some straw. I asked General Phillips, who came up to me, why we did not continue our retreat while there was yet time, as my husband had promised to cover our retreat and bring the army through. "Poor woman," he said, "I admire you! Thoroughly drenched as you are, you still have the courage to go on in this weather. If only you were our commanding general! He thinks himself too tired and wants to spend the night here and give us a supper." In fact, Burgoyne liked having a jolly time and spending half the night singing and drinking and amusing himself in the company of

---

Stone, trans., *Mrs. General Riedesel*, 123, and *General Riedesel*, I, 201–2; Hadden, *Journal*, 367–72; Ford, *British Officers*, 143. It has been observed that he had in his veins "noble blood enough to have inoculated half the kingdom." Hadden, *Journal*, xlix.

the wife of a commissary, who was his mistress and, like him, loved champagne.[21]

On the 10th at seven o'clock in the morning I refreshed myself with a cup of tea, and we now hoped from one moment to the next that we would at last proceed. In order to cover the retreat General Burgoyne ordered fire set to the beautiful houses and mills in Saratoga belonging to General Schuyler.[22] An English officer brought a very good bouillon, which on his urgent entreaties I had to share with him, and after drinking it we continued our march; however, we got only to the next village, not far away. The greatest misery and extreme disorder prevailed in the army. The commissary had forgotten to distribute the food supplies among the troops; there were cattle enough, but not a single one had been slaughtered. More than thirty officers came to me because they could stand the hunger no longer. I had coffee and tea made for them and divided among them all the supplies with which my carriage was always filled; for we had a cook with us who, though an arch-rogue, nevertheless always knew how to get hold of something for us and, as we learned later, often crossed streams at night in order to steal from the farmers sheep, chickens, and pigs, which he sold to us at a good price.

Finally my own supplies were exhausted, and in my desperation

21. It is not established who Burgoyne's companion was. Mrs. Tharp, *The Baroness and the General,* 176, speculates on the possibility that it might have been Mrs. Foy, whose husband was a commissary in Canada. However, this is very questionable; in view of what Madame de Riedesel had to say about Mrs. Foy and her sister on other occasions, she would certainly have mentioned either of them by name.

22. Philip John Schuyler (1733–1804), a great New York landowner, who participated in the Seven Years' War became a member of the Second Continental Congress, before being appointed a major general in 1775 in charge of the Northern army in New York. After the British recapture of Ticonderoga, he was replaced by Gen. Horatio Gates in Aug. 1777, two months before Burgoyne's surrender. Gates received the credit for defeating the British, but much of the credit really belongs to Schuyler. It was in Schuyler's house that Burgoyne had been making merry. After Burgoyne surrendered, Schuyler made the trip to Saratoga where he met Burgoyne and Mrs. Riedesdel. For a sketch of Schuyler, see John H. G. Pell, "Philip Schuyler: The General as Aristocrat," Billias, ed., *George Washington's Generals,* 54–78. There is a recent full-scale study of *Philip Schuyler and the American Revolution in New York, 1733–1777* (Lincoln, Neb., 1964), by Don R. Gerlach. On the burning of Schuyler's house, see the Marquis de Chastellux, *Travels in North America, in the Years 1780, 1781 and 1782,* ed. Howard C. Rice, Jr., 2 vols. (Chapel Hill, 1963), I, 218, 354–55.

at no longer being able to help the others I called to Adjutant-General Petersham, who was just passing by, and, as I was really very much worried, I said to him vehemently: "Come and look at these officers who have been wounded in the common cause and who lack everything they need because they are not getting their due. It is your duty to speak with the General about this." He was very much moved, and, as a result, about a quarter of an hour later General Burgoyne himself came to me and thanked me most pathetically for having reminded him of his duty. He added that a commander is very much to be pitied if he is not properly served and his orders correctly executed. I asked his pardon for having interfered in matters which I well knew were not a woman's business, but said that it had been impossible for me to keep still when I saw how these gallant persons were in need of everything and I, myself, had nothing more to give them. Thereupon he thanked me yet again (although I believe in his heart he never forgave me for this interference) and went to the officers and told them how sorry he was about what had happened; that he had, however, taken care of all by an order; but why, he asked them, had they not come to him for food, as his kitchen was at their disposal at all times? They replied that English officers were not accustomed to visiting the kitchens of their general, and that they had taken each morsel from me with pleasure, being convinced that I had given it to them from the heart. Thereupon he gave strict orders that the provisions be properly distributed. This only delayed us still further and availed us nothing. The General resumed his place at the table, and our calashes were harnessed and made ready for departure. The whole army was in favor of making a retreat, and my husband said it could be done, if only we lost no time. General Burgoyne, however, who had been promised an order if he succeeded in joining General Howe's army, could not make up his mind to leave and lost everything by tarrying.

Toward two o'clock in the afternoon we heard cannon and musketry again, and alarm and confusion prevailed. My husband sent me word to get immediately to a house which was not far away. I got into the calash with my children, and just as we came up to the house I saw five or six men on the other side of the Hudson, who were aiming their guns at us. Almost involuntarily I thrust my children onto the floor of the calash and threw myself over them. The same instant the fellows fired and shattered the arm of a poor English soldier behind me, who had already been wounded and was retiring into the house. Immediately after our arrival a terrifying cannonade began, which was directed principally at the house where we sought shelter,[23] presumably because the enemy, seeing so many people fleeing thither, got the idea that the generals themselves were there. But, alas, the house contained only the wounded and women! We were finally forced to seek refuge in the cellar, where I found a place for myself and the children in a corner near the door. My children lay on the floor with their heads in my lap. And thus we spent the whole night. The horrible smell in the cellar, the weeping of the children, and, even worse, my own fear prevented me from closing my eyes.

Next morning the cannonade went on again, but from the other side. I suggested that everyone leave the cellar for a while so that I could have it cleaned, because otherwise we would all become sick. My suggestion was carried out, and I got many to help, which was highly necessary for this extensive task; the women and children, afraid to go outside, had polluted the entire cellar. When everybody had gone out, I examined our place of refuge; there were three fine cellars with well-vaulted ceilings. I suggested that the most seriously wounded men be put into one cellar, the women in another, and all the others in the third, which was nearest to the door. I had everything swept thoroughly and fumigated with vinegar, when, just as everyone was about to take his place, renewed, terrific cannon fire created another alarm. Many who had no right to enter threw themselves against the door. My children had already gone down the cellar steps, and we would all have been crushed if God had not given me the strength to keep the crowd back by standing in front of the door with outspread arms; otherwise surely someone would have been injured. Eleven cannon balls flew through the house, and we could distinctly hear them rolling about over our heads. One of the poor soldiers who lay on a table, and was just about to have his leg amputated, had the other leg shot off by one of these balls.[24] His comrades had run away from him, and when they returned they found him scarcely breathing, lying in a corner of the room, where he had rolled himself in his agony. I was more dead than alive, not so much on

23. For this house and Benjamin Lossing's sketch of it, see Stone, trans., *Mrs. General Riedesel*, 128.

24. According to Stone, *ibid.*, 129, this was an English surgeon named Jones. Ford, *British Officers*, 103, lists 23 Joneses, but no surgeon. A certain John Jones, a chaplain attached to a hospital in 1776, might possibly be the one.

account of our own danger as for the danger that hung over my husband, who kept inquiring how we were and sending me word that he was all right.

Major Harnage's wife, Mrs. Reynell, who had already lost her husband, the wife of the good lieutenant who had been so kind as to share his bouillon with me the previous day, the wife of the commissary, and myself were the only ladies with the army. We were just sitting together and bewailing our fate when someone entered, whispered something to the others, and they all looked at each other sadly. I noticed this and that all eyes were upon me, although nobody said anything. This brought the horrible thought to my mind that my husband had been killed. I screamed; they assured me, however, that such was not the case but indicated with a nod that it was the poor lieutenant's wife to whom this misfortune had befallen.[25] She was called outside a few moments later. Her husband was not yet dead, but a cannon ball had torn his arm away at the shoulder. We heard his moaning all through the night, doubly gruesome as the sound re-echoed through the cellar; the poor fellow died toward morning. However, we spent this night just as we had the previous one. In the meantime my husband visited me, which lightened my anxiety and gave me renewed courage.

Next morning we started putting things in better order. Major Harnage and his wife and Mrs. Reynell made a room for themselves in one corner by partitioning it off with curtains. They wanted to fix up another corner for me just like it, but I preferred staying near the door so that in case of fire I would be able to get out as quickly as possible. I had some straw put down, laid my bedclothes on it, and slept there with the children, with my serving women not far away. Opposite us there were three English officers who had been wounded, but who were determined, in case of retreat, not to stay behind. One of them was a Captain Green,[26] aide to General Phillips, a very estimable and polite man. All three assured me on oath that in case of a hasty

25. This lieutenant was probably Adjt. George Tobias Fitzgerald of the 62nd Regiment, the only British officer listed as killed in the skirmishes after Oct. 7. Stanley, ed., *For Want of a Horse*, 179; Baxter, ed., *Digby's Journal*, 336, 344. His position on the staff might have enabled him to share the cup of bouillon with the Baroness.

26. Capt. Charles Green, an aide to General Phillips and an officer of the 31st regiment. Stone, *Visits to the Saratoga Battle Grounds*, 123–34; Ford, *British Officers*, 85.

retreat they would not forsake me, but that each of them would take one of my children with him on his horse. One of my husband's horses stood saddled and ready for me all the time. My husband often wanted to send me to the Americans, in order to put me out of danger, but I told him it would be worse than anything I had had to bear heretofore to be with people to whom I should have to be polite while my husband was fighting them. He promised me, therefore, that I could continue to follow the army. Many a time in the night, however, I was seized with the fear that he had marched away, and I crept out of my cellar to see; when I saw the troops lying by the fire, as the nights had already grown cold, I was able to sleep more tranquilly again. The things which had been entrusted to me for safekeeping also worried me. I had put them all in the front of my corset because I was constantly afraid of losing part of them, and I made up my mind never again to take such a responsibility upon myself. On the third day I found the first opportunity and a moment to change my underclothing when the courtesy of a small corner was allowed me. Meanwhile, my three above-mentioned officers stood sentry not far off. One of these gentlemen could imitate most realistically the mooing of a cow and the bleating of a calf. Whenever my little daughter Frederika cried at night, he made these sounds for her, and she would become quiet again immediately, at which we all had to laugh.

Our cook brought us food, but we had no water, and I was often obliged to quench my thirst with wine and even had to give the children some. Moreover, it was almost the only drink my husband would take. This finally began to worry our faithful Rockel, who said to me one day, "I fear that the General drinks all this wine because he is afraid of being taken prisoner, and that he is tired of living." The constant danger which surrounded my husband kept me in continuous anxiety. I was the only one among all the women whose husband had not been either killed or at least wounded, and I often said to myself, "Should I be the only lucky one?"—particularly as my husband was in such great danger day and night. He did not spend a single night in the tent, but lay outside by the sentry's fire all night long. That, alone, was enough to cause his death, as the nights were so damp and cold.

Because we were badly in need of water, we finally found the wife of one of the soldiers who was brave enough to go to the river to fetch some. This was a thing nobody wanted to risk doing, because the enemy shot every man in the head who went near the river. However, they did not hurt the woman out of respect for her sex, as they told us themselves afterwards.

I tried to divert my mind by busying myself with our wounded. I made tea and coffee for them, for which I received a thousand blessings. Often I shared my dinner with them. One day a Canadian officer came into the cellar, so weak that he could hardly stand up. We finally got it out of him that he was almost starved to death. I was very happy to be able to give him my own dinner, which gave him renewed strength and won me his friendship. When we returned to Canada later on, I became acquainted with his family.

One of the worst things we had to bear was the odor which came from the wounds when they began to fester. At one time I was nursing a Major Bloomfield,[27] aide to General Phillips, who had a bullet shot through both cheeks, smashing his teeth and grazing his tongue. He could not keep anything in his mouth; the pus almost choked him, and he could not take any nourishment at all except a little bouillon or other liquid. We had some Rhine wine. I gave him a bottle, hoping that the acid would cleanse his wounds. He took a little of it in his mouth, and this alone had such a fortunate effect that his wounds healed entirely, and I gained another friend. Thus even in these hours of suffering and sorrow I had moments of pleasure which made me very happy.

On one of these unhappy days General Phillips wanted to visit me and accompanied my husband, who came to me once or twice every day at the risk of his life. He saw our plight and heard me beg my husband not to leave me behind in case of a hasty retreat. He took my part when he saw how I hated the thought of being left with the Americans. When he left me he said to my husband, "No! I would not come here again for ten thousand guineas, for my heart is absolutely broken."

On the other hand, not all the men who were with us deserved pity. Some of them were cowards who had no reason whatever for staying in the cellar, and who later when we were taken prisoners, were well able to stand up in line and march. We were in this dreadful

27. Capt. Thomas Bloomfield (1744–1822) (Blomefield) (Blomfield) (or Plumpfield, as Madame de Riedesel spelled it) returned to England in 1779. He became a member of Parliament, a lieutenant general, a baronet, and marshal to the King. Hadden, *Journal*, 361–66; Ford, *British Officers*, 29; Stone, trans., *General Riedesel*, I, 147, and Stone, trans., *Mrs. General Riedesel*, 132.

position six days. Finally there was talk of capitulation,[28] as by delaying too long our retreat was now cut off. A cessation of hostilities took place, and my husband, who was completely exhausted, could sleep in a bed in the house for the first time in a long while. In order that he would be absolutely undisturbed I had a good bed made for him in a small room and slept with my children and the maids in a large hall close by. At about nine o'clock in the morning someone came and wanted to speak to my husband. With the greatest reluctance I found it necessary to wake him. I noticed that he was not pleased about the message he received and that he immediately sent the man to headquarters and lay down again, much annoyed. Shortly afterwards General Burgoyne sent for all the other generals and staff officers to attend a council of war early in the morning, during which he suggested, on the basis of a false report, that the capitulation which had already been made to the enemy be broken. However, it was

28. Putnam had warned Gates that Clinton had broken through defenses farther down on the Hudson, and therefore Gates should be prepared for the worst. For this reason, largely, Burgoyne was able to negotiate a "convention" rather than make an outright surrender, even though British delay and the destruction of the pontoon bridge made impossible any escape. Moreover, Clinton had no intention of trying to head that far north. The council Burgoyne called debated whether there were military precedents for surrender under such circumstances, whether such a capitulation would be consistent with honor, and whether the army was actually in such a position as to have to capitulate. After first refusing, Gates finally accepted terms of a convention whereby the British and Brunswick troops would be sent to Boston for transportation to England, terms that the Congress finally did not ratify, partially because of Lafayette's influence. General Riedesel was satisfied that the capitulation was with honor, but he resented Burgoyne's complaints to Lord Germain about the role of the Germans, and also his failure to give the Brunswickers credit for saving the day on Sept. 19. He particularly resented Burgoyne's report saying that of his 3,500 men, "scarcely 2,000 were English." Riedesel would not surrender the Brunswick flags, which Madame de Riedesel dramatically had sewn into a mattress (below, pp. 72–73, and Eelking, *German Allied Troops*, 142). Technically the capitulation (as Riedesel himself called it, Stone, trans., *General Riedesel*, I, 187) was called a convention; nevertheless, as events proved, it was really a capitulation. The German edition of Madame de Riedesel's *Journal* (1801) contained the essence of the military memoir her husband wrote (pp. 32–62), and this account was preserved in subsequent editions. I have omitted this account, however, since it is technical from a military point of view and tangential to her personal account. It is, of course, an important part of General Riedesel's papers, and it may be consulted in Stone, trans., *General Riedesel*. For the council and the terms, see *ibid.*, I, 175–86.

finally decided that this would be neither practicable nor advisable, and that was a lucky decision for us, because the Americans told us later that, had we broken the capitulation, we would all have been massacred, which would have been an easy matter, because there were only four to five thousand of us, and we had given them time to get more than twenty thousand of their men together.[29]

On October 16 my husband had to go back on duty, and I had to return to my cellar. That day the officers, who until then had received only salted meat, which was very bad for the wounded, were given a lot of fresh meat. The good woman who always got the water for us cooked a tasty soup with it. I had lost all appetite and had eaten nothing the whole time except a crust of bread dipped in wine. The wounded officers, my companions in misfortune, cut off the best piece of beef and presented it to me with a plate of soup. I told them it was impossible for me to eat anything. Seeing, however, how much in need of nourishment I was, they declared that they would not eat a bite themselves until I had given them the pleasure of joining them. I could no longer resist their friendly pleading, whereupon they assured me that it made them most happy to be able to share with me the first good food they had received.

On October 17 the capitulation went into effect. The generals went to the American Commanding General, General Gates, and the troops laid down their arms and surrendered themselves as prisoners of war. The good woman who had fetched water for us at the risk of her life now got her reward. Everyone threw a handful of money into her apron, and she received altogether more than twenty guineas. In moments like this the heart seems to overflow in gratitude.

At last my husband sent a groom to me with the message that I should come to him with our children. I got into my beloved calash again, and while driving through the American camp I was comforted to notice that nobdy glanced at us insultingly, that they all bowed to me, and some of them even looked with pity to see a woman with small children there. I confess that I was afraid to go to the enemy, as it was an entirely new experience for me. When I approached the

29. Harrison Bird, *March to Saratoga, General Burgoyne and the American Campaign* (N.Y., 1963), 285, 287, says Burgoyne's army numbered 4,693 men on Oct. 17, 1777; and Gates had 6000 Continentals and anywhere from 1200 to 3000 militia. William M. Dabney, *After Saratoga: the Story of the Convention Army* (Albuquerque, 1954), 27, gives a figure of 5,756, of whom about 1,100 returned directly to Canada.

tents a very handsome man came towards me, lifted the children out of the calash, hugged and kissed them and then, with tears in his eyes, helped me out. "You are trembling," he said. "Don't be afraid." "No," I answered, "I am not, for you look so kind and were so affectionate to my children that you have given me courage."[30] He led me to the tent of General Gates, where I found General Burgoyne and General Phillips, who were on very friendly terms with the former. Burgoyne said to me, "Have no fear, for your sufferings have now come to an end." I replied that, of course it would be wrong to be afraid any longer if our leader were not and after seeing him on such good terms with General Gates. All the generals stayed with General Gates for dinner. The same man who had welcomed me so kindly came up to me, saying "It would embarrass you to take dinner with all these gentlemen; come to my tent with your children, and although I can only give you a frugal meal, it will be given gladly." "Surely," I replied, "you are a husband and father, because you are so good to me." I learned then that he was the American General Schuyler. He treated me to delicious smoked tongue, beefsteaks, potatoes, and good bread and butter. No dinner had ever tasted better to me. I was content. I saw that all about me were likewise, and, most important of all, my husband was out of danger.

When we had finished eating, he offered to let me live in his house, which was near Albany, and told me that General Burgoyne would also come there. I sent my husband a message, asking what I should do. He told me to accept the invitation, and as it was a two-days' journey and was already five o'clock in the afternoon, he suggested that I go on ahead and spend the night at a place about three hours from there. General Schuyler was kind enough to let a French officer take me there, a very polite man, the one in command of the troops who had reconnoitered the area and whom I have already mentioned. When he had brought us to the house where we were to spend the night, he returned to camp.

I found a French doctor at this house with a mortally wounded Brunswick officer, who had been put in his care and who died a few days later. The patient was full of praise for the doctor's treatment, and perhaps he was a skilled surgeon, but otherwise he was a young fop. He was very pleased to hear that I could speak his language and began to say all sorts of sweet things and impertinences to me, among

30. For Schuyler's account of his encounter with the Baroness, see Chastellux, *Travels,* ed. Rice, I, 220, 355–56.

which, that he could not possibly believe that I was a general's wife, because a woman of such high rank would never have joined her husband. I should, therefore, stay with him, as it would be better to stay with victors than with the defeated. I was furious over his boldness but did not dare to show how much contempt I felt for him, because I was without protection. When night came he offered to let me share his room with him. I replied, however, that I would sit up in the room of the wounded soldier, whereupon he made me a lot of silly compliments, when suddenly the door opened and my husband and his aide entered. "Here, sir, is my husband," I said to him with a withering glance, whereupon he departed shamefacedly. Nevertheless, he was polite enough to give us his room.

The next day we arrived in Albany, where we had so often longed to be. But we did not come as victors, as we had thought. We were welcomed by good General Schuyler, his wife, and daughters not as enemies, but in the friendliest manner possible, and they were exceedingly kind to us as well as to General Burgoyne, although he had had their beautifully furnished houses set on fire, needlessly, it is said.[31] Their behavior was that of people who can turn from their own loss to the misfortune of others. General Burgoyne, too, was very much touched by their magnanimity and said to General Schuyler, "You are so kind to me who caused you so much damage." "Such is the fate of war," the gallant man replied. "Let us not talk about it any more." We stayed with them three days, and they assured us that they regretted seeing us go.

Our cook had stayed in town with my husband's equipment. The second night after our arrival all our things were stolen, in spite of the American guard of ten to twenty men, who had been ordered to keep watch. We had nothing left except my own and the children's

31. See above, footnote 22. Henry C. Van Schaack, *The Life of Peter Van Schaack* . . . (N. Y., 1842), 93–94, recounts this incident: "Not long after their arrival, one of Madam de Riedesel's little girls, after frolicking about General Schuyler's spacious and well-furnished mansion, ran up to her mother, and with all the simplicity of youthful innocence, inquired in German: '*Mother, is this the palace father was to have when he came to America?*' The blushing Baroness speedily silenced her child. The teeming question, which was asked in the presence of some of General Schuyler's family, by whom German was understood, as may be imagined, was well calculated to disconcert her." The Convention troops met Van Schaack at Kinderhook on their way to Cambridge, and presumably this is where he heard this anecdote. Ray W. Pettingill, trans., *Letters from America, 1776–1779* . . . (Boston, 1924), 115.

bedding and the few household articles which I kept with me—and this in a country where nothing could be bought at any price, and at a time when we so badly needed many things; for my husband had to furnish board for all his aides, quartermasters, and others. Our friends, the English, of whom I speak truly as friends, because throughout our stay in America they have always treated us as such, each made us a present of some article. One gave a couple of spoons, another a few plates. It was all we had for a long time, because not until three years later in New York did we have the opportunity of replacing at great cost the things we had lost. Fortunately, I had kept my little conveyance containing my own things. As it was late in the fall, and the weather was getting raw, I had made for my calash a top of coarse linen painted with oil paint. Thus we drove to Boston—a tedious and difficult journey.[32]

I do not know whether it was my vehicle which aroused the people's curiosity, for it really looked like a wagon in which rare animals were being transported, but I was often obliged to stop, because the people wanted to see the German general's wife with her children. In order to prevent them from tearing the linen top off the carriage, I decided it was better to alight frequently, and thus I got away more quickly than otherwise. But even so, I cannot deny that the people were friendly and were particularly pleased to hear that I could speak their native language, English.

In all my suffering God blessed me with His help, so that I lost neither my gaiety, nor my courage; but my poor husband, who was consumed by sadness over everything that had happened and by his captivity, was very much annoyed by such episodes as these, and could scarcely endure them. His health had suffered greatly, especially from the many nights spent outdoors in the cold and dampness, and, accordingly, he often had to take medicine. One day when he was very weak from the effects of an emetic, he could not sleep on account of the noise made by our American guards, who never left us, and who were drinking and feasting outside our door and who became even noisier when he asked them to be quiet. I decided to go out myself, and I told them that my husband was ill and begged them, therefore, to be a bit less noisy. They ceased at once and all was quiet. Here is proof that this nation also has respect for our sex.

32. According to Stone, General Riedesel left Albany on Oct. 22, 1777, and arrived in Boston Nov. 7. *General Riedesel,* I, 10.

Some of their generals who accompanied us were shoemakers by trade, and on days when we rested made boots for our officers and also repaired the shoes of our officers. They very much prized coined money, which for them was very scarce. One of our officers' boots were completely torn. He saw that an American general was wearing a good pair and jestingly said to him, "I would gladly give you a guinea for them." The general immediately jumped off his horse, took the guinea, gave the officer his boots, and wearing the officer's torn pair, mounted his horse again.

VI

Massachusetts and Virginia

———◦◦———

We finally reached Boston, and our troops were quartered in barracks not far away, on Winter Hill.[1] We were put up at a farmer's house, where we were given only one room in the attic. My maids slept on the floor, and the men in the hall. Some straw on which I had spread our bedding was all we had for a long while on which to sleep, since I had nothing other than my field bed. Our host allowed us to eat downstairs in his room, where his whole family ate and slept together. The man was good, but his wife, in revenge for the bother we caused her, deliberately chose to vex us during our mealtime by combing her children's hair, which was full of vermin, often making us lose every bit of appetite, and when we asked her to do her combing outside, or at some other time, she replied, "It is my room; I see fit to stay and to comb my children now." We had to hold our silence, for otherwise she might have turned us out of the house.

1. These barracks on Winter Hill were wretched wooden structures erected by the Americans in 1775 while besieging Gage in Boston. The rule was to put four officers or twenty men in each. According to a contemporary description: "They are built of boards, and the windows are of paper, so that we have had plenty of fresh air this winter." Actually the Brunswickers were better off than the British on the more promising-sounding Prospect Hill. General Riedesel bought a carriage, and the life of his family was not bad, considering the circumstances, but the General ran into debt, and Clinton had to forward him money. See Stone, trans., *Letters of Brunswick and Hessian Officers*, 153, 166, 173; Dabney, *After Saratoga*, 45, 49; Ray W. Pettingill, trans., *Letters from America, 1776–1779* . . . (Boston, 1924), 130; Stone, trans., *Mrs. General Riedesel*, 138, and *General Riedesel*, II, 52–53. For a description of the Convention troops entering Boston, see Hannah Winthrop to Mercy Warren, Nov. 11, 1777, *Warren-Adams Letters*, II (Massachusetts Historical Society, *Collections*, 73 [1925]), 451–53.

One day, our gentlemen, disregarding this filth, celebrated the birthday, I believe, of the Queen of England, by drinking a good deal of wine. My two elder daughters, little Augusta and Frederika, having noticed that the wine left over had been stowed away under the stairs, helped themselves to some of it so that they could also drink to the Queen's health. They sat outside by the door and drank so many toasts that their little heads could stand no more and Frederika even developed a fever, which frightened me terribly, because she had cramps, and I could not possibly think what had caused them. When nature finally came to aid by causing her to vomit, I saw the whole trouble came from wine and scolded the little girls severely, whereupon they replied that they also loved the King and the Queen and, therefore, could not refrain from wishing them happiness.

We stayed in this place three weeks before we were then taken to Cambridge, where we were put up in one of the most beautiful houses, previously the property of royalists [i.e., loyalists].[2] I have never seen a lovelier location. Seven families, partly relatives and partly friends, had leasehold estates here with gardens and magnificent houses and orchards nearby. All these estates were only about an eighth of a mile apart from one another. The owners gathered every afternoon at one of the homes or another, where they enjoyed themselves with music and dancing, living happily in comfort and harmony until, alas, the devastating war separated them all, leaving all the houses desolate with the exception of two, whose owners shortly thereafter were also obliged to flee.

None of our gentlemen were permitted to go to Boston.[3] My curiosity and the desire to see General Schuyler's daughter, Mrs. Carter,[4]

2. "The Riedesel house in Cambridge is still standing, Number 149 Brattle Street. . . . The house has been moved across Riedesel Avenue from its original site, and extensively remodeled." Tharp, *The Baroness and the General*, 432. Brattle Street was known as "Tory Row" from the allegiance of so many of its residents, who are identified in Lucius R. Paige, *History of Cambridge, Massachusetts, 1630–1897* . . . (Boston, 1897), 167–69, 427. The Riedesels lived in the Lechmere-Sewall House.

3. Lieutenant Anburey called it "the grand *emporium of rebellion*" in his *Travels*, I, 56.

4. Angelica Schuyler, the Schuylers' eldest daughter, married John Barker Church, known in America as "Mr. Carter." Thus, to Madame de Riedesel, her friend was "Mrs. Carter." Harold C. Syrett and Jacob E. Cooke, eds., *The Papers of Alexander Hamilton* (1961 ———), II, 599.

impelled me to go, and I had dinner with her there several times. It is quite a pretty city, but inhabited by enthusiastic patriots and full of wicked people; the women, particularly, were horrid, casting ugly looks at me, and some of them even spitting when I passed by them. Mrs. Carter was gentle and good, like her parents, but her husband was a bad and treacherous person. They often visited us and ate with us and the other generals. We did our utmost to reciprocate their kindness. They seemed to feel very friendly toward us too, but it was during this time that this horrible Mr. Carter made the gruesome suggestion to the Americans, when the English General Howe had set fire to many villages and towns, to behead our generals, put the heads in small barrels, salt them, and send one of these barrels to the English for each village or town which they had set on fire. This beastly suggestion fortunately, however, was not adopted.

While in England I had become acquainted with a Captain Fenton of Boston,[5] whose services the Americans had wanted when the war broke out, but who, being faithful to his King, had refused to obey. Hereupon the women among the embittered mob grabbed his wife, a most respectable lady, and his pretty fifteen-year-old daughter, and disregarding their goodness, beauty, and embarrassment, undressed them to the skin, tarred and feathered them, and paraded them through the city. What may one not expect from people of this sort, animated by the most bitter hate!

There was also the case of two brothers who loved each other dearly, but the one espoused the King's party, the other the republicans. The former, desiring to see his brother again, took leave and went to him. The other welcomed him joyously and said, "I am so happy to see that you have returned to the good cause." "No, my brother," the royalist replied, "I shall continue to be faithful to my King, but that cannot prevent me from loving you." Thereupon the American jumped up in rage, took a pistol, and threatened to shoot him if he did not leave the house immediately. All his good brother's assurances that a difference of opinion in politics could not injure their love were in vain. The other only cried, "It is only my old love for you which prevents my shooting you immediately, because every royalist is my enemy." And he would really have done it, had not his brother finally departed. Almost all families were thus divided, and

5. See Chap. 2, n. 4, and text, where the Baroness speaks of the "fourteen-year-old" daughter.

this made it clear to me that there is nothing more terrible than a civil war. With such people we were obliged to live or to see nobody at all. I naturally preferred the latter choice.

General Phillips continued to be our good and sincere friend, and we saw much of him. Furthermore, our house was always filled with Englishmen after we learned that in England it is customary to ask the guest, when parting, to call again. Before we knew this, we noticed to our amazement that a certain kind of people, whom we had to be sure entertained well, never returned. Later on we followed the English custom and found it very convenient, because it enabled one to choose those people with whom one liked best to associate. However, some people were, as the English called it, brazen.

In Cambridge I saw a whole house being moved on long logs to the ends of which wheels were attached. A house is jacked up, the logs pushed under it, and it is then readily moved.

On June 3, 1778, I gave a ball and supper in celebration of my husband's birthday. I had invited all the generals and officers. The Carters also came, but General Burgoyne sent his apologies after having kept us waiting until eight o'clock in the evening. On one pretext or another he refused every invitation of ours until he left for England. Before his departure he called on me to make his apologies personally, to which I merely replied that I should have been sorry if he had put himself to any inconvenience for our sake. There was much dancing, and my cook had prepared an excellent supper for more than eighty guests. Moreover, our court and the garden were illuminated. As the King's birthday was on the 4th, the day after, we decided not to part until we could drink to the King's health, which was done with the most sincere loyalty, both toward his person and toward his cause.

Never, I believe, was "God save the King" sung with more enthusiasm or greater sincerity. Even my two elder daughters were brought downstairs to join us and see the illumination. All eyes were filled with tears, and everyone seemed proud of having the courage to celebrate thus in the midst of the enemy. Even the Carters had not the heart to hold themselves aloof. When the company left, we saw that the house was entirely surrounded by Americans, who, upon seeing so many people enter and observing the illumination, had grown suspicious, fearing that we were planning a revolt, and had there been the slightest noise, we should have had to pay dearly for it.

Whenever the Americans want to gather their troops together, they set up lighted torches on every hilltop, at which signal everyone hastens to assemble. One day we witnessed General Howe's attempt to land in Boston in order to release the captured troops.[6] As usual, the enemy had learned of this plan well in advance, set up their burning tar barrels as signals, and for three or four days we saw a mob most hastily assembled without shoes and stockings and with guns on their backs. In a short time so many had gathered that it would have been too difficult to make a landing.

We lived in Cambridge quite happily and would have liked to stay there as long as our troops were held prisoners,[7] but as the winter drew near, we got orders to go to Virginia.[8] I had to conceive some means now for bringing the flags of our German regiments into safety. We had told the Americans in Saratoga that they had been burned, which annoyed them very much at first, but they said nothing more about it. In fact, only the staves had been burned, and the flags themselves had been hidden. My husband entrusted me with this secret and assigned me the task of keeping the flags concealed. I got a trustworthy tailor, locked myself up in a room with him, and together we made a mattress, in which we sewed up all the flags. Captain O'Connell was sent to New York on some pretext and took the mattress with him as part of his bedding. He left the mattress in Halifax, where we got it and took it with us when

6. For the British attempt to land at Boston in Dec. 1777, on the orders of General Howe, see Stone, trans., *General Riedesel*, I, 227; Christopher Ward, *The War of the Revolution*, ed. John R. Alden, 2 vols. (N. Y., 1952), II, 541; and William Abbatt, ed., *Memoirs of Major-General William Heath* (N. Y., 1901), 134–37.

7. For a contrast of the situation of the Riedesels and that of the Brunswick troops, see Stone, trans., *General Riedesel*, I, 217–18, II, 32; Eelking, *German Allied Troops*, 144–47.

8. The Convention was never carried out, and the troops taken at Saratoga were treated like any other prisoners. The Congress feared that if they were sent back to England, they would simply go into garrison duty, releasing fresh troops for America. Lafayette, asserting that the British had violated their agreement at Kloster Seven in the Seven Years' War, was influential in persuading the Congress to do likewise. As the expenses in Boston became very high, it was decided that the Convention troops should be removed to Virginia, a less expensive area. See Eelking, *German Allied Troops*, 152; Alden, *The American Revolution*, 149; Dabney, *After Saratoga*, 35.

we went from New York to Canada.[9] In order to avoid all suspicion, if our ship should be captured, I took the mattress into my cabin and slept on these badges of honor all through the rest of the trip to Canada.

When we were ready to depart I found that our cook, who fortunately had given me receipts every day for the money I had given him, had paid no one at all. I was presented with unpaid bills amounting to a total of a thousand reichsthalers. My husband had him arrested. He escaped, however, and was engaged by General Gates, but he did not keep him long because he was too extravagant. He then went to General Lafayette, who told us afterwards, "He would be fit only for a King." My husband was inclined to be lenient with him on account of his good cooking, but the rascal hated me, because I watched him closely. I still believe that he had a hand in the theft of my husband's baggage in Albany. Later on we met him again in New York, where he was living in great poverty. He had seduced the wife of an American, eloped with her, and then left her because he was so poor that he could not support her.

My husband frequently suffered from nervousness and depression. The only thing that helped him in this mood was to go walking, or to work in the garden, so whenever we were obliged to move, I always managed to have a garden prepared for him, which was no great difficulty and cost very little, because almost all our soldiers could do garden work and were glad to earn a bit extra. I thanked God more than ever that he had given me courage to join my husband! The misery of being kept a prisoner, the unfortunate position of our troops, and the lack of news from home all made my husband depressed. How much greater would his misery have been if he had had no one to divert his thoughts during the six months and more he would have been without news from us. How happy I am, even now, when I recollect those times, that I had paid no attention to the people who wanted to prevent me from doing my duty and following the call of my heart, and that I faithfully shared all his suffering and his sorrow.

9. Capt. Laurentius O'Connell was an engineering officer who served on Riedesel's staff. He had been taken prisoner at Bennington. See Stone, trans., *General Riedesel*, I, 66, 135–36; II, 265; Hadden, *Journal*, 398–400. For the trip from New York to Canada, and the Halifax stopover, see below, pp. 111–17.

It was during the month of November 1778 that we received orders to go to Virginia. Fortunately my husband found a pretty English carriage, which he bought for me so that we were able to travel more comfortably than before.[10] On the way my little Augusta had begged one of my husband's aides, Captain Edmonstone,[11] not to leave us. Touched by the child's confidence, he gave her his promise and kept it faithfully. I always traveled with the army, often over quite impassable roads. The Captain, who was very strong and always kept near us, dismounted from his horse whenever we reached a dangerous spot and held our carriage. Our good old Rockel, who was with me and to whom such assistance was very welcome, because he was already quite worn with fatigue, often remained quietly seated in his box and only called, "Captain!" Immediately the Captain would get off his horse. I did not want Rockel to take this liberty, but the good Captain was so amused that he begged me not to pay any attention to it.

I always had provisions with me, but in another wagon. As this other conveyance could not be driven as quickly as ours, we were often without food. One time when we were passing through a town called [New] Hartford, where we intended resting for one day, which we did every fourth day, we met General Lafayette, and my husband invited him to dinner, because he had been unable to find a place to eat. I was terribly embarrassed, because I knew that the General liked a good dinner. By using up all the provisions we possessed, I finally succeeded in having a pretty good dinner made after all. He was so polite and pleasant that we all liked him very much. He had a number of Americans in his party, who almost jumped out of their skins because we always talked French. It may be that they were afraid that, being on such friendly terms with

10. See General Riedesel to Major General Gates, Nov. 21, 1778, where the General discusses the plans for their departure from Cambridge on Nov. 26, 1778; Stone, trans., *General Riedesel*, II, 238–39. *Ibid.*, 56, gives the actual departure date as Nov. 28.

11. Captain Edmonstone was a young English aide assigned to General Riedesel. He had studied at the Caroline College in Brunswick not long before the outbreak of the American Revolution. He was a great help to Madame de Riedesel on this hard trip and became a favorite of the children. She even hoped he might marry her younger sister and was greatly distressed by his death. Stone, trans., *General Riedesel*, I, 39–40; II, 59, 64; Stone, trans., *Letters of Brunswick and Hessian Officers*, 178 (note by Schlözer); and below, pp. 88, 202, 204.

him, we might win him over to our side, or that he might tell us things which they did not want us to know.[12] He talked much of England and how the King had been so kind as to have him shown everything. I could not forbear asking him how he could have had the heart to accept so much kindness from the King just as he was about to leave for the purpose of fighting against him. He seemed rather embarrassed by my remark and said, "It is true that this thought also passed through my own mind one day when the King offered to let me see his fleet. I said that I hoped to see it some other time and then quietly retired in order to be relieved of the embarrassment of having to refuse his offer again." Others, however, accused the General of being in England as a spy, whence he departed directly for America.[13]

One evening we came to a very pretty place, but our extra wagon had not been able to keep up with us, and we were almost famished. As I had noticed a quantity of meat in the house where we stopped, I asked the woman of the house to let me have some. "I have all kinds of meat," she said. "There is beef, veal, and mutton." My mouth watered. "Give me some," said I, "and I will pay you a good price for it." She snapped her fingers almost under my nose saying, "You shall have none of it. Why did you leave your own country to come here and kill us and waste our goods and possessions? Now that you are our prisoners it is our turn to torment you." "Look at these poor children," I replied. "They are faint with hunger." She remained unmoved. However, when my three-and-a-half-year-old daughter Caroline went up to her, took her by the hand and said in English, "Good woman, I am very hungry," she could no longer

12. During this Hartford interview, Lafayette made a very favorable impression on General Riedesel. Stone, trans., *General Riedesel*, II, 58; compare Dabney, *After Saratoga*, 54. Lafayette was on his way to Boston early in Dec. 1778. The Baroness called this "Hartford," but the necessity of providing dinner for Lafayette, as well as the itineraries given for the march south, indicate that this was New Hartford, which Du Roi described as "a place of about 8 houses." Epping, trans., *Journal of Du Roi*, 135. Chastellux also found accommodations at New Hartford inadequate; Chastellux, *Travels*, ed. Rice, I, 227. J. Bennett Nolan, *Lafayette in America Day by Day* (Baltimore, 1934), 94.

13. Shortly before his departure for America Lafayette went to London, presumably to visit his uncle, the Marquis de Noailles, who was ambassador, and while there he spent three weeks in the highest society. He gives his own version of his visit with George III in his *Mémoires*, 6 vols. (Paris, 1837–38), I, 13–14.

resist. Taking the child into her room, she gave her an egg. "No," the good child said, "I have two sisters." This touched the woman, and she gave her three eggs saying, "I am vexed with myself, but I cannot refuse the child." She became more friendly then and offered me bread and milk. I made some tea for us. The woman watched us greedily, for the Americans loved tea very much, but had decided not to drink any more, because the tea tax was the cause of the war. I offered her a cup and made her a present of a small bag of tea. This won her over completely, and she invited me into her kitchen, where her husband sat chewing a pig's tail, and, much to my joy, she brought up from the cellar a basket of potatoes for me. When she came back her husband offered her his delicacy. She gnawed on it a bit, then gave it back to him, and he continued feasting on it. I beheld this strange reciprocal entertainment with amazement and disgust. But the man seemed to think that my own hunger made me envious, and he offered me the tail, now thoroughly gnawed. What was I to do? If I refused it, I thought, he would be insulted, and I would not get the precious basket of potatoes. So I took it and pretended to gnaw on it. Then I slipped it into the fire. Thus we were finally at peace with one another. They gave me the potatoes, and I made a good repast of them with butter. Moreover, they gave us three pretty rooms with good beds.

The next morning we went on, and wherever we passed we excited the curiosity of the inhabitants. When we reached the Hudson River we stopped at the house of a boatman, who favored us with a half-finished room without a windowpane. We hung a blanket over the opening at night and slept on straw, because our luggage cart had broken down and therefore we had no bedding, coffee, tea, or sugar, which was sometimes all we had to live on during this trip. The woman of the house was a perfect fury. She finally allowed us the next morning, when our things had arrived, to eat breakfast in her room, as it was December and we could not make a fire in our room. However, we could not persuade her to give us a table for ourselves, and she did not let us sit at her table until she and her children and the servants had finished their breakfast, which consisted of the leavings from the previous night's supper, cabbage, ham and the like, and coffee with coarse sugar; she left all her dirty dishes on the table, so that we had to wash them before we could use them. After we had finished she insisted that we wash everything again and give the dishes back to her clean. At the slightest protest on our part she offered us to the door. She did everything she could to torment us, because she was an arch-anti-royalist.

Unfortunately, a storm came up, and it was so windy that the boatman assured us it would be dangerous to make the crossing. His wicked wife insisted that we go, and only after much pleading did she allow us to stay two days longer. On the third day the man came to us very much embarrassed and told us we would have to go. I begged him to consider the danger we would be in and at least to accompany us, because that would give me more courage to make the crossing. He promised to take us over himself, and we got into a small boat with one sail. As we put off from shore the boatman jumped out and left us only one of his men, who did not even know how to handle the rudder properly, with the result that, because of his inefficiency and the adverse wind, we sailed up and down the river in great anxiety for more than five hours before we finally reached the other shore. Even then we had to wade through a morass up to our knees to get to the house of Colonel Osborn,[14] a very wealthy man with whom we were to stay.

I was given two small but nice rooms for myself, my husband, the children, and my two maids, but in these rooms we and the aides-de-camp as well, had to eat breakfast, dinner, and supper. As my stockings were soaking wet, I asked our officers to leave the room while I changed them. They wanted to warm themselves in the kitchen in the meantime, but the man of the house took them by the arm and thrust them out, saying, "What, you horrid royalists! Isn't it enough that I have given you rooms? Can you not sometimes leave me in peace?" He had just returned from the field, and in his coarse cloth suit with his long beard and dirty linen he looked like a bear, so that he made us shudder. His wife, however, was good. On the following day, which was a Sunday, she invited me to have coffee with her after dinner. I had just sat down when the man entered, looking a bit better after having shaved, and wearing his Sunday shirt. Not having been able to forget the scene of the day before, I immediately rose and wanted to leave the room. But he closed the door and asked me, "Are you afraid of me?" I replied, "I am afraid of nobody, not even of the devil, whom you resembled very much yesterday." "But

14. The 1801 German edition has it Hoxborn, but this most likely was simply Madame de Riedesel's misunderstanding of a bad English accent. Colonel Osborn was a blunt anti-royalist, but a friendly man. General Riedesel had a letter to him from General Gates. Stone, trans., *General Riedesel*, II, 63.

I look better today, do I not?" he asked. "Yes," I said. "But I always try to avoid discourtesy." My demeanor seemed to please rather than anger him; he took me by the hand and insisted that I sit down again. "I am not as bad as you think," he said. "I like you, and if I did not have a wife already, I would marry you." "But how do you know that I would have you?" I replied. "That we should soon see," he said. "I am very wealthy, and the whole countryside around here belongs to me. My wife is already old, and I should think it would be best for you just to stay here." From that moment on I could have had anything I wanted in the house, for the good woman was willing to share with me everything she was accustomed to have.

We had to stay there a week in order to give our troops time to cross the river, which was a slow procedure, because of the scarcity of boats. Our third stop was with a German, where we were comfortably put up and also had good food. It happened that the old man was the son of a coachman who had been in the service of Count Goertz in Germany.[15] When he was twelve years old his father had punished him for some mischief. Thereupon he decided to run away and somehow had reached London. As people were frequently sent to the American colonies, he happened to be among one of these groups. His lucky star led him to a good master, who grew very attached to him, had him educated, and after a few years' service, as is customary, he gave him some land to cultivate. He had worked very hard and was soon able to rent a farm from his master, who, seeing what a good worker the man was and how well he took care of everything, gave him his daughter in marriage. Now the man had sons who also rented farms, and the only thing that prevented him from being completely happy was the thought of having left his father, whom he often sent money. Knowing that the Riedesel family were neighbors and friends of the Goertz family, he was most kind to us and was sad when we left.

At another time we spent a night with a Colonel Howe, whom I wanted to compliment by asking him whether he was related to the

15. Count Karl Friedrich Adam Goertz (1733–97), who had been in the Hessian army from 1750 to 1762 and who eventually became a Prussian general, was the titleholder at that time. Several prominent members of that family were in the Prussian service. The Count was one of those who were educated at the Caroline College in Brunswick, and undoubtedly a number of circumstances threw them into contact with the Riedesels. *Allgemeine deutsche Biographie*, IX, 393–96.

English General. "God forbid," he replied, very much insulted. "He is not worthy of me." The Colonel had the reputation of being a worthy man. When he was at home rather than in the army, he plowed his land himself and thoroughly busied himself with his domestic affairs. He had a fourteen-year-old-daughter, who was pretty but of a wicked character. I was sitting by the fireside with her when she looked at the burning coal and said, "Ha! If I had the King of England here, what a pleasure it would be to cut open his body, tear out his heart, fry it over these coals, and eat it!" Horrified I looked at her and said, "I am almost ashamed to belong to a sex which is capable of expressing such a hideous desire." I have never been able to forget this abominable girl and was glad to get away from that house, even though we had been very well treated there.

Before crossing the Blue Ridge Mountains we had to make another week's halt in order to give our troops a chance to reassemble. [16] Meanwhile there had been so much snow that four of our men had to ride ahead of my carriage and make a path for us. We passed through picturesque country, but so rough and wild that it was frightening. Often our lives were in danger when we passed over breakneck roads, and we suffered terribly from the cold and, what was even worse, from lack of food. When we arrived in Virginia and had only another day to go before reaching our destination, we had nothing left but tea and some bread and butter, nor could we get anything else. One of the natives gave me a handful of dried fruit. At noon we arrived at a house where I asked for some food, but it was refused harshly with the remark that the people had nothing to give to the royalist dogs. I saw some Turkish flour [17] and begged for a couple of handfuls so that I could mix it with water and make some bread. The woman replied, "No, that is for our Negroes who work for us; you, however, wanted to kill us." Captain Edmonstone offered her a guinea or two for it because my children were so hungry, but she replied, "Not for a hundred would I give it to you; and if you die of hunger, so much the better." The

16. Anburey's *Travels*, II; Epping, trans., *Journal of Du Roi;* and Dabney's account of the Convention Troops at various points give a vivid picture of the difficult progress from Boston to Charlottesville. See Stone, trans., *General Riedesel*, II, 49–62, which traces Madame de Riedesel's dread of leaving, their hardships, and such military factors as the desertions that occurred, especially in Pennsylvania.

17. Indian meal.

Captain was so angered that he wanted to take some of the flour by force, but in order to avoid a scene, I begged him earnestly to keep quiet, adding that perhaps we would soon meet some kinder people. Unfortunately, however, we did not. We did not even come across a cabin. The roads were abominable, the horses tired out, my three children pale and exhausted from hunger, and I, myself, for the first time absolutely without hope. Captain Edmonstone was so extremely moved by this sight that he went from man to man, trying to get something to eat, and from one of the drivers of the luggage cart he finally got a piece of dry bread weighing about a quarter pound, the outside of which had been gnawed off all around because it was too hard to bite off a piece. When he brought this to me, the children's eyes beamed. Caroline being the youngest, I wanted to give her the first piece. "No," the good child said. "My sisters are hungrier than I am." Moreover, neither little Augusta nor Frederika would take it, because they wanted their little sister to have it. So I divided it and persuaded all three to partake of it. The tears rolled down my cheeks, and the good Captain was so moved that he could not bear the sight any longer. Had I ever refused a beggar a piece of bread, I would have thought that this was God's punishment. The good driver, who had so willingly given us his last bit of bread, received a guinea for it from Captain Edmonstone, and on arrival at our destination a lot of bread for his return journey.

Our destination was called Colle, in Virginia, where my husband had gone on ahead with the troops and now awaited us with impatience and longing. We arrived there the middle of February 1779, having gone from Boston through the provinces of Connecticut, New York, New Jersey, Pennsylvania, and Maryland, traveling 678 English miles, in about twelve weeks. The house where we lived and the whole property belonged to an Italian,[18] who let us live there

18. Philip Mazzei, an Italian horticulturist who became an agent of the State of Virginia during the Revolution, had arrived in 1773 for the purpose of introducing the culture of grapes, olives, and other Mediterranean plants. He carried on his experiments east of Charlottesville on land adjacent to Monticello. These were not crowned with success, and he was appointed by Gov. Patrick Henry to serve in Europe as an agent of the revolutionary government. After being captured by the British and interned on Long Island for three months in 1779, he found his efforts in Europe were blocked by Franklin, who opposed the practice of the states' sending out their own commercial agents. In Virginia again in 1783, he failed to receive the consular post he was seeking and returned in 1785 to Europe, going first into the

during his absence, since he intended to be absent for a while. We looked forward longingly to his and his wife's and daughter's departure because the house was small, and, moreover, the scarcity of provisions annoyed them. Under the circumstances, the man preserved a kind of guardianship over us. For instance, on the first day, when he had had a ram killed, he gave us only the head, the neck, and the giblets, even though I pointed out to him that it would have to do for more than twenty people. He assured me it would make very good soup, and gave us two heads of cabbage and a partly spoiled ham, and thus we had to content ourselves.

The troops had been expected sooner, and therefore a number of cattle and pigs had been killed, and as salt was very scarce, holes had been dug in the ground, and the meat, cut in quarters and sprinkled with ashes—which is said to be just as good a preservative as salt—was buried therein. However, as the sun is often very warm there even in January, the top layers of meat were spoiled. The meat was brought to us in wheelbarrows. Sometimes we had to throw all of it away, but sometimes it could be washed off, salted, and then smoked. The first day, when I hardly had enough to eat for ourselves, I was alarmed to see eight of our officers approaching shortly before dinner. There was nothing to do but to share with them what little we had. The troops were in Charlottesville, [19] two hours away. One had to go through a beautiful forest to get to them.

service of Poland and then of Russia. His four-volume *Recherches historiques et politiques sur les Etats-Unis de l'Amérique Septentrionale . . . ,* 4 vols. (Colle, 1788) is a monument to his American years. For Mazzei, see Howard Marraro, trans., *Memoirs of the Life and Peregrinations of the Florentine, Philip Mazzei, 1730–1816* (N. Y., 1942); Richard C. Garlick, *Philip Mazzei, Friend of Jefferson: His Life and Letters* (Baltimore, 1933); E. C. Branchi, "Memoirs of the Life and Voyages of Philip Mazzei," *Wm. and Mary Qtly.,* 2d Ser., 9 (1929), 161–74, 247–64; and Armistead Churchill Gordon, Jr., "Mazzei, Philip," *DAB.* See also, above, p. oo.

19. A report of Aug. 16, 1780, showed there were at or around Charlottesville 77 German officers, 142 non-commissioned officers, 25 drummers, 809 privates, and 94 servants, making a total of 1147 persons. On Dec. 1, 1781, this number had shrunk to 1053. These figures do not include the British troops. Stone, trans., *General Riedesel,* II, 88, 116. The prisoners' barracks were about four miles from Charlottesville. Dabney, *After Saratoga,* 60. See description in Jefferson to Patrick Henry, Mar. 27, 1779, Julian P. Boyd, *et al.,* eds., *The Papers of Thomas Jefferson* (Princeton, 1950 ———), II, 241–42.

At first they were very uncomfortable there. They had log cabins, but these were not plastered, and they lacked doors and windows, so they suffered terribly from the cold. They worked very hard to build better houses for themselves, and in a short time the place became a pretty town. Each of the barracks had a garden in the back and a nice little fenced-in yard for poultry. [20] When the old supply of provisions had been eaten up, they received another lot of fresh meat and flour enough to make bread; moreover, Indian meal served for making pancakes and dumplings. The only thing they lacked was money. The English sent very little money, and it was hard to get anything on credit, which particularly troubled the private soldiers.

By the middle of February the fruit trees were already in bloom, but all of them were killed by the night frosts. As soon as the weather permitted, we had the garden and the farm land planted, and as our landlord left three weeks later, we then took over everything, the pigs, wild turkeys and so on. [21] The latter weighed over fifty pounds apiece and were quite tame. When spring came they all flew away in order to hatch their eggs, which they had laid in the woods. We thought they had gone for good, but they all came back, bringing a flock of young ones with them.

We had a large house built with a big room in the center and two smaller rooms on each side, which cost my husband a hundred guineas. [22] It was very pretty. A number of Negroes brought us everything they had in the way of poultry and vegetables. Every week General Phillips and we ourselves took turns in slaughtering an ox and two pigs. In a word, we had everything we needed. But in the summer we suffered terribly from the heat and lived in constant

20. General Riedesel was disturbed over the bad conditions in which the troops had to live, particularly their barracks. General Riedesel to Duke Karl I, Mar. 22, 1779, Stone, trans., *General Riedesel*, II, 188–89; and Anburey, *Travels*, II, 323–24.

21. For the daily life of the Riedesels at Colle, see Stone, trans., *General Riedesel*, II, 69–70, which describes their gardening and so on. Life, however, was not all gardening and horsebackriding (Madame de Riedesel amazed some of the Virginians by "Amazonian" characteristics, including riding as a man would). The entire Riedesel family enjoyed their acquaintance with the Jeffersons although the Baroness, for some strange reason, makes no reference whatever to them. See the introduction, above, pp. xxxiv–vi; Henry S. Randall, *The Life of Thomas Jefferson* (N. Y., 1858), 235–36; Dabney, *After Saratoga*, 62–63; Stone, trans., *General Riedesel*, II, 71; and Boyd, ed., *Jefferson Papers*, II, *passim*.

22. See above, the introduction, pp. xxxiii–iv.

fear of rattlesnakes, and the fruit was completely ruined by three
sorts of insects. We had heavy thunderstorms, sometimes five or six
a day, and the wind was so terrific that a hundred trees or more were
uprooted. [23] None of the trees were very firm in the ground, their
roots being hardly covered because the heavy wind blew the soil,
which was very sandy, away from the roots. Furthermore, the
Negroes and the cowherds often set fire to the trees, which are not
considered of much value there. All this made it an easy matter for
the wind to blow them down. Frequently a whole forest was set on
fire in order to gain more farming land. We could not sleep at night
without leaving our windows wide open so as to get fresh air.
During the night we were often awakened by three or four horrid
bats, three times as large as ours at home, and it would take us half
the night to get rid of them. One night my husband was called out
of bed because the new stable was almost blown down by the wind.
Everyone came running to help support the stable, and I stayed in
the house alone with the children and maids. The wind grew worse
and worse. Big pieces of the chimney fell into the room. The whole
house shook, and half the night I was in fear of being hit by something and killed. We had a number of similar frights.

We had no chairs at all, only treestumps on which to sit, and these
were also used for tables by laying boards across them. We lived in
this manner quite content for three or four months. Only my husband
was always sad, and, what was more, he could not stand the heat at
all, which went as high as 103 degrees and was most oppressive. We
tried our best to cheer him up. When the vegetables in our garden
began to come up, he got a lot of pleasure from the garden work.
However, as he would not wear a hat for this work, he suffered a
great deal from headaches, and the heat bothered him. Thus he suffered a sunstroke, about which I shall tell, which was the beginning
of my greatest grief.

I was busy setting our new home to rights and putting my husband's things in his room when I heard a commotion outdoors. I ran
to the window and saw some men carrying my husband into the
house. His face was blue, his hands white, his eyes rigid, and beads
of perspiration covered his forehead. He had had a sunstroke! I was

23. Jefferson recorded a thunderstorm of Apr. 17 which brought severe
winds and frost and damaged the Convention army's gardens. Edwin Morris
Betts, ed., *Thomas Jefferson's Garden Book* . . . (Phila., 1944), 86–89. See
also Epping, trans., *Journal of Du Roi*, 160–61.

more dead than alive myself, and the children uttered penetrating screams. We laid him down at once, tore off his clothes, and fortunately the surgeon of the regiment, who lived with us, was at home at the moment, so that he could bleed him immediately. He began to gain speech again and told us that while walking through the garden he had felt the sun burning hot on his head. He had hardly been able to reach the house, when his aides arrived, without whose help he would have been lost. Good Lord, what would have become of me and my little children among the captives so far from home in the enemy's country! My hair still stands on end when I think of it. After my husband had regained consciousness, he took my hand in his and looked at me lovingly. It was obvious that he felt very ill. If I left him for only a moment, he would immediately grow uneasy and follow me with his eyes. The doctor for whom we had sent arrived, and after everything possible was done to help him, God finally let my husband recover. But for many years after he still suffered a great deal from headaches and weakness, which made him even more distressed over our predicament.

The doctor prescribed a cure at a spa in Virginia called Frederick's Springs, so we went there. It was my opinion, however, that this cure made him worse rather than better, because he always moistened his head before taking the baths, and afterwards, in spite of every effort to dry it, his hair always stayed damp.[24] His melancholy mood continued, and the thought of our captivity worried him more than ever. He could not sleep at night. I would try to soothe him by reading aloud to him in a drowsy manner, and this would finally put him to sleep. His hands and feet were always blue, and cold as ice. Whenever I thought I might venture to lie down, his anguish would immediately awaken him again. Everything annoyed him. One day a Virginian came into the room, saying that he was curious to see a German woman, and looked me over from head to foot. I was very much amused about this, but when I took the man to see my husband, he became so excited over the thought that his position made him subject to the whims of other people that the tears came to his eyes. I was filled with regret over this thoughtlessness.

While at this place we were introduced to General Washington's

24. Contrary to what Madame de Riedesel says, the General himself expressed the view that he was helped by this treatment. Stone, trans., *General Riedesel*, II, 73. Frederick Springs, or Berkeley Springs, was in Berkeley County, later West Virginia.

family,[25] and to Mrs. Carroll, a very pleasant woman, and her husband.[26] She was a very enthusiastic, but reasonable patriot, and we became great friends. She spent almost every forenoon with us. Captain Geismar played the violin, and I sang Italian arias, which she enjoyed immensely.[27] One day a farmer came to our house, whom we had frequently asked with many kind words to bring us fresh butter. As most Americans love music, he listened attentively, and when I had finished, he told me I would have to sing again. I asked him jestingly what he would give me for singing, as I did nothing without being paid. He immediately replied, "Two pounds of butter." That amused me very much, and I sang another song. "Sing another," he said when I had finished, "but something jolly." In the end I had sung so much, that the next day he brought me four or five pounds of butter. He had brought his wife with him and begged me to sing again. I won their affection, and after that I always had everything I needed. The best of it was that he really thought I wanted to be paid for my singing and was very much astonished when I paid them for the butter before they left.

The Virginians are mostly indolent, which is ascribed to their hot climate, but with the slightest inducement they are ready in an instant to dance; and if a reel (an English or Scottish folk-dance) is played, the men immediately catch hold of the women, who then spring up as though possessed. But as soon as they are led back to their chairs, they sit there like blockheads again. What we had heard about the morals of the people in this part of the country does not make a favorable picture. For instance, we were told that two girls had been made pregnant by their own father, and that while this created a lot of gossip, it had remained unpunished. Another man, who found his daughter-in-law more attractive that his own wife, made his son an

25. There is no record of Martha Washington visiting Berkeley Springs in 1779. By "General Washington's family," Madame de Riedesel could have meant his brother and first cousin, Samuel and Warner Washington, who were on the board of trustees of the bath and buildings at the resort, or members of their families. See Carl Bridenbaugh, "Baths and Watering Places of Colonial America," *Wm. and Mary Qtly.*, 3d Ser., 3 (1946), 164.

26. Madame de Riedesel calls this woman "Madame Garel." Louise Hall Tharp identifies her as Mrs. Charles Carroll of Carrollton. Tharp, *The Baroness and the General*, 328–30, 434–35.

27. Jefferson also enjoyed the musical talents of Captain Geismar. Marie Kimball, *Jefferson: War and Peace, 1776 to 1784* (N. Y., 1947), 18, 19, 20, 38, 40–45.

offer to exchange wives, to which the son agreed on the condition that, in addition to getting his own mother for his wife, he also be given two cows and two horses, which was done, and nothing further was said about the affair.[28]

The plantation-owners in Virginia have numerous Negro slaves and do not treat them well.[29] Many of them let the slaves walk about stark naked until they are between fifteen and sixteen years old, and the clothes which they give them afterward are not worth wearing. The slaves are in the charge of an overseer who leads them out into the fields at daybreak, where they have to work like cattle or suffer a beating; and when they come home completely tired out and sunburnt they are given some Indian meal called hominy, which they make into baked stuff. Often, however, they are too exhausted to eat and prefer sleeping a couple of hours, because they must go back to work. They look upon it as a misfortune to have children, because these, in turn, will also be slaves and unhappy men. As they have no time to cultivate their own bit of land that is given to them, they have no money whatever, except what they can get from the sale of poultry, with which to buy their clothes. But there are, of course, good masters too. One can recognize them immediately, because their slaves are well dressed and housed. These Negroes are very good servants, very faithful to their master, and very much attached to him. It is not surprising that the brutal type of masters have ill-disposed slaves.

During our stay at the spa my husband received the good news that he and General Phillips and their aides had permission to go to New York to be exchanged there. My husband, accordingly, went back to Colle to make arrangements for the maintenance, in his absence, of

28. For another discussion of life in Virginia, not flattering to Virginians, see Anburey, *Travels,* II, 293–99. The Marquis de Chastellux discusses Virginia extensively; Chastellux, *Travels,* ed. Rice, II, 377–468.

29. For a comparison between the condition of the Negroes in the South and those in New England, who "reside in good houses, are in comfortable circumstances, and live as well as their white neighbors," see Stone, trans., *Letters of Brunswick and Hessian Officers,* 142. Chastellux found that many of the Virginians "treat their Negroes with great humanity," while describing and deploring the institution of slavery. Chastellux, *Travels,* ed. Rice, II, 439 and *passim.* Many travelers commented on the slaves' lack of clothes; see Epping, trans., *Journal of Du Roi,* 147, 157; Chastellux, *Travels,* ed. Rice, II, 585; Anburey, *Travels,* II, 295.

the troops, which he put in Colonel Specht's command,[30] and for the sale of all the things we would no longer require, particularly of our new house into which we had not even moved as yet. This happened to us again several times later. We were frequently put up very uncomfortably when we reached a new place, and hardly would we succeed in fixing things up with effort, when we would get orders to leave, which often made me very unhappy. This time, however, all of us rejoiced.

30. Col. Johann Friedrich Specht, who died in 1787 as a pensioned colonel in Brunswick, had commanded the Specht Regiment, one of the three infantry regiments under Riedesel, before replacing the General as commander of the German troops in the Convention Army. Stone, trans., *General Riedesel,* II, 271.

VII

Removal to New York

In August 1779 I left this spa to join my husband in York, Pennsylvania.[1] Mrs. Carroll, the nice woman whom I mentioned previously, had invited me to visit her on her plantation in Maryland, should I ever come into that vicinity. I decided to do so now.[2] Captain Freeman, one of my husband's English aides, stayed with us.[3] Captain Edmonstone, through the intervention of his father, had been exchanged. He was so much attached to my husband, and it distressed him so to leave him, that my husband had to urge him to return to England. We grieved to see him depart, particularly as he said "I feel certain that I shall never see you again."[4]

1. The General himself, much concerned about the American attempt to keep the captured troops as separated as possible from their officers, did not leave Virginia until Sept. He met his family at York, or "Yorktown," as Madame de Riedesel called it. Stone, trans., *General Riedesel*, II, 71–72. For a description of Lancaster and York at that time, see Anburey, *Travels*, II, 271–72, 274–75, and Epping, trans., *Journal of Du Roi*, 141–43.

2. Mrs. Tharp speculates that this was Mary Darnall Carroll's plantation, "Doughoregan." Mrs. Carroll was the wife of Charles Carroll of Carrollton and the daughter-in-law of Charles Carroll of Annapolis. She died in 1782 at the age of 33. Tharp, *The Baroness and the General*, 328–30, 434–35; see above, p. 85.

3. Captain Freeman had been brigadier-major or adjutant to General Fraser. Along with Captain Willoe he was assigned by Lord Germain as an adjutant to General Riedesel. He drew maps of the engagements at Freeman's Farm and Bemis Heights. During this period he regularly dined with the Riedesels. Stone, trans., *General Riedesel*, II, 137.

4. Captain Edmonstone carried a letter from Madame de Riedesel to her mother with him. The entire Riedesel family mourned his death on this trip home. See below, pp. 202, 204.

88

During our journey to Mrs. Carroll's plantation, Captain Freeman saw a black snake (said to be a harmless variety) swallow a frog. He said jestingly, "I hereby declare myself the frog's rescuer." He took his sword, cut open the snake, and, lo and behold, much to the surprise of all of us, the frog hopped out quite alive. Before we reached our destination our coach overturned, but fortunately nobody was hurt. I had notified Mrs. Carroll of our coming, and she sent a man on horseback to meet me. After driving through a very pretty village, inhabited entirely by Negroes, each of whom had his own garden and had learned a trade, we came through a large court to a very handsome house, where the whole family welcomed us joyfully. The family consisted of the eighty-four-year-old father-in-law, an old gentleman in the best of health, and in the most charmingly merry mood, scrupulously clean and tidy, and on whose venerable face one saw the happiest contentment stamped—and four darling grandchildren and their dear mother, our amiable hostess. Our meals were served on silver platters, without elegance, to be sure, but prepared with taste, and nothing was lacking. They said that as they hoped that I would stay with them for a long time, they would treat me as one of the family.

The garden was magnificent, and the next day they drove us out to show us their vineyard, which was very elegant and surpassed our expectations. At first we drove through a large orchard. Then we climbed up a winding path to the vineyard. The grapevines were planted alternately with hollyhocks and amaranths. The view from both sides of the hill and looking down from the top was the most beautiful sight I had ever beheld in the whole part of America I had visited. Mrs. Carroll's husband had traveled a great deal and had gotten his ideas for such planting in England and France. In other respects he was not such a lovable man, but rather brusque and stingy, and not at all a suitable mate for his wife, who, although she would not let any of this be noticed, did not seem to be very happy. Her father-in-law loved her dearly.

Not far from the plantation there was a city called Baltimore, which I was told was very pleasant and that various nice families lived there. We were visited one day by a close friend of our hostess, a polite and cheerful woman. These two women reminded me of Rousseau's Héloïse and her friend, and the old father of Héloïse's husband. Mrs. Carroll was loving and affectionate like Héloïse, and I feel sure would have liked to have had a husband like Saint Preux.[5] We built a temple for her, decorated with flowers, in accordance with plans sketched by Captain Freeman, dedicated to friendship and gratitude. A few years later she wrote me that her family always kept the flowers fresh. The dear, good woman has since passed away, and her family, particularly her children, miss her terribly. We stayed with her a week or ten days, and our parting was very sad. We were given the best of provisions, enough to last us for a long time, although we did not need these things now, as the royalists, partly as an expression of their friendship and partly as a matter of habit, were very kind to us and gave us plenty of everything we needed. It would be considered a crime in this country not to receive a traveler.

When we were not far from the place where we were to meet my husband, a heavy thunderstorm caught us while we were in the woods. One of the trees blew over and fell between the driver's seat and the horse. We were caught fast and could not move from the spot, and none of our men was strong enough to lift the fallen tree. In the meantime the thunder was heavy, the lightning struck several times around us, and another big tree threatened to crush us. I begged that we be gotten out of this predicament, but the driver, who had completely lost his head, insisted that it was impossible to move. Finally my little Augusta, who was then eight years old, said, "Why don't you unhitch the horse from the front and hitch him onto the back of the carriage to pull it back!" That worked immediately, and we asked ourselves why the thought had not occurred to us sooner.[6] Thus we finally arrived safely at York in Pennsylvania, where we met my husband, who had been exceedingly worried about us on account of the heavy storm.[7]

We drove through magnificent country where, among other places, we came through a very well-cultivated district inhabited by Moravian Brethren. One of the towns was called Holy Sepulchre, another district was called Holy Land, and the town there, Bethlehem. We found

5. Saint Preux is the main figure in Rousseau's *Nouvelle Héloïse* (1761). In this sentimental and highly moralizing novel, he is the *séducteur "vertueux."* *Larousse du XXe Siècle,* VI, 142.

6. The account given by Anburey, *Travels,* II, 346–47, sounds as though it were the same accident. Perhaps it should have been mentioned a bit later in his account, or somewhat earlier in Madame de Riedesel's.

7. For a description of York's reception of the Convention Army on their march *to* Virginia, see Epping, trans., *Journal of Du Roi,* 143.

a very good inn, where we waited for the rest of the party, who had not yet arrived.[8] I had brought two gorgeous birds with me from Virginia. The male bird was scarlet with a darker red tuft of feathers on his head, about the size of a bull-finch, and it sang magnificently. The female bird was gray with a red breast and also had a tuft of feathers on its head. They are very tame soon after they are caught and eat out of one's hand. These birds live a long time, but if two male birds are hung in the same room they are so jealous of each other that one of them dies soon afterwards. I saw black birds in Virginia of the same size, which always cry "willow." This amused us very much because one of my husband's aides was named Willoe. One of my servants discovered a whole nest of these red birds and fed and raised them. Knowing how much I loved them, he left Colle with two cages full on his back, but they all died before he reached me, much to our sorrow.[9] I also had a collection of very beautiful butterflies and had packed them carefully in a box. However, the wagon in which they were transported was upset, and the box broke. This happened to me twice, which discouraged me from making another collection.

After our whole party had gathered and we had all rested, we proceeded on our journey and stopped with a family which was very kind to us and told us they were royalists. Their name was Van Horne.[10] They were most hospitable and asked us to give their regards

8. Joseph M. Levering, in *A History of Bethlehem, Pennsylvania* (Bethlehem, 1903), 492, says the Riedesels stopped at Bethlehem for two days, Sept. 25 and 26, 1779. The Riedesels had also stayed there on their trip to Virginia, on Jan. 5, 1779. *Ibid.*, 490. Levering on p. 493 comments on the "singular information"—or misinformation—about the existence of a town of "Holy Sepulchre" and a district of "Holy Land" which Madame de Riedesel picked up. For descriptions of this section of Pennsylvania, see Anburey, *Travels*, II, 250–52, 254–60, 450–51. See also pp. 93–94.

9. The birds of America made a great impression on Anburey. For his description of humming birds, mocking birds, and others, see *Travels*, II, 178–87, 247–48. Anburey's impressions of the birds and other natural wonders of America may have been vicarious, via Peter Kalm's *Travels into North America*, 3 vols. (Warrenton and London, 1770–71), and Chastellux's *Travels*. See Whitfield J. Bell, Jr., "Thomas Anburey's 'Travels through America': A Note on Eighteenth-Century Plagiarism," Bibliographical Society of America, *Papers*, 37 (1943), 23–36.

10. This was the family of Philip Van Horne, uncle of Mrs. Harriet Van Horne Foy. Chastellux also visited the Van Hornes. See above, chapter I, n. 15; Tharp, *The Baroness and the General*, 421; Chastellux, *Travels*, ed. Rice, I, 118–20, 286–87.

to the English General Cornwallis, who, like General Clinton, was a friend of General Phillips and had arranged for our return from Virginia.

We also stopped at a very pretty place called Elizabeth Town [Elizabeth, New Jersey] opposite Staten Island, where we met a number of royalists, who were happy to have us stay with them. Being so near New York and sure of my husband's exchange, we thought that we had now reached our immediate goals and ate our dinner there happily in the thought that, as we intended crossing over to New York directly afterwards, we would be set free that same evening. But suddenly the door opened and an officer, who had been sent by General Washington, entered and handed General Phillips a letter, containing orders to return, as Congress had not given its approval to the exchange. The eyes of General Phillips, who was a very violent man, sparkled with fury. He hit the table with his fist, exclaiming, "This is pleasant! [11]—and we should have expected it from these people, who are all rascals!" I was petrified and unable to speak a word. He took my hand and said, "Now, my friend, do not lose courage. Follow my example. See, I am quite composed!" "Everyone," I replied, "has his own way of expressing sadness. I conceal mine in my heart, and you express yours by violence. In my opinion, however, you would do better not to show these people how angry you are, because they only scoff at you, and besides it may only cause you still further trouble." He admitted I was right and assured me that he would bear his sorrow like I, with resignation, and was thereafter quiet.

I was pregnant and felt badly all the while, so the journey exhausted me exceedingly. I had hoped to be able to live quietly among people who would take care of me; but in vain! After only one day of rest, which had been granted us, we had to start on the return journey, and we stopped with the Van Hornes again. This time we met a nephew of General Washington there [12] with a number of American officers,

11. Madame de Riedesel used English in the original. Her words were: "This is pleasant!"

12. Washington's nephew Bushrod enlisted as a private in 1778 at the age of 16. George W. Goble, "Washington, Bushrod," *DAB*. His nephew George Augustine Washington was serving as a secretary to his uncle in the fall of 1779 and was officially detailed to the Guard in April 1780. John C. Fitzpatrick, ed., *The Writings of George Washington*, 39 vols. (Washington, 1931–44), XVI, 392. The latter seems more likely to have been the Van Hornes' guest. Levering, *History of Bethlehem*, 505, identifies the nephew, who visited Bethlehem on July 28, 1779, as "Col. William Augustine Wash-

who during the three days of their stay had succeeded in so changing the minds of these people (they were of the turncoat type), that not only did we find the daughter of these so-called royalists on the friendliest of terms with these anti-royalists, whom she allowed all sorts of liberties, but in addition, as they no longer felt that they needed to spare our feelings, we heard them singing all through the night "God save great Washington! God damn the King!" It was difficult for me to conceal my annoyance about this when we departed next morning.

We now returned to Bethlehem,[13] where my husband and General Phillips had been given permission by the Americans to stay until the delayed exchange of prisoners should take place, and as our previous innkeeper had given us excellent service, we all stopped with him again. And, indeed, there were sixteen of us and four servants. The servants received money for their board. We had twenty horses. The innkeeper did not want to make a definite agreement, and as none of us had much money, we were glad that he was willing to wait until we had received some. We were even more inclined to regard him as an honest man, as he belonged to the Congregation of the Moravian Brethren, and the inn was the so-called Congregation Inn.[14] But great was our horror, after staying there six weeks, when we were finally allowed to go to New York, on being presented with a bill for $32,000, American paper money, of course, which was around the sum of four hundred guineas. If it had not been for a royalist, who was passing through and who wanted to exchange coins at any price, we would have been greatly embarrassed and could not have left. Through this man we were fortunate enough to get eighty dollars in paper money for one piaster.

During this whole period my husband still suffered from headaches, and at night had difficulty in breathing. This being the case, he began

---

ington," but Gen. Washington recorded no relative of that name. Jared Sparks, ed., *The Writings of George Washington . . .*, 12 vols. (Boston, 1837), I, 549–50.

13. On Oct. 10, 1779, the Bethlehem Diary records "General Riedesel and his family also arrived today." Information provided by Vernon Nelson, archivist of the Moravian Church, Bethlehem, Pa. See also Levering, *History of Bethlehem*, 493.

14. This inn was known as the Sun Inn; the innkeeper was the Norwegian sailor, Jost Jansen. Levering, *History of Bethlehem*, 493 and 494, where Levering defends the high prices. Chastellux stayed at the same inn on his travels. Chastellux, *Travels*, ed. Rice, II, 522, 649; see also, Stone, trans., *General Riedesel*, II, 75.

to use snuff, a thing which he had earlier abhorred. I first persuaded him to take a pinch of snuff. He thought I was joking, but when he found a few moments later that it had actually relieved him, he gave up his pipe for a snuff-box.[15] Our little Caroline was very ill with whooping cough, and my pregnancy was more and more advanced, so we were all filled with longing to get to New York as quickly as possible, in order to have better care, comfort, and necessary help closer by when needed.

In Bethlehem, as in all Brethren Congregations, there was a "brother house" and a "sister house." In the latter lovely embroidery and other pretty needlework were made, and we bought various pieces. A young German woman named Gersdof, who later went to Herrn-hut, taught the sisters all this kind of work. The houses of the congregation were well built, and there were all sorts of manufacturing establishments there. Among others, there was a tannery which produced as good leather as the English at half the price. Our gentlemen bought a lot of it. There were good carpenters, cabinetmakers, steel-workers, and very good blacksmiths.[16] We would have liked very much to have seen Philadelphia, which was only twelve to fifteen miles distant, over a thoroughly good road, but as my husband and the other gentlemen were not permitted to go, and as I preferred sharing everything with my husband, the pleasant as well as the unpleasant, I gladly gave up going. While in Bethlehem we often went to church and enjoyed the lovely singing.[17] The wife of the preacher died while we were there.[18] Her coffin was set up in a special place made for this purpose with a fence around it, as the dead are not kept in the house here.

Finally at the end of November 1779 we left Bethlehem. My husband, General Phillips, and their aides were not exchanged, but they

15. General Riedesel had been much opposed to the use of snuff. His story checks with his wife's. Stone, trans., *General Riedesel,* II, 76.

16. For Susanna Charlotte von Gersdof and the general industriousness of the Moravians, see Chastellux, *Travels,* ed. Rice, II, 522–23, 644, 650–51.

17. On Oct. 13 General Phillips, General Riedesel, the Baroness, their chaplains, and the other English officers attended a church service which included the baptism of a Negro woman. Bethlehem Diary, information provided by Vernon Nelson, archivist of the Moravian Church, Bethlehem, Pa. For Moravian music, see Chastellux, *Travels,* ed. Rice, II, 523, 644–45, 651–52.

18. This was the wife of the Rev. Paul Muenster. Levering, *History of Bethlehem,* 493.

were given permission to go to New York on parole.[19] I did not want to visit with the Van Hornes again, because I detest two-faced people, but we had the misfortune of having our carriage break down almost before their door, so we were forced to stay with them until the damage had been repaired. But I did not spend the night with them, and when they asked us again to give their regards to the King and assured us of their loyalty to him, in whose army the head of the family had been a colonel, I replied dryly that I did not believe he needed our recommendations, an answer he could take as he chose.

We again passed through Elizabeth, where again we were very well received, crossed the Hudson, and reached New York late at night, my husband having gone on ahead.[20] A soldier, who had been sent with us to show us the way, lead us to a large, handsome house, where everything had been prepared for our coming, even a good supper. I was too busy putting the children to bed and too tired, myself, to ask where we were and thought it was an inn. My husband, who had eaten supper with General Cornwallis, came home late. The next morning I was asked what I should like to have to eat. I replied that, as my husband would not take his meals at home, I should not need more than three dishes for six people; that is, for myself, my children, my maids, and Pastor Mylius,[21] the chaplain of my husband's regiment, who traveled with us and taught my children. He was a very

19. The Bethlehem Diary for November is missing, but according to an extract of the Diary Generals Phillips and Riedesel left for New York on Nov. 22. Information provided by Vernon Nelson, archivist of the Moravian Church, Bethlehem, Pa.

20. The General arrived at New York on Nov. 29, 1779. See General Riedesel to Duke Ferdinand, Dec. 8, 1779, Stone, trans., *General Riedesel,* II, 201. Adj. Gen. Carl Leopold Baurmeister noted in a letter of Dec. 13, 1779, that: "Generals Phillips and von Riedesel finally arrived here at the end of November with seven officers. They were brought over from Perth Amboy to Staten Island. General Riedesel had his wife and three merry daughters with him. I cannot keep from remarking that the baroness speaks German only with difficulty and that the children speak English only and do not know a word of their mother tongue." Bernhard A. Uhlendorf, trans., *Revolution in America; Confidential Letters and Journals 1776–1784 of Adjutant General Major Baurmeister of the Hessian Forces* (New Brunswick, N. J., 1957), 327.

21. Pastor Johann August Mylius (Milius) was chaplain for the Riedesel Regiment. He regularly dined with the Riedesels in Virginia. He became pastor to a congregation at Salder in Germany, dying in 1819, Stone, trans., *General Riedesel,* II, 70, 271.

pious man of excellent character, always in good spirits, much beloved by the children and all of us. I was told that orders had already been given to serve us six large and four small dishes every day. Still thinking that we were in an inn, I protested against such excess, as I feared the size of the bill. I learned then that we were in the home of the Governor, General Tryon,[22] who had forbidden that I be told where I was being taken, because he was afraid that I would not accept his hospitality. In addition, this noble-minded gentleman had left for Long Island,[23] where he had temporary command, in order to avoid our expressions of gratitude. Every wish of mine was anticipated, and I was ever fearful of taking advantage of so much kindness. General Pattison, commandant of the city, called on me and said that a house was being furnished for us, where we should make our real home.[24] Lord Cornwallis and General Clinton also both visited me. The former departed on an expedition soon afterwards;[25] the latter offered to arrange for my stay at a country estate, which he had at his disposal, and where my children should be inoculated against smallpox, which would be too dangerous a procedure in the city, where there was an epidemic of this disease at the time. I gladly accepted this offer and made all necessary preparations to move there. I gave our cook ten guineas to buy all sorts of supplies. When he returned soon after and

22. William Tryon (1729–88), became governor of North Carolina in 1765, where his abilities as well as his severity were shown. In 1771 he was appointed governor of New York. Although recalled in 1775, he returned after New York City was taken by Howe. He became commander of the New York district, and in this capacity led expeditions into Connecticut. Leonard W. Labaree, "Tryon, William," *DAB*. Tryon was occupying the William Walton house in New York City. Tharp, *The Baroness and the General*, 337–38, 435–36.

23. For a description of Long Island as it must have appeared to Madame de Riedesel, see Anburey, *Travels*, II, 478–80.

24. Gen. James Pattison (often spelled Patterson) was commandant of New York City from July 5, 1779, to Aug. 12, 1780. Oscar T. Barck, *New York City During the War for Independence* (N. Y., 1931), 53. The house furnished by General Pattison was the home of John Marston. Tharp, *The Baroness and the General*, 342, 435–36.

25. Maj. Gen. Henry Clinton, commander in chief of the British army, sailed with Cornwallis on Dec. 26, 1779, for the South and returned to New York on June 17, 1780. Ward, *The War of the Revolution*, ed. Alden, II, 696, 706; Eelking, *German Allied Troops*, 194. For a recent study, see William B. Willcox, *Portrait of a General: Sir Henry Clinton in the War of Independence* (N. Y., 1964).

asked for more money, I learned to my horror that this was only enough to last for two days, everything being so expensive there, even the most simple food. For instance, one pound of meat cost, in our money, twelve groschen; one pound of butter, eighteen groschen; a turkey, four reichsthalers; a chicken, twenty groschen; one egg, four groschen; one quart of milk, six groschen; a bushel of potatoes, two reichsthalers; one-half of a bushel of turnips, two gulden; ten oysters, eight groschen; six onions, one reichsthaler. But there was nothing else for me to do except bear it with patience![26]

One day a general was announced. I received him, and he asked me among other things whether I was satisfied with my stay in this house. My heart was so filled with gratitude for all the kindness extended to us, that I could not say enough in praise of everything. I finally expressed the desire to meet my noble benefactor, who had shown so much delicacy. He smiled, and at that moment my husband entered saying, "This is the man who has shown us so much goodness!" I was so glad to see him, that I could find no words to express my feelings, which touched him very much. As time went on, he continued to give us more and more proof of his great friendship for us.

The country home of General Clinton, where we were to stay, was an hour from the city.[27] The estate was very lovely, as was also the house, but the house had been built more for a summer residence, so that, as we were there in December, I suffered a great deal from the cold. However, the inoculation was a success. When it was over, and we henceforth no longer had to fear contagion, we prepared for our return to the city and sent our cook and the rest of the servants on ahead to get everything ready for our arrival the next day. However, we had such a terrible storm that night, that we thought the house would be blown down. In fact, an entire balustrade actually was torn off and fell to the ground with a dreadful crash, and when we woke up the next morning we saw that four to five feet of snow had fallen in the night, and in some places there were snowdrifts eight feet deep,

26. The high prices of New York also made an impression on her husband. Stone, trans., *General Riedesel*, II, 78–79.

27. This country house occupied by Clinton was the Beekman mansion, "Mount Pleasant," where Nathan Hale was tried, convicted, and condemned. Philip L. White, *The Beekmans of New York in Politics and Commerce, 1647–1877* (N. Y., 1956), xviii, 484, 493; Tharp, *The Baroness and the General,* 339, 435–36. The house made a great impression upon the Germans, particularly because it was carpeted, which was regarded as extraordinary in Germany. Stone, trans., *General Riedesel*, II, 79.

so that it would be impossible for us to leave without sleighs. I tried therefore to get together whatever food I could for our dinner. An old chicken which had been forgotten was used for soup, and this with a few potatoes given us by the gardener and some corned meat, which was the last of our supplies, formed our whole dinner for fourteen people. In the afternoon, as I was sorrowfully looking out of the window, thinking of how we could get along, I saw our cook approaching on horseback. Full of joy I turned around to tell the others about this. When I looked out again the cook was nowhere to be seen. Horrified at his disappearance, the gentlemen ran out and found him with his horse buried so deep in the snow that he could never have gotten out alone and probably would have died. Our people in the city had become uneasy when we did not come, and knowing that we had no supplies, the cook brought us some food for supper. It was impossible for a carriage to drive to the city. The next morning Captain Willoe brought us two large sleighs. We got in, and I was rather worried about the children, because their inoculation had not yet entirely healed on account of the awful cold. But the trip did not hurt them a bit. While their inoculations were healing, Caroline did not have her whooping cough, but it set in again immediately afterwards and hung on for a whole year.

When we had returned to New York I was very much surprised to find our new home furnished throughout with mahogany furniture. I was frightened to think how much this would cost. Captain Willoe told me, however, that everything had been bought at the government's expense, and that the commandant, General Pattison, had been happy thus to be able to justify my faith in the English nation. I had told him when we discussed the furnishing of our house that I would leave that entirely to the English, who heretofore had never been other than kind and polite to me, and I felt confident that inasmuch as they had sent for us to come to New York, they would continue to treat us well.

We were overwhelmed with expression of honor and friendliness, which were due chiefly to General Phillips, who was very popular, and whose friendship for us was so great that he had declared that any kindness shown to us would be appreciated by him more than if it were extended to himself. As a consequence, I was so fortunate as to have many friends.

As the birthday of the Queen of England drew near (which is actually in the summer, but which is celebrated in the winter in order to give the tradespeople more business, as the King's birthday is also in the summer, and on these two occasions it is customary to appear at Court in gala dress), it was decided to celebrate the day, as usual, with a big fête; and desiring to honor me—partly to please General Phillips, who wished it, and partly to help me forget all the trouble I had gone through—they chose me to be queen of the ball.[28] In order to accomplish this the wife of General Cornwallis' aide, who, as an English noblewoman ranked higher than I, and should, therefore, have been chosen, was persuaded to stay at home because she soon expected to be confined.[29] When the festive day arrived, all the ladies went to General Tryon's home, where I was received with all ceremony. The General presented all the ladies to me, some of whom plainly showed their jealousy at my having been thus honored. I declared immediately that I would only accept this distinction for that day alone, as they had wanted to do me the honor of letting me represent the Queen, but that afterwards I would give place to the ladies who were older than I. As there were a number of them older than I, and some of them felt complimented by this remark, their faces brightened up and I was soon on cordial terms with them.

At six o'clock I got into the coach with General Tryon and General Pattison and drove to the ball, where I was received with drums and trumpets.

28. The *New-York Gazette and the Weekly Mercury*, Jan. 24, 1780, reports: "The Anniversary of her Majesty's Birthday was celebrated here on Tuesday the 18th instant, with uncommon Splendor and Magnificence, at Noon a Royal Salute was fired upon Fort George, and repeated by His Majesty's Ships of War at one o'Clock. The Public Rooms were on this Occasion entirely new painted and decorated in a Stile which reflects Honour on the Taste of the Managers. A Doric Pediment was erected over the principal Entrance, enclosing a transparent Painting of their Majesties at full Length. . . . The Ball was opened at eight o'Clock by the Baroness de Riedesel, and Major General Pattison . . . Country Dances commenced at half past Nine, and at Twelve the Company adjourned to Supper. . . . The Company retired about three in the Morning, highly satisfied with the Evenings Entertainment."

29. This noblewoman's identity is elusive. George, Lord Chewton, Cornwallis's only titled aide, was not married at this time. Charles Ross, ed., *Correspondence of Charles, First Marquis Cornwallis*, 3 vols. (London, 1859), I, 135. She may have been Elizabeth Elliot, daughter of the New York Loyalist Andrew Elliot, who married Sir William Schaw Cathcart, aide to General Clinton, on Apr. 10, 1779. If she was Lady Cathcart, the child presumably did not live to maturity. See H. M. Stephens, "Cathcart, Sir William Schaw," *DNB*; Ford, *British Officers*, 45.

As my own pregnancy was pretty far advanced, I did not want to dance, but could not refuse to open the ball by dancing a minuet with one of the generals. Because of my condition, as well as my shyness, I felt that my dancing was not very good, but to encourage me the others said I did very well, so that I had to dance another minuet, and finally even some English dances as well.

At supper, as I represented the Queen, I was seated under a canopy and had to drink the first toast. I was very much touched by all the kindness shown me, but I was very tired. However, I wanted to show my appreciation by staying as long as I possibly could, so I did not leave until two o'clock in the morning. Thus, not only on this day, but all during my stay I was overwhelmed with kindness, and the rest of the winter was most pleasant, except that we suffered a great deal from the cold. The commissary had not had enough wood chopped because, in order to save money, he had wanted to have this done by his Negro slaves. However, the winter had come earlier than usual, and as the rivers were half frozen, it was impossible to transport the wood either by boat or by sleighs, and the garrison was greatly in need of fuel.[30] We received our tickets for wood, to be sure, but what good were they when there was none to be had? Frequently we had to borrow wood from General Tryon for Saturday and Sunday, which we returned to him on Monday, if we got some ourselves. The cold was so fierce that I often kept the children in bed, and often wood could not be bought at any price, and when it was sold it cost ten pounds a cord. I, myself, had to pay a piaster for one log, which is equivalent to a laubthaler in our money. The poor people burned lard to warm their hands and to cook over.

One day I was visiting the lady who was the wife of General

30. The General wrote to Duke Karl I, Feb. 24, 1780, that "A cold spell, the like of which is not remembered by the oldest inhabitant, has frozen over the North [Hudson] and East rivers so that they can be crossed with wagons and artillery." Stone, trans., *General Riedesel,* II, 190. The *New-York Gazette and the Weekly Mercury,* Jan. 31, 1780, reported "The Severity of the Winter to the Northward has been inconceivable, and the Snow so deep that travelling has been very difficult. The Weather has been very cold to the Eastward, attended with uncommon high Tides." Thomas Jones, in his *History of New York During the Revolutionary War,* I, 320–21 says "The winter of 1779 was the severest ever known in the middle colonies," with the harbors and rivers of New York City frozen solid. In fact the winters from 1776 to 1782 were severely cold. See Anburey, *Travels,* I, 151; Stone, trans., *General Riedesel,* II, 119; and Hadden, *Journal,* 39–42.

Cornwallis' aide, who had given birth to her child, and complained bitterly about our lack of wood; whereupon she promised to send me some coal, which I could return to her at my convenience. I was so delighted about this that Major Brown,[31] a member of the commissary, who happened to be present and who had listened to my tale of woe with pity, went away very much touched.

The next day when I looked out of the window I saw four wagons stop in our street, loaded with big tree trunks, each wagon containing about two cords of wood. I went into the room where Pastor Mylius was sitting with the children by the fireplace, where our last log was burning, and said to him, "I have never known envy before, but I am so unhappy now to see how the children are suffering from the cold that I cannot help feeling envious; for someone next door to us is just being delivered four wagons full of wood. How happy I would be to have only one of them!" Hardly had I finished speaking when one of the servants brought me Major Brown's regards and the message that he was sending this wood to us, and that should we ever be short of wood again, we should let him know immediately. My joy can readily be imagined and my desire to thank our guardian angel. I had hardly been able to see his face, as Milady's bedroom was so dark. One day I attended a ball, where he was also said to be present. He had been described to me as having a pug nose, so I looked about for a man with a nose of this sort, but could find none for a long time because he always kept out of my way to avoid my thanks. Finally I found him after all and thanked him with all my heart. He said that he had not known of our difficulty until he heard me speaking of it, and that he had been unable to sleep that night for fear that his orders to procure wood for us would not be carried out promptly. For he had given orders that some trees in the large avenue on the outskirts of the city be chopped;[32] even had someone tried to stop him by saying that it was a pity to chop down these trees, he would have answered that it is better to do without a few trees than to let the family of a general, who had served with such zeal, suffer from want; and in all things that depended on the commissary, if we should need something, we should call on him.

31. The General was also impressed with the obliging nature of the upper class of New York, and he particularly mentioned this Major Brown. Stone, trans., *General Riedesel*, II, 79.

32. Stone, trans., *Mrs. General Riedesel*, 175, guesses that these trees were on Wall Street.

This acquaintance was a great help to us. My husband received a lot of supplies, wheat flour, which we used for baking bread and other things, and salted meat, which was useless to us because we had more than we could eat, and often it was not good, so that we had to give it away in order to get rid of it, particularly as our servants also got their own share. The Major now suggested that we do as the other generals—exchange the meat for cases of tallow candles and spermaceti candles, which give a better light than wax candles, and for butter. This was gladly done, as the soldiers had to be provided with meat, and thus we saved a great deal of money. We did not lack for wood now, as old, useless ships were taken apart in order to give us wood, and after that time we regularly received two cords a week.

Shortly before my confinement I had an awful fright. One of my servants brought me something, and I noticed that he rolled his eyes and could hardly speak. I was terrified and wanted to run away, but he ran in front of me, fell down, slamming the door shut as he fell, and threw a severe fit. As he lay in front of the door, and I could not get out, I screamed. The others tried to get in, but the lock had snapped shut when the door slammed and had to be broken, and then the poor man had first to be pushed a bit aside just to get in. Finally, I had to step right over him to get out, while he gnashed his teeth frightfully and flung his arms about. However, I had long since grown so accustomed to all sorts of sad and terrible sights, that fortunately this incident did not harm me, in my condition.

Early in March 1780 an old friend of ours came to New York, the Hessian General Loos,[33] who knew me when I was a young girl. "Oh!" he said, "What has become of the slender waist, the lovely complexion, and the pretty white hands? They are gone, but you have seen many countries, and when you get back home your people will let you tell about this and that concerning yourself; after a moment your tale will probably tire, perhaps out of envy, the ladies who first asked to hear it. They will play with their fans and say, 'The woman can talk about nothing else except America.'" Knowing it to be a habit of his to tell an unpleasant truth in jest, I replied that I was grateful to him for the warning, and that I would endeavor to refrain from continually speaking about this journey, a bad habit which I might

33. This blunt old soldier commanded the Lossberg Regiment after May 1778. He was godfather for the Riedesels' second child born in America. Stone, trans., *General Riedesel*, II, 220, 230–31.

have gotten into otherwise. On the other hand, I, on my part, advised him not to speak to other women about their lost charms, as he had done with me, because he might come across many who would not listen so goodnaturedly.

The following day, which was March 7, I gave birth to a daughter.[34] My husband had wished for a son, but the little one was so pretty, that we were reconciled over its not having been a boy. We had intended naming the boy Americus, but the name now had to be changed for the little daughter into America. The christening was such a hurried affair, since General Phillips (who, with the Hessian General Knyphausen and Colonel Wurmb,[35] were the only godfathers) had to go away on a little expedition,[36] that the name America was forgotten and later on had to be entered in the church register.[37] On the day of the christening my eldest daughter was taken ill with a very dangerous disease called *asthma infantile,* and a few days later my third daughter also became ill, so that I lay in my bed between two of my children, who almost died. Although my heart suffered just as intensely from every sorrow, my body had become hardened, and I bore it all well, although it was in the very first days of my confinement.

Six weeks later my husband persuaded me to go to a dinner given by General Tryon. This plan had been arranged by them so that during my absence my husband could have the baby inoculated by an English doctor, because the smallpox was raging so in the city. He did this therefore, without my knowledge to save me anxiety, and he

34. The General wrote to Duke Ferdinand that America was born on March 8. Letter of Mar. 25, 1780, Stone, trans., *General Riedesel,* II, 203.

35. Baron Wilhelm von Knyphausen (1716–1800), commanded the Hessian troops in America. *Allgemeine deutsche Biographie,* XVI, 343–44. Colonel Wurmb could have been either Col. Friedrich Wilhelm von Wurmb, commander of the Hessian Guard Regiment, who was promoted to Major General in Nov. 1780, or Lt. Col. Ludwig J. Adolph von Wurmb, commander of the Hessian Jaegers, who later was promoted to colonel. Both were in New York at this time. See Eelking, *German Allied Troops,* 294, 332, and *passim.* Stone, trans., *General Riedesel,* II, 85, also includes General Haldimand, governor and commander in chief of Canada, in the list of America's godfathers, but Haldimand was of course in Canada at this time. H. Manners Chichester, "Haldimand, Sir Frederick," *DNB.*

36. General Phillips' "little expedition" was to Perth Amboy as one of the British commissioners for exchange of prisoners. Uhlendorf, trans., *Baurmeister Journal,* 336–37, 347; Sparks, ed., *Writings of Washington,* VII, 1–3.

37. It is interesting that the Baroness did not immediately let her mother back in Germany know the child's unconventional name. See below, p. 000.

would have succeded in concealing it from me, had his fatherly uneasiness not betrayed him. He came every few moments to see how the baby was and soon was saying, "How pale she is!" or "She must be ill," so that I finally began to grow anxious and told him he must have a reason to be so uneasy and asked whether he had had her inoculated. Right away I drew back the sleeves and saw two spots on each arm. I must admit that for a moment I was very angry, but I appreciated my husband's good purpose. The little one became so ill that we feared we might lose her. My poor husband was inconsolable, because he blamed himself for it all, and I had all I could do in sustaining his spirits. But, God be praised, all went well. However, it did not turn out that way for a certain lord, who also followed our example, and was so unfortunate as to lose his child.

Through the whole winter General Phillips, General Tryon, and General Pattison were our constant friends and guests, and every week we gave a dinner for the gentlemen. That was all we could manage, because everything in the city had grown dreadfully expensive. At the end of the winter General Tryon left for England, and before his departure, without telling me about it beforehand, he sent me magnificent furniture, rugs and curtains, and a silk tapestry that would cover an entire room. I shall never forget the numerous tokens of friendship which I received from almost everyone of this excellent nation, and it will always be a pleasure to me to be able to assist the English, for I know from experience how wonderful it is to be treated so well in a strange country.

At this time began our friendship with General Clinton, who was commander in chief of the English army in the southern provinces of North America. Like all Englishmen, it was difficult at first to make friends with him. His first visit was merely a matter of form, paid to us in his capacity as commander in chief, attended by his whole staff. Since his manner and conversation were pleasant, I told his friend, General Phillips, that I was sorry that he treated us so ceremoniously, and that I would much rather associate with him on more friendly terms. Later on he offered us his country home for the summer, which we gladly accepted. It was magnificent. The location was the most beautiful, there were orchards and meadows, and the Hudson River flowed past the house.[38] Everything was at our disposal, including more fruit than we could eat. Our servants ate enormous quantities

38. She must have meant to say the East River.

of peaches, and our horses, which grazed under the fruit trees, ate the fruit right off the trees and spurned to eat that which had fallen to the ground. We had this fallen fruit gathered every evening and fed it to the pigs. It would seem incredible that we fattened six pigs, whose meat was excellent, on this fruit alone, and only the fat was a bit flabby. Peach and apricot trees grow here that are exactly like other fruit, and are never grown on espaliers, their trunks being just as thick as those of ordinary trees.

Not far from us were the Hell-Gates [39]—dangerous breakers for ships sailing on the river. We often saw ships in danger, but only one of them was wrecked while we were there.

General Clinton often came there to visit us, but dressed only in his hunting clothes and accompanied by a single aide, and said, "I know you prefer having me visit you as a friend, and as I feel the same, I shall always come to you that way." The last time he came he brought with him the unfortunate Major André, who became so well known, and who, on the following day, went on the fatal expedition where he was caught by the Americans and later hanged as a spy.[40] It was very sad, because this excellent young man was the victim of his zeal for service and his good heart, which had made him take upon himself a mission which had been assigned to another officer, too old and well known, whose turn it really was, and whose life, therefore, was in greater danger and whom he wanted to save.

We spent our time as pleasantly as possible. Our peace, however, was disturbed by the fever epidemic in New York at the time.[41] Twenty in our house alone grew ill, and eight of them were in great danger; among these eight were my husband and my daughter, little Augusta.[42] My sorrow and anxiety can be imagined! I did nothing day

39. See Anburey, *Travels*, II, 472–73.

40. Maj. John André (1751–80) was a protégé of General Clinton, who made him adjutant general and entrusted him with the negotiations with Benedict Arnold over the betrayal of West Point to the British. André left New York on Sept. 20, 1780, on his fatal mission. Richard Garnett, "André, John," *DNB*. William Abbatt dates André's departure as Sept. 19, in *The Crisis of the Revolution, being the Story of Arnold and André . . .* (N. Y., 1899), 2. See also, White, *The Beekmans of New York*, xviii, 493.

41. There had been small pox in New York, but this epidemic was cholera. See Stone, trans., *General Riedesel*, II, 87.

42. See letter of Sept. 8, 1780, from General Riedesel to Duke Ferdinand, where he says "I have been very ill and my recovery was doubted. I now begin to gain a little, but am still very weak." Stone, trans., *General Riedesel*, II, 206.

and night but divide my time nursing my husband and daughter. My husband was so ill, that we often thought he would not live through the day, and little Augusta had such fever attacks, that when she had a chill she begged me to lie on her, and although she was only nine years old, she thoroughly shook me and the whole bed. It was during chills like this that the patients usually passed away, and I was told daily that fifty or sixty more people had been buried, which, of course, did not help to make me more cheerful. Also temperatures during this fever were so frightful that pulses were 135. All our servants were ill, and I had to do everything myself. I was nursing my little America at the time, and my care of the sick left me neither the time nor the desire to lie in bed, except while I was nursing the baby. Then while doing this I lay down in my bed and slept. At night I was usually busy making lemonade for my patients, which I made with absinthiated salts, lemon juice, sugar, and water. In the space of two weeks I used two cases of lemons containing five hundred each, as all my patients were given this drink.

One day we were impatiently awaiting the doctor from New York. My husband had such a bad case of diarrhea and constant vomiting and was so ill that we lost all courage. He slept all the time, and when I wanted to give him some tapioca water, which I had been advised to give him to drink frequently, he pleaded with me to leave him alone and let him die, for he could stand it no longer. At this moment the doctor arrived, and I insisted that he tell me honestly whether there was any hope. He assured me, "Yes." Hereupon my three older children, reading the good news from my face, jumped out from under the table, where they had hidden themselves without our noticing it and covered their ears, fearing that the doctor's verdict might be bad. They threw themselves at the doctor's feet and kissed his hands, which touched everyone who saw it and brought tears to the eyes of the doctor, who was a man of much feeling. He had come as quickly as he could, but after this he made an even greater effort to help us and arranged to have his dinner with us every day, in order to save time, as he had to call on so many sick people. He particularly recommended to me a drink made of tapioca powder. At first my husband could keep it in his stomach only three minutes, then five, then a quarter hour, and finally a whole half hour. I always had my watch in hand, and I was beside myself with joy at this, which everyone with me shared. Pastor Mylius and our good footman Rockel, who had stayed well, took turns caring for the others all night with me.

Of the thirty persons in our house, only ten stayed well. The cook, the kitchen maid, and so on, all became sick and could only alternate in performing their duties on their better days. And besides all this we had horribly hot weather. It is amazing what a human can bear, and what all I endured, but I was well and blessed with a happy, cheerful temperament, which let me receive every moment of comfort with gaiety and the heartiest of joy. Really, though, I believe periods of this sort gradually undermine one's health, but nevertheless it makes me happy to think that I have been useful, and that without my efforts my dear ones, who now make me so happy, perhaps would no longer be with me.

At last all of our household who had been sick became well again, and not one had died, which was a rich reward for my efforts. We spent the whole summer of 1780 at this most lovely country seat. Two Misses Robinson came to share our loneliness and enliven us. They stayed with us until a fortnight before our return to the city, where the news of the arrival of ships bringing new fashions from England drew them back. When we came back to the city, I scarcely recognized them in their strange and really laughable attire, which a very pretty woman, who had come from England, had palmed off on them along with the other New York women.

This English lady was pregnant and wished to conceal it. She informed them, therefore, that in England corsets were being worn which were parted in the middle with the points sticking upwards, with whalebone skirts like barrel hoops and very short coats which were tied up in ribbons. All this was believed and imitated.

We were received in the most friendly way on our return to New York, and people vied with each other to make the winter pass in the most pleasant way for us.[43] My husband, General Phillips, and their aides were finally exchanged in the autumn of 1780, but the rest of the army taken at Saratoga was not. General Clinton, partly through friendship for my husband and partly out of devotion to our present Duke, wanted to place my husband on active service, which would be to his advantage. He, therefore, in accordance with the power of an English general in command of his own army, appointed him lieutenant general in his army and gave him the English pay it entailed, which was most welcome, since with the rising prices we had hardly

43. On the social prominence of Madame de Riedesel in New York, see Thomas J. Wertenbaker, *Father Knickerbocker Rebels* (N. Y., 1948), 199.

been able to get along.[44] At the same time he gave him command of Long Island, which lies opposite New York, being separated only by a narrow stretch of water called the East River. I was unable to follow him thither in the winter, since I could not live in the house in which he had his headquarters, only a few rooms of which could be heated. Therefore my husband traveled back and forth, which during the winter was done easily enough, since all was quiet.

In the autumn, before he had obtained this post, he had suffered a severe attack of his malady, having bathed in the ocean after becoming overheated, and then presumably having taken cold. All at once he became completely stiff and speechless, and had it not been for his friend, Colonel Wurmb, who luckily was in the room, it might perhaps have been all over for him. The doctor immediately opened a vein and vigorously massaged him, and once again God gave him back to me. However, his cramps, oppression, headaches, and sleeplessness increased, and all the physicians agreed that the climate thoroughly disagreed with him, and that he could never hope for recovery so long as he remained in these southern [*sic*] provinces of North America. However, there was nothing else to do, and my husband could not think of taking leave, but had to remain at his post.[45]

In the spring of 1781 I, too, settled on Long Island, where we would have had a good, though rather lonely, life, had we been able to remain in peace. But since the river was no longer frozen over, the Americans [46] made all sorts of attempts to take prisoners. They seized

44. Although Clinton promoted General Riedesel to lieutenant general, Riedesel did not sign himself this way in letters to Brunswick, since he remained a major general in the Brunswick forces. Eventually in 1787 he reached this rank in his own army. Undoubtedly the additional money was most welcome to the Riedesels, but whenever they were short of spending money, it was because of their frugal ways. General Riedesel was definitely of "an economical turn of mind," and was said to have saved 15,000 thalers during his years in America, some of which money probably came from forage funds. Stone, trans., *General Riedesel*, II, 89, 208; Eelking, *German Allied Troops*, 17–18.

45. On Jan. 26, 1781, the General reported to Duke Ferdinand that "my headache still continues; my mind is feeble and unable to work; and a genuine hypochondria causes me to spend my days in sadness." Stone, trans., *General Riedesel*, II, 209.

46. As early as Feb. 24, 1780, General Riedesel stopped calling his adversaries "rebels" and started calling them "Americans." Stone, trans., *General Riedesel*, II, 190.

Major Maybaum from his bed,[47] and we knew they intended to do the same thing for my husband, since our house was quite isolated and stood near the river. Had they surprised the watch, they could have carried him off without anyone noticing the deed. For this reason the slightest noise he might hear at night set him on the alert, thus making him lose sleep. I, too, grew so accustomed to staying awake that often daylight surprised me, and only then would I sleep a few hours, for my husband would only sleep when he thought I was awake, so dreadful to him was the thought of becoming a prisoner again. We had a magnificent view from our house. Every evening I saw from my window New York all lighted up and the reflection in the river, since the city is built right on its bank. We heard also the beating of drums, and, if all were quite still, even the challenges of the sentries. We had our own boat, in which we could reach New York in a quarter hour or so.

One day I saw from my window a fleet of thirty-five vessels under full sail approaching, and from another window I saw these vessels lying at anchor between us and the city. My husband had many Englishmen under his command, and among others the light dragoons. Although English troops are proud and, as the common belief has it, difficult to keep in submission, yet they liked my husband and were satisfied with him. The first time the English officers had dinner with us my husband told them he would accompany them to their camp, whereupon they politely begged me to do them the same honor. So I got into my carriage, and I arrived before they did. But I believe that they had sent word ahead, for, to my great embarrassment, an officer came and bade me alight and march along the line with him, at which full military honors with the sounding of music were rendered me, which made me quite flustered. I remarked to the officer that all this was not due me, and that we German ladies were not accustomed to such, but he answered very courteously that their entire corps could not honor sufficiently the wife of a general who commanded them so well, and that in addition none of them would ever forget what I had done for their comrades at Saratoga. Although all

47. This Major Maybaum (Maibom, Maiborn) has been described as "not in good health" and as having taken to drink from boredom. In any case, he was captured. His capture occasioned an exchange of letters between Riedesel and Washington, who paroled Maybaum (Maibom, Maiborn). *Ibid.*, 94–98, 243–44. See also, Fitzpatrick, ed., *Writings of Washington*, XX, 75–76.

this was very flattering and inspiring, I nevertheless seized the first favorable moment to get away.

During our stay there I often saw people buried up to their necks in the earth and in this manner cured of scurvy. We had a hospital at that place in which were many wounded and sick sailors. When one would lament their fate, these good people would answer, "We have fought for our King and are satisfied, and once we get back to Chelsea we shall be sufficiently rewarded!" This is an excellent naval hospital near London, where there is the best food, clothes, and care.

Around this time General Phillips was sent on an expedition to Carolina. Parting was painful on both sides. We never again saw this excellent friend, for he died there of a high fever, which was brought on through a dreadful cold. We have constantly mourned his loss. He was a very fine man, and a real friend to his friends.[48]

As my husband's health did not improve one bit, and since, in addition, his presence was useful and necessary to that part of his corps which had remained in Canada, General Clinton was finally induced to send him thither, although he did not gladly part with a friend of whom he had been so fond, and even after parting this friendship lasted until the death of this general.[49]

Because of the uncertainty as to when we would depart, I had not wanted to wean my little daughter America, and I nursed her fourteen whole months. At last she had grown so large that I feared I could not stand it any more, and, therefore, at the beginning of May weaned her. But right away I developed something which caused me much more trouble, a skin irritation, which almost everyone, even if in good health, suffers from in this warm climate. Little pimples come out over the whole body, which itch so dreadfully that one cannot get any rest. They come with the heat and go with the cold weather. Otherwise one is perfectly well.

48. Gen. William Phillips died in Petersburg, Va., on May 15, 1781. General Riedesel to Karl Wilhelm Ferdinand, June 6, 1781, Stone, trans., *General Riedesel*, II, 193. See also Madame de Riedesel's letter to her mother, below, p. 207.

49. Henry Clinton died on Dec. 3, 1795, at Gibraltar, where he was governor. H. M. Stephens, "Clinton, Sir Henry," *DNB*. This reference to his death gives some indication that the Baroness did not prepare the final version of her journal until many years after her "tour of duty."

VIII

Assignment in Canada

‹——◄◖◆◗►——›

Our departure was set for July 1781. I had received my wood coupons for ever so long a time, and during our stay on Long Island I had saved thirty cords, which I now wanted to give back to my excellent commissary major, who had helped me so faithfully, but he would not have it and bade me either sell it or distribute it among the poor. "I know you," said the good man. "You will find more satisfaction alleviating misery." This was indeed the case and the way my husband and I felt. We gave twenty cords to a very worthy royalist family, who had already lost much and later had to emigrate, and divided the remaining ten cords among other poor.

When we wanted to return the borrowed furniture before leaving, it was not accepted, and we were told that it was ours and that we should take it with us to Canada, for otherwise we certainly would have none. But we did not want to abuse such kindness, and we sent it all back to the royal warehouse, except for a single English bedstead, which we kept as a remembrance. Nevertheless I must confess that I later regretted a bit not having taken the furniture, partly because there was none in Canada, and partly because this splendid royal warehouse was later plundered and burned by the Americans.

Finally we departed, or, rather, we boarded ship,[1] for we lay at anchor about an hour's sail from New York for more than a week. General Clinton had explicitly ordered the transport-agent, whom he had carefully chosen for us, thinking him an active and capable man, to seek out a very comfortable but at the same time good-sailing ship,

1. Stone in *Mrs. General Riedesel* says the ship was named the *Little Seal* (p. 186). In his edition of General Riedesel's memoirs, however, he calls it the *Little Deal!* This, however, appears to be a typographical error. Stone, trans., *General Riedesel*, II, 105.

on which we would not run the risk of being captured on the way. But here was more evidence of how superiors are deceived, for this agent was a lazy, rude, and ignorant fellow, who either out of laziness had not inspected the ship, or, as often is the case, allowed himself to be bribed by the ship's captain. Suffice it to say, we drew one of the smallest and worst ships in the whole fleet, on which we often ran the danger of being left behind, so that the captain of the second man-of-war convoying us often had to take us in tow. For this purpose a large cable was let out from the towing ship and fastened to the other, thus drawing it along, which was very unpleasant and even dangerous, for if there was a calm, one ship would strike against the other, or if we were so unlucky as to meet an enemy ship, we would have been in the midst of the fight. Moreover, the ship's crew was not large enough, which made us run the additional danger of capsizing, were a sudden wind storm to arise, since with our small crew we could not have taken in our sails quickly enough, especially since the ship leaked, and we also had to station men at the pumps. And to cap it all, our ship was badly loaded and listed to one side, so we had to fill empty barrels with seawater to maintain an even keel, which is something that always has to be taken into consideration.[2] In addition to all this, the company of the above-mentioned agent was most unpleasant, and we had to pay his expenses and have him around us, where he was a real burden with his grumbling and his howling yawns, by which he woke people from their sleep, even ourselves, although we were in another room.

At the moment of our departure we met with another vexation. Our good Negroes, a man, his wife, and a young kinswoman of theirs, were reclaimed by their first owner, from whom, as a rebel, they had been taken, on the grounds that he had again become a royalist, and just as the signal for departure was given, he actually arrived with the order that the Negroes be returned to him. Since they were much attached to us, and this man was also an evil master, who had treated them badly, the horror and lamentation of these poor people were extremely great. The young girl, named Phyllis, fainted, and when she regained her senses would not hear of leaving us. She threw herself at my feet, and, clutching, had to be withdrawn by

2. Her husband's memoirs indicate that Madame de Riedesel was sick on this voyage. Although going ashore at Halifax must have been something of a break, the second part of the voyage was also stormy. Stone, trans., *General Riedesel*, II, 105–7.

force. My husband offered their master money, but since he noticed how much we wanted to keep them, he demanded thirty guineas for each, which my husband would not pay him. Had all this not happened at the moment of our departure, I believe that we yet would have kept them. We gave them all their things, even the mattresses we had had made for them for the voyage. At this they grew all the more excited, and Phyllis cried, "If I do not die first, I will come back to you, even if it be at the other end of the world!" The good girl had later actually begged two or three persons to take her with them and bring her to me, always adding, "Milady will be very glad to pay my passage." She was quite right, but as no one was assured of this, nobody would burden himself with her. My husband would have paid the money for her alone, but her greedy master would not sell her separately, since he was trying to force us to take them all. But this was too stiff for our purse. We regretted our decision later, however, because maidservants in Canada are poor and especially difficult to find.

On the first day of our voyage my skin trouble disappeared, over which I rejoiced, but unfortunately it had a bad effect on my health for the rest of my life, for three days afterwards I developed such pains in my head and my teeth, that I could neither eat nor sleep, and I had to endure this day and night. The sharpness was penetrating, and my feet were so cold that they could not be warmed even with hot water. They gave me opium, which made me doze a bit but not sleep, because my pains were too severe. Thus I suffered during the whole voyage.

We had all sorts of experiences on this voyage. Among others, a ship came too close to us during a calm and gave us a bad jolt, and we had to push it off with poles. On another occasion a ship swept us with its stern, tearing away our lavatory, and it was only good fortune that no one was using it at the time.

One day, when a thick fog enveloped us, we thought we saw land. Fortunately at this moment a gust of wind parted the fog like the raising of a curtain. Our captain was horrified to see that we were at a place called Dusky Bay and hard by a dangerous rock there which, on account of its shape, is called the "Old Woman," and which really looks like an old woman sitting out there with a bent back and bowed head. He immediately called to the captain of the man-of-war which had us in tow, who was making this voyage for the first time and therefore did not know the danger, and as a favorable wind arose at this very moment, we took full advantage of it, and in less than half an hour we had left this bay, which is quite full of rocks and the site, therefore, of many shipwrecks. On this voyage we touched Halifax, in Nova Scotia, and even went ashore. We were given the best sort of welcome there. The governor and his wife, both amiable people, invited us to luncheon, and we found there a very agreeable company of seven or eight families, who continually visited each other.[3] The next day they not only showed us the town, but the surrounding countryside as well, which I found very pleasing. One lives there most inexpensively, and the seafood is especially good. It was remarked on as a curious circumstance, that lobsters or large sea-crabs were caught, which was not the case before the Revolution, but that now they were leaving the mainland and coming to Nova Scotia. The popular joke, therefore, was that the lobsters were good royalists, and for this very reason also wore the English (red) uniform.[4]

Since I suffered so the whole time there from my toothache, I decided to have one of my teeth drawn. In order to spare my husband and children all care and unrest, I arose at five in the morning, sent for our surgeon, who was considered a skillful man at this kind of operation, went into a room somewhat apart from the rest, where he had me sit on the floor, and with a nasty, blunt instrument he gave me such a jerk, that I thought the deed was done and asked for my tooth. "Just be patient another moment," he said, going at it again and giving me another jerk. Now, I thought, I was at last freed of it. But not at all. He had, on the contrary, taken hold of and pulled at a good tooth, without completely extracting it. I was extremely angry at this, and although he advised pulling this one now as well as the bad tooth, I neither could nor would put myself in his hands again. I have had reason to regret this attempt for a long time, for this tooth which was now out of place prevented me for more than

3. Sir Andrew Snape Hamond arrived at Halifax with his wife and two children on July 30, 1781, and the next day was sworn in as lieutenant governor of Nova Scotia. Beamish Murdoch, *A History of Nova-Scotia or Acadie,* 3 vols. (Halifax, 1866), II, 618. At Halifax the Baroness picked up the German regimental flags, concealed in a mattress, and slept on them for the rest of the voyage to Canada. See above, p. 72–73.

4. One story was that the lobsters forsook New York after the 1776 cannonading there. This general claim is, in any case, corroborated elsewhere. Anburey, *Travels,* II, 471. See Bell, "A Note on Eighteenth-Century Plagiarism," Bibliographical Soc. of America, *Papers,* 37 (1943), 23–36, where this story is traced to Peter Kalm.

two years from closing my teeth together. Moreover, this experience was so dreadful, that I was never able again to bring myself to undergo such an operation.

On the remaining part of our voyage, we yet had to experience a few storms, and when we had already reached the St. Lawrence River, we had the disagreeable misfortune of losing two anchors. We dropped anchor in this river every evening because of the ebbing of the tide. Unfortunately our anchor was dropped on a reef, and since our ship was in constant motion with the wind, the line was cut. A second anchor was dropped, which, however, had the same fate. We had but one small anchor left, and had we lost that one, we would have been helpless in the wind, and so we spent a very miserable night. Moreover, we ran out of provisions, and a boat we sent ashore brought us only a few chickens and eggs. All this drove my husband to the decision that we would not spend another night aboard ship, and, accordingly, that evening when the anchor was being dropped, he ordered that the large boat be lowered, and we—my husband and I, our children, the two aides, my maidservants, and the two man-servants—seated ourselves in it and went ashore. We came upon a pretty farmhouse, where we were received in a very friendly way. The captain of the ship brought us there himself together with our pilots. Such pilots came aboard when a ship enters a stretch of the St. Lawrence. These people are well paid, and often receive as much as twenty guineas. Since all ships are insured, every captain is bound to take one. But on the other hand, the captain's responsibility is ended as soon as a pilot is aboard, and the latter guides the ship, taking full responsibility for all danger.

My husband traveled on to Quebec that same evening with one of his aides, and I followed the next day, not arriving, however, until three days later.[5] The region through which we passed was like a picture indeed. Every inhabitant has a good house, which he takes the pains to clean every year. This gives them a very immaculate look, and makes them glisten in the distance.[6] When sons marry, they build their houses close to their parents, as do also sons-in-law, with the result that handsome settlements spring up, for which reason these people are called *habitans* [settlers], and not peasants. These

5. The General arrived in Quebec on Sept. 12, 1781. See his letter to General Knyphausen, Sept. 29, 1781, Stone, trans., *General Riedesel*, II, 247.

6. The glistening white appearance of these houses was also noted by Lieutenant Anburey, *Travels*, I, 62.

dwellings, to each of which adjoins a stable, an orchard, and a pasture, are situated along the St. Lawrence, and make a very picturesque sight, especially to those who sail up and down the river. Each house has an ice cellar, which is made with little difficulty. A hole is dug in the ground and lined around with boards, and it is filled with ice. Then water is poured in, which in freezing fills the crevices and makes all smooth as glass. Over this the inhabitants place a very clean board on which to put the items to be preserved, observing the greatest cleanliness and taking special pains to keep out of the ice cellar any straw or hay, which, they say, causes the ice to melt more quickly. These ice cellars are all the more indispensable, since everyone slaughters his own cattle, which otherwise would not keep in the heat of summer there. Ordinarily these ice cellars are dug under the barns.

These people keep a lot of livestock in the summer, which at the start of winter they slaughter and bring to the city for sale. The smaller stock—beefs, sheep, and swine—which they keep for themselves, they drive into the forest in the morning to graze, and only in the evening do they give them fodder in the stable. In this part of the country they also have a small fish, called small cod, which are caught under the ice. This is done by cutting large holes in the ice, three or four hundred paces apart.[7] Into these are placed nets of stout cord fastened on strong beams. In this manner they sometimes catch five or six sledges full. They throw the fish onto the ice where they are frozen in a moment and where they remain until they are needed. Then they are gotten, thawed out, thrown directly into the kettle, and eaten. These fish taste particularly good when fried in butter.

The dwellings are very comfortable, and one finds the beds remarkably good and clean. All people of property have curtained beds, and as their living rooms are very large, they have their beds in them. They have large stoves, in which they also cook. Their soups are very substantial, and for the most part consist of bacon, fresh meat, and vegetables, which are cooked together in a pot and served as a side-dish. The Canadians make their sugar themselves from maple trees, which for this reason are called sugar-maples. Early in the year they go into the woods with kettles and pots, in which they catch the sap from cuts made in the trees. This they boil, and the part that

7. They also had to cut these holes for their cattle and sheep to have water to drink. *Ibid.*, I, 151.

comes to the top, which is the best, they particularly use. The only thing wrong with maple sugar is that it is brown; otherwise it is very good, especially for [troubles in] the chest. The natives are hospitable and jovial, singing and smoking all the time. Frequently the women have goiter. Otherwise the people are healthy and live to an old age. Not infrequently one sees people, old as the hills, living with their great-grandchildren, who take the best of care of them.

It was in the middle of September 1781 after an eight-week trip that we reached Quebec, where we were welcomed in the most friendly way. My husband soon gained the favor of the English Lieutenant General Haldimand, who was governor of the province and commanding general of the troops in Canada, although he had been represented as a man with whom it was difficult to get along and whom no one satisfied.[8] I not only had the satisfaction of being warmly received by him, but of having won his friendship, which lasted as long as he lived. People tried to make us distrustful of him, but we did not listen to them. We were frank and sincere in our relations with him, for which he was all the more grateful to us, since he was little accustomed to such treatment there. Great changes had been made in the governor's mansion, since formerly it had appeared very much like a barrack. He had furnished and decorated it in the English style, and although he had only been there five years, his gardens already were full of excellent fruit and exotic plants, which one would not have believed could be grown in this climate. He had, however, taken advantage of a good southern exposure. The house was on high land, almost at the summit of a hill.

We remained in Quebec for four weeks, during which time General Haldimand went to Sorel with my husband, and showed him his post there. While there he expressed to him in the most friendly way his regrets about the poor quarters we would have, but

8. Sir Frederick Haldimand (1718–91), at first lieutenant governor and then governor of Canada, was commander of all the British forces in Canada. He was born in Neufchâtel, and there is some question as to his early career. He was definitely in the Sardinian army and then in the service of the Dutch. During the Seven Years' War, he served with the Royal Americans (English 62nd) with distinction, and then commanded the British forces in Florida. He replaced General Carleton in 1778 and remained in Canada until 1784. He never spoke or wrote English well, and he was regarded as a harsh governor. H. Manners Chichester, "Haldimand, Sir Frederick," *DNB*. General Riedesel, who was fond of him, noted himself that Haldimand was of a morose character and kept to himself. Stone, trans., *General Riedesel*, II, 108.

he pointed out that the post was of the greatest importance, and that he knew of no one better able to fill it. Since he could not build a house for us there, he bought one that was just being built, of which only the walls were finished.[9] He gave orders that all be finished by Christmas, and begged us to say how the rooms were to be divided. Until we could move into the place we lived with a resident of the area. Our plan was presented, and, to our great surprise, we were able to eat our Christmas pie—with which the English always celebrate Christmas—in our new house, although the timber for the building was felled and sawed into boards only after our arrival. Pretty paper was hung on the walls, and we were really very well lodged. We had a large dining hall, a nice room for my husband, next to which was our bedroom, a nice room for the children with a special little room for our oldest daughter, and finally yet another large and handsome salon, which we all used as a sitting room. The entry was like a nice room, with benches along the walls. In it stood a large stove with stout pipes running up to the ceiling to heat the entire house. Upstairs were four large rooms, one for the maidservants, one for the men, and the other two guest rooms.

In the spring of 1782 two covered passageways were built onto the house, one of which led to the kitchen and the other to our laundry, over which was the guard room. We did not live in the village of Sorel itself, but about a quarter of a mile away, and so near the outposts that, in order that my husband not be captured, six men slept on the benches in the entry every night. The great stove which stood there gave off so much heat that the house was constantly kept warm, and despite the bitter cold of Canada, nothing was frozen in the house. One unpleasant circumstance, however, confronted us; namely, our walls became warped during the winter, which tore our pretty wallpaper, and even caused us to have drafts.

During the summer of 1782 my husband took a trip of three weeks, during which time I bade the English artisans, who in accordance with the orders of the Governor were all at our disposal, to bring all to rights for his return. Carpenters, painters, and paperhangers were all put to work. The walls were repaired, doors, windows, chairs, and tables were painted with oil paint, and the cracks in the wallpaper were mended with new paper for which I had sent. On his return my

9. General Riedesel complained that the walls of this house were too thin. The house was about a fifteen-minute walk from Sorel. Stone, trans., *General Riedesel*, II, 118.

husband, to his great amazement, found everything ready and in order, a house quite like new, and all this at little cost, as we were only allowed to give the artisans food and drink, for which they worked with the best will. Our company consisted solely of men. What we lacked here, however, was made up to us during both the winters we spent in Canada by the invitations we received from General Haldimand to Quebec, where both times we spent six weeks at the home of Doctor Mabane,[10] a trusted friend of the General. We dined each midday at the home of the General, who even sent for the children to dine. In the evening he would come to the house of our host to play cards and have supper, and he told us that he did this in order not to keep me from the children. He often played cards until midnight, and even until one o'clock, but he was so kind as not to embarrass me about this, and I could retire whenever I chose. I have almost never seen a man who was so kind and friendly toward those to whom he had once given his friendship, and we could flatter ourselves that we were included in this number.

In the spring of 1782 he had asked us to come to Montreal, where he had business, on which occasion he assured us that his fondest moments were those he spent with us. I traveled there on the frozen St. Lawrence River on a sleigh. We remained there a week, and I returned home in the same manner, which, however, was not only imprudent but risky in the highest degree, because during this time it had begun to thaw, and on the whole route, which was marked with logs (as one does there every winter so that the many sleighs will make a well-beaten course), water was already found over the ice everywhere. Our Canadian guides themselves seemed to be afraid, but they did not want to look for a firmer way nearby, however, because they said one was always in less danger on the beaten course. At last, around five in the afternoon, we safely reached Sorel, almost in water however, which came into our sleigh from all sides. The next morning I saw to my horror when I awoke a ship under full sail proceeding down the river.

10. Dr. Adam Mabane (1734–92), Scottish surgeon, was a leader of the "French party" in Quebec, member of the governor's council, judge of the provincial court of common pleas, and an intimate friend of Governor Haldimand. See Hilda Neatby, "The Political Career of Adam Mabane," *Canadian Historical Review*, 16 (1935), 137–50. Mabane and his sister became close friends of the Riedesels. Several of his letters to them are in the McCord Museum, McGill University, Montreal, Canada.

The winters there are very healthy, though severe,[11] for since the weather is not changeable, one can take good precautions against the cold. Thus one takes cold there less than in our country. At the beginning of November people lay in their winter provisions. I was very surprised when people asked me how much fowl, and particularly how many fish, I wanted and where I should like to have the latter left, since I had no pond. In the attic, I was told, where they would keep better than in the cellars. Accordingly I took three to four hundred, which kept very well through the winter. All that had to be done when a person wanted meat, fish, eggs, apples, and lemons for the midday meal was to put them in cold water the day before. Thus the frost is thoroughly removed, and such meat or fish is just as juicy, even more tender than that we have at home. In addition to this, poultry is packed in snow, which forms such a crust of ice that one must chop away with a hatchet.

There is a fruit in Canada called ottocas. It grows in water, is red, and of the size of a small cherry, but without the stone. They are bought without stems, and are carefully gathered, especially by the Indians. It makes a very good preserve, especially after a hard frost.[12] All other fruits are very rare there, and only in Montreal are there good, yes, even excellent, apples, but only *reinettes* and apples of a variety called *bourrassas* that is large, red, and good-tasting. They are packed in barrels, which have to be carefully sealed and covered with paper, for they remain good to the last apple. But they use small barrels, for once they are broken open they no longer preserve the apples. Fruit is very expensive, especially pears, which are far scarcer there than apples and which also do not keep as well. I ordered six barrels of apples and half a barrel of pears. One can imagine my horror when I had to pay twenty-one guineas for them. To be sure, I had asked the price beforehand, but they had not been able to tell me the exact price then. My husband had a large piece of land behind our house plowed up for a garden and had twelve hundred fruit trees planted there, which made a very pleasant and at the same time very useful garden, especially as few vegetables could be raised there. All grew excellently in our garden, and every evening we went into it and plucked one hundred and fifty to two hundred cucumbers, which I made into pickles, which were not known there

11. The winter of 1781–82 must have been a cold one. *Ibid.,* 119.
12. This fruit is today called the cranberry.

and of which I made presents to all the people, especially our good General Haldimand, who found them excellent.

It was as though I were upon a magnificent farm. I had my cows, a great many fowl, and Virginia hogs, which are black and smaller than ours and are especially short-legged. I also made my own butter. For the soldiers this was truly a promised land, for they had nicely furnished barracks, near to each of which were gardens. My husband gave them seeds, and it was a pleasure to look in on their housekeeping, especially their cooking, an amusement we often had, especially when we were strolling. They exchanged half of the salted meat which they received for fresh meat, then put both together in a large kettle along with all kinds of vegetables and dumplings; [and then] there was rivalry among them then as to who was the best cook. All work was regularly divided among them. Some tended the gardens, others looked after the kitchen, still others cleaned the barracks, while still different ones went to cut wood, which they brought back themselves on little carts made especially for this purpose. My husband had fish nets made, and every company in its turn went fishing, and each time they were so considerate as to send us something of their catch. In this way they had fish to eat two or three times a week, and every six days they received a bottle of rum, rice, butter, and twelve pounds of flour for bread, and every day a pound of salt pork or a pound and a half of beef. In spite of all this, most of them longed for their native land.

My husband also had Indians under his command in Canada and became much beloved by them. His straight-forward ways won him their hearts. Even before I arrived in Canada one of his Indians, named Hansel, once heard that he was sick, that he had a wife, and that he was very uneasy that she had not yet arrived. Therefore, he came to my husband with his own wife and said to him: "Listen. I love my wife, but I love you too, and as an indication I give her to you." My husband answered, "I thank you, and I recognize your love, but I already have a wife whom I love, and therefore I beg you to keep yours." He seemed sad over this refusal and almost offended, and only with effort could be persuaded to take back his wife, who was quite pretty and whom I often saw later. To be sure, this Hansel was not born an Indian, but a German. However, he had been captured in his fifteenth year along with others in a battle with the Indians. All the others were killed, but his appearance and his brave resistance had so delighted the savages that they spared him his life, under the condition that he marry one of them and accept their customs and dress, which he then did.[13] The life of the Indians must have something very attractive about it, since a nephew of General Carleton lived for a long time among them, even marrying an Indian, and became so accustomed to the restless but free and merry life, that not until after many years and repeated entreaties did he return to his uncle, whose sister-in-law, a pretty and pleasant person, he then married. But, I was told, he clung to his old ways and longed for his first wife, whom he had had when among the Indians, but whose marriage was later annulled. He served in the army, I believe as a major, and was a very pleasing person.[14]

It was just at this time that I saw the famous Indian chief, Brant,[15] of whose likeness an engraving had been made. Since he showed much intelligence and many talents while still very young, General Carleton sent him to England to the King, whom he pleased so very much that he had him educated and promised to take care of him. He took advantage of the instruction he received, but when he was between twenty and twenty-four years old he begged to be sent back again to his people. At that time, when we were there (in Canada), he was chief among the Indians. His language was good, his manners the best, and, moreover, he was held in high esteem by General Haldimand. I have dined with him at the General's table. He was dressed half as a soldier and half as an Indian, and his countenance was manly and clever. His character was very gentle.[16] My husband also was once invited to a meeting of Indians, where they first made a speech to him and then bade him be seated among them. Then they offered him a pipe of tobacco, which is their highest token of honor and an indication of their high esteem and friendship. They also gave him a name, which in their language meant

13. See Stone, trans., *General Riedesel*, I, 50.

14. Governor Carleton's nephew was Maj. Christopher Carleton. Tharp, *The Baroness and the General*, 422; Hadden, *Journal*, 19–21.

15. For this Mohawk Chief, Joseph Brant (1742–1807), see especially William L. Stone, Sr., *Life of Joseph Brant—Thayendanegea . . . ,* 2 vols. (N.Y., 1838), I. For a good brief description, see William L. Stone, ed., *Orderly Book of Sir John Johnson during the Oriskany Campaign, 1776–1777* (Albany, 1882), 196–203. In *Mrs. General Riedesel*, 200, Stone says Madame de Riedesel is in error about Brant's first trip to Europe, this taking place in 1775 at the age of thirty-three.

16. Stone, ed., *Orderly Book of Sir John Johnson*, presents Brant's cruel side.

"The Sun." He, in turn, invited them to visit him and entertained them in accordance with the custom of the land with tobacco and rum.

One of them in particular was decorated with medals, which are the signs of bravery. We invited him to dinner and pressed him to have some drink, but he drank very little and said to us in broken French, "The savage is a good child as long as he is sober, but when he's had too much to drink—a ferocious animal!" My daughter, little Frederika, won his friendship. He begged her for a new ribbon on which to hang his medals, assuring her that he would then prize them the more highly for it. He really was a very good man, kind and courteous.

The Indians are great believers in dreams. Before our arrival a certain man named Johnson became rich because of this. The Indians often would come to him and say: "We have dreamed that we came to you and that you gave us rum and tobacco." He would then reply, "In that case I must make your dream come true," and give them as much as they wanted. This pleased them, and they often came back, repeating their dreams. But one day he went to them, saying, "My brothers, I dreamed that I came to you, and you were so satisfied with the friendship and frequent good hospitality that I have shown you, that you presented me with a large piece of land," at the same time describing just which tract of land this was. "How can it be," they exclaimed quite shocked, "that you dream this?" They immediately went out and held a council, the result of which they expressed on their return: "Brother Johnson, we give you the piece of land, *but dream no more.*"

The Indians customarily treat their bodies very cruelly, making cuts and marks on their faces, which they then paint with various colors to make themselves look more like warriors.

One day a youth was chosen chief of a tribe. This caused grumbling among the other tribes, and at a general council so many abusive things were said to him by another chief that after much exchange of words his anger was so aroused that he sprang up and split open the head of his antagonist with his tomahawk. But later after reflecting upon the consequences of his rash act, which among the Indians was cause for feud and bloody revenge between the tribes of the murdered and the murderer, he went to the house of the English commander, called for a black ribbon, pierced holes through both his arms, through which he drew the black ribbon, with which he had his arms tied at his back, and thus gave himself over to the tribe of the man he had killed, exclaiming that he acknowledged his guilt in killing one of their number in a rage. In order to prevent the bloodshed which could result between these two tribes, he had rendered himself defenseless and delivered himself to them in this condition. At this noble behavior and at his evident penitence and courage, the Indians of the aggrieved tribe were so moved and touched, that they not only forgave but adopted him into their tribe in the place of the man who was slain, and later even chose him for their chief.

The Indians behave bravely in battle as long as victory is on their side. But on retreats, for example before our capture at Saratoga, I saw them first running and then hiding themselves. But this conduct was, to be sure, probably prompted by fear of being captured and then killed.[17]

In the summer of 1782 we spent several very pleasant weeks in Quebec. General Haldimand had a house built on a hill, which he named Montmorency, after the famous waterfall of that name hard by. There he took us. It was his pet, and certainly nothing could equal its location. The celebrated Montmorency Falls plunge from a height of one hundred and sixty-three feet with a dreadful deafening noise through a cleft between two mountains.[18] While the General was showing us this magnificent spectacle, I accidentally made the remark that it would be wonderful to have a cottage right above the Falls. Three weeks later he took us there again, and had us climb by a steep path over rocks which were linked by little bridges, just as in descriptions of Chinese gardens. When at last we had reached the top he offered me his hand to lead me into a little hut which hung directly over the waterfall. He was amazed at my courage in entering it directly without any hesitation. But I assured him that I would never be afraid with a man so considerate as himself. Thereupon he showed us how the little house was fastened. He had had eight strong beams extended over the chasm through which the water cascaded. A third of their length rested upon the rocks, and on these

17. For another account of the Indians as warriors, see Anburey, *Travels*, I, 258–64. For Burgoyne's opinion, see Hadden, *Journal*, 14–15.

18. Anburey was deeply impressed by the beauty of Montmorency Falls. He estimated the width at ten to twelve yards, but the height at 120 feet The fog, the spray, and the noise particularly struck him. Anburey, *Travels* II, 82–83. Bell attributes Anburey's description to Peter Kalm in "A Note on Eighteenth-Century Plagiarism," Bibliographical Soc. of America, *Papers*, 37 (1943), 23–36.

beams stood the hut. It was a terrifying but majestic sight. One could not remain in there for long, since the din was dreadful. Above the Falls excellent trout are caught among the rocks, which, however, once cost an English officer his life. He was jumping from rock to rock in order to catch them, but his foot slipped out from under him, and he was swept away by the force of the water. Only a few of his shattered limbs were later found.

We were also there once in the winter, where the different and strange forms the ice had taken offered a magnificent spectacle, but the roar was missing then. It was so cold then that the General's Madeira wine froze in its bottles, from which, however, it does not suffer, keeping the same excellence when thawed out again. The General let us drink that day the quintessence of it, which had not been frozen, and we found it extraordinarily good.

In the fall of 1782, just when I was in a most advanced stage of pregnancy, my husband received orders to go to the Isle aux Noix to have a fort built to cover us against surprise attacks.[19] I felt very lonely during this time, and my only comfort was that he came to see me every three or four weeks. For his part, he, too, spent his time in an unpleasant way. He made a short trip from there to a place called Pointe au Fer, which was situated at the point where the Sorel River emptied into Lake Champlain, in order to visit the outposts. He was nearly burned to death in a barrack in which his quarters for the night had been established. In the middle of the night he heard a commotion, and since it was an advanced post, he thought the Americans had learned he was there and sought to capture him. Hereupon an English non-commissioned officer entered, asking whether the General was there. In reply to his answer, "Yes!" he called out to him: "For God's sake, General, save yourself, for the barrack is burning up!" This non-commissioned officer did not even give him time to try to get his things together, and undressed and bare-footed on the ice he had to run through the flames. The danger really was great because of the barrels of powder stored in the bar-rack and the cannons loaded with canister, which easily could have been touched off by the fire. However, my husband turned back again when he saw that the soldiers were remaining, keeping busy putting out the fire, and he dressed himself by a sentry's fire.

In the meantime I was taken sick on November 1. I wanted to

19. For a description of Isle aux Noix, see Hadden, *Journal*, p. 16.

distract myself during the absence of my husband and to drive away my melancholy thoughts and uneasiness, and for this reason I went out on a ride. But the pains, which I had already felt, grew stronger and compelled me to return. To be sure, they urged me to take my place at the table, but I felt that I had a more important expedition to make. I had hoped, since my husband was expected back on the 5th, that I might delay my confinement that long, but I was deceived in my expectation, and happily was delivered of a beautiful little daughter.[20] I did so well, that I was able to write to my husband about it myself. But since he wanted a son so badly, he thought I was only joking, and when at dinner the health of his newborn daughter was proposed, he sought again to discover in my letter that he really had a son. Finally he had to resign himself, but on his return on the 5th he found the little girl so pretty, that he thus found solace, and she was our mutual joy, which, however, sadly did not last long, for we were only able to keep her for five months. I nursed her myself, but suffered so badly in the breasts, that I even had to have an operation performed on them.[21] I was strongly advised against nursing the child any longer, and I finally gave in, though with the greatest reluctance, for I almost had a foreboding that things would not go well, and in the very first night after I had weaned my little daughter, my powers of imagination were so very much seized by it, that I thought I heard a voice calling to me: "You were wrong to have weaned her. She will die." Half asleep and terribly frightened, I sprang out of my bed and wanted to tear off the bandages that had been put on my breasts to drive away the milk and take my dear little Canada (for so we had named her) to my breast again. But I was not allowed to do so and was told that it would do the child harm, since she had

20. This little girl was named Canada. Ironically General von Loos was a godfather, who sent a gift of one hundred louis d'or. He, too, regretted the child was not a boy. Since it was a girl, he suggested Jeannette or Lozina as names. He was also afraid that Madame de Riedesel was angry with him. Stone, trans., *General Riedesel*, II, 230–31. As for the General's comments on his family at this period, these were his words to the Hessian Colonel Romrod from Quebec, Oct. 16, 1782: "My wife has been well of late. She is in good spirits, and is near her confinement. May fortune grant that it may be a son! Gusta is my milkmaid, and her sister does nothing but collect the news of which she keeps [in] a diary. All the children, thanks to God, are well." *Ibid.*, 250.

21. See *ibid.*, 152, for his mention of the operation. General Haldimand expressed his sympathy for her in a letter to Riedesel. *Ibid.*, 148.

already been weaned. Three days later she developed diarrhea, and five days later she was very sick. I was not allowed to nurse her, since I was myself very sick with milk-fever. But I can never forgive myself for not having done so, for I later heard that the baby had received no nourishment at all. To be sure, I finally succeeded in having our cook, who fortunately was a wet-nurse, give her the breast anew, which she eagerly took, but probably it was already too late. We summoned a distinguished English physician by the name of Kennedy from Trois Rivières,[22] who, as soon as he saw the child, said it was dying from weakness. He had some old hens killed and removed the entrails, which were cooked without being cleaned. Of this he gave her clysters every half hour, which at first seem to infuse new life into her, but she had already lost too much of her strength, and we had the sorrow of losing her. My oldest daughter, Augusta, who loved her very much, became sick from her sorrowing, and also my youngest daughter, America, who almost died even before her sister was buried. But since the physician, who was still with us, made such good use of his remedies, she was yet spared to us.

My husband was so beside himself over all this that he would not even come into the house again until the doctor assured him that all the patients were out of danger.[23]

Our beloved little dead one was buried in Sorel, and the officers promised me that they would place such an inscription on her tombstone as would restrain the inhabitants, who were fanatical Catholics, from removing her as a heretic child from consecrated ground.

In the summer of 1783, in order to distract me from my sorrow, General Haldimand invited us to visit him in Quebec. We received at this very time news of the death of my father-in-law,[24] and my husband longed more than ever to return to Europe, for more than

22. Dr. Hugh Alexander Kennedy dispensed many remedies to the ailing Riedesels, and on the birth of his seventh child, asked the Baroness to be the sponsor for "little Louise." His letters to the General are in the McCord Museum, McGill University, Montreal, Canada.

23. On July 2, 1783, the General told Duke Ferdinand of this sad event: "I have had the misfortune to lose in the month of March, my youngest daughter, who was born on the 1st day of November of last year. But, thank God, my wife is very well." Stone, trans., *General Riedesel*, II, 213.

24. The General received letters from his brother on May 18, 1783, telling of the death of their father at the age of 77 at Lauterbach on Sept. 5, 1782. Stone, trans., *General Riedesel*, II, 169. See also General Riedesel to Mrs. Riedesel, June 9, 1783, below, p. 211.

ever his health was uncertain, and although the climate of Canada agreed with him better than that of New York, he was never free from an unpleasant ringing in the ears and violent headaches. I, for my part, also longed to see my mother and brothers and sisters again. Had it not been for this longing, I would have been quite satisfied there, for the climate agreed very well with the children, there were those who loved us, and we were on a very pleasant footing. There were some reports that our troops would perhaps be recalled to Europe that same year, since the preliminaries of peace were already signed. General Haldimand himself also very much wanted to return to England, and had even sought it. We had often planned together to make this voyage on the same ship. One day when we were with him, strolling in the garden, we saw a large number of ships arrive, among which was a very fine one lying at anchor by the foot of a mountain. The General said: "Those are certainly the ships to pick up your troops and carry them back. Perhaps we will go back together." My little daughter Frederika, who was standing next to me, said to him: "Now then, if we go, give us this ship. It is so beautiful!" "My child," he answered, "very gladly, if it is a transport, but what would the King of England say if I were to hire a ship for this purpose, for this would come too dearly?" "Oh," she replied, "the King loves his wife and children, so he would certainly be pleased to see Papa bring his family home safely; and you, would you be delighted to see that your little wife did not perish?" (The good General always called my eldest daughter "his little wife.") He laughed at this sally and said, "Well, we shall see."

Two days later he called on us in the morning and said to me with tears in his eyes: "We must part! You are to go, but I must remain. I shall miss you terribly. In your husband I had a man on whom I could rely, and in your whole family I had friends such as one seldom finds. I had hoped that we would return together, but the King has decided otherwise, and I must obey. Meanwhile, I have thought over what your daughter said to me, and since I am most anxious that you return to Europe safely, I myself have inspected the ship that was chosen for you, but found it bad. The ship, however, which pleased your daughter so much is just what I should want for you, and therefore, although it is not among those designated for the transport of the soldiers, I took it upon myself to have it chartered and fitted out for you. Now go and look at it, and order whatever you wish to have. I have already given orders that everything shall be done as you desire. Your husband is going to Sorel, and it would be well if you also went there to make all your arrangements for your departure. But come back soon and share with me the moments which still remain before your departure."

At this he left me much affected. How could one do other than give such a man one's complete friendship? An hour later Major Twiss[25] came to take me to the ship. It was a large West Indian three-decker in good condition. Also, the captain was extolled as an excellent seaman and a courteous and upright man. I was shown over the entire ship and asked what space I would need, for I would certainly have need of a dining room and a sitting room. I laughed and asked, "Where could you find such accommodations?" "Let me worry about that," replied the Major, and he gave orders to clear away the cannons that were on a gun-deck, a large window to be cut above it, and rooms on either side of it for the gentlemen, in which their beds, tables, and chairs were all made fast. We kept for ourselves the large cabin, and my husband and I had a stateroom with two beds, and right next to it another room for our children. In short, everything was as good as could be had in such a floating prison.

On the next day I went to Sorel. I was advised to travel by boat in order to arrive there more quickly. This I did, but we found that the water was too shallow, and we were told accordingly that we must again take to land. "But how can we do this," I asked, "for there is nothing here but a morass and stones?" The proposal was made to carry us, which was a dreadful undertaking, for our bearers were continually slipping. When we finally reached dry land, we found a new difficulty; namely, we had to climb a high and steep mountain. I protested that I should never be able to climb it, but the Canadians, who are accustomed to this and climb like Alpine goats, gave assurances that this was a mere trifle for them, and that, moreover, there was nothing else that we could do but to climb there. People carried my children, and two of them seized me under the arms and dragged me up. The mountain was so steep that it seemed as though those who were ahead of me would fall on me, and from all this we were unbearably hot. Finally, after much toil and trouble, we reached the

25. Lt. William Twiss was Burgoyne's chief engineer during the Saratoga campaign. Bird, *March to Saratoga*, 34, 285; Stone, trans., *General Riedesel*, I, 94–96, II, 121, 132, 158, 255. Adam Mabane to the General, June 22, 1783, mentions the elaborate outfitting of the *Quebec* for the Riedesels. McCord Museum, McGill University, Montreal, Canada.

top, and not a moment too soon, for I was so worn out that I had to sit down, and all my veins throbbed so from this violent overheating that my poor children became very disquieted over it. We were obliged to spend a night on the way. But I found a good bed and some refreshment, which restored my strength, and on the next day we set forth again on our journey.

At our arrival in Sorel I found my husband already very busy, and for my part I bestirred myself also to such purpose, that in nine days I was able again to return to Quebec, where my husband also followed me shortly. Prior to this I was anxious to talk to the parish priest, who was a good man, about the grave of my little daughter who died there, and to express to him the concerns I mentioned above, that one of the very bigoted people living there might, out of blind religious zeal, violate the child's grave because she was not Catholic. He assured me, however, that since the child had only been christened and not yet confirmed, she would be regarded as an angel and her ashes would not be disturbed, and he gave me his word, moreover, that he himself would watch over them.

When we were back in Quebec, I heard that the refitting of our ship was already far advanced, and that its appearance was entirely different. General Haldimand himself had already been there several times to inspect it, and he had had a cow with its calf brought aboard the ship, so that we might be supplied with fresh milk. Topside he had ordered a place on the deck be covered with soil in which he had had greens planted, which was not only very pleasant but also very healthy on a sea voyage. We also bought much poultry, mutton, and many vegetables, for I was much concerned that we not run short of anything, since there were so many of us, and every day twenty-two people were at our table.

Doctor Kennedy, our physician, on our passage through Trois Rivières, begged us to arrange it so that his family, namely his wife and three daughters, two maids, and a manservant, could travel to Europe with us. We promised him to speak to the General about it, for since he was so skillful, we would have liked to have such a man with us. The General answered me, when I asked him about it: "The ship is yours, do with it what you like, but you do not know how pretentious these people are; they will make a lot of trouble for you." I learned later from experience that he knew his people well. Still another cabin for Mrs. Kennedy, two of her daughters, and a maid was fitted out next to ours, and my children took the third daughter, who was ten years old, in their cabin. The doctor was given a cabin in the large area next to the wardroom.

At our departure my husband gave the General as a present his favorite horse and a beautiful foal, and he gave me in return a magnificent muff and cape of sable as a remembrance of the country where we had stayed so long, of which one of the finest products is furs. English merchants enrich themselves by sending over the commonest wares; these they trade at a good price for furs, which they then have dressed in England.

The General also presented my daughter Augusta with a beautiful dog. Moreover, he took every opportunity he could to show his friendship for us, and he was so moved at our departure, that we ourselves were quite affected. Two days before our departure the English officers paid us the attention in a performance, which they put on twice a week (and the receipts of which, deducting costs of lighting up, were given to the poor), of adding at the end of the piece a truly touching song about the departure of our troops, which ended with thanks to my husband for the kind treatment he had given each and every one of them and with wishes for our safe voyage.

After my husband had taken care of the embarkation of the troops, we had dinner and supper with the General. Then he escorted us aboard ship, where we took a very affectionate and sad leave of him as well as various other persons who had shown us friendship.

IX

Return to England and Brunswick

It was around the middle of the month of August when we set out on our return voyage to Europe. As I have already said, we traveled together in the same ship, my husband, myself, and our children. The morning after we boarded ship, the signal for setting sail was given. Everyone laid in as large a supply of fresh meat as he could, and within an hour our whole fleet was under sail. We sailed as far as the Isle of Bic at the mouth of the St. Lawrence,[1] where we had to lie two whole weeks, waiting all the while for favorable winds, which was all the more tedious for us since our provisions of fresh meat and vegetables were consumed during this time, and because the surrounding countryside did not have these items in good quality or in such quantity as to be able to afford fresh provisions in accordance with the needs of an entire fleet. Also we learned that we would not be able to reach Europe before the autumnal equinox, during which one runs great danger of storms along the English coast.

While we were in this frame of mind, Chaplain Mylius of my husband's regiment was holding one of his regular Sunday services, and just as he was very fervently praying that God soon grant us favorable wind for our voyage and a safe return to our fatherland, the ship, which had lain motionless during the calm, once again began to move, and just as the chaplain said "Amen" there rang out the cry that the English commodore who commanded the fleet had just given the signal for departure. Half an hour later he passed our ship, and the whole fleet sailed.

1. The Isle of Bic is not far from where a ship would turn to pass by Cape Race and head for Europe.

Since sailing with a fleet is always a slow matter, and often with delays, my husband wished very much to be able to sail ahead of the fleet, the sooner to be able to bear to the King the letters which General Haldimand sent by him. The captain of the ship also wished to leave the convoy and sail ahead faster, but he did not dare do so without the permission of the commodore who commanded the fleet. Two days later one of the ships gave the signal that it had something to say to the commodore, at which all the ships shortened sail. The commodore, however, was so courteous as to call through a speaking trumpet: "General, go on!" Our ship's captain took advantage of this, acting as though he took it for a general order not to wait for the other ships. He spread full sail, and in a short time we saw no more of our fleet. At first we were well pleased, but later, seeing ourselves so isolated, I became fearful that something untoward might befall us.

At our separation a strange circumstance occurred, which deserves to be mentioned in this connection, since it seemed to our captain to be an infallible and favorably auspicious omen of a happy end for our voyage. Two pigeons, which belonged to the commodore's ship, flew over to our ship, from which they would not return. As I said, our captain took this for a very significant and favorable omen, but the crew of the commodore's ship regarded it as a bad sign for them. Incidentally, this foreboding turned out to be right, since the poor commodore had the misfortune of becoming insane on this very voyage. Never have I seen such superstition as prevails among sea-faring people. They give heed to the slightest circumstance, and draw conclusions and omens from it.

Soon after we had sailed on ahead, we noticed a great flock of blackbirds and an astoundingly large number of porpoises gathering around our ship, while the horizon became a pale yellowish color. From this our captain prophesied a severe storm, which, to be sure, came up that very evening, and, with the exception of a single day's calm which we had on the Newfoundland Banks, continued uninterrupted with the same fury, day and night, for three weeks. Since fortunately we were sailing with the wind, we made the passage from the Isle of Bic to St. Helen's Bay in eighteen days,[2] which is unheard-of speed, of which there is only one other example, that of a French frigate, which made the passage in nineteen days, one day longer indeed than we took.

2. St. Helen's Bay is at the northeast corner of the Isle of Wight, just opposite Portsmouth.

One evening one of our sails was torn away by the wind, and since it was very dark, this made bad work, and our ship received a terrible pounding and was tossed completely on one side. Before night, however, the damage was repaired.

A few days later we noticed a smell of something burning, and we were all the more anxious to discover its source, because the powder magazine was under our cabin. After searching long in vain, I finally found that in Mrs. Kennedy's cabin a rope, from which a lantern hung, had caught fire and had already burned up close to a beam, which, as is customary on ships, was smeared with tar, and consequently could have caught fire all the more easily. I hastened to point this out, and the captain was very glad it was discovered. He informed Mrs. Kennedy of the danger in which she had placed us all, and begged her in the future to be more careful. However, instead of acknowledging gratefully that she herself had escaped the danger, she took offense and sulked toward me for more than a week, and she even went so far as to place a nightlamp on her floor, which slid back and forth from the motion of the ship, giving us much anxiety.

My husband and I could sleep little because of the violent storm, and he spent the greater part of the nights up on deck. Once I told our captain that what I feared the most were the so-called dead-lights, which are wooden window-pieces placed in the windows of the ship during violent storms to keep the water from coming in. The captain, a kind and amiable man, sought to comfort me, saying that since our ship was very high, a storm would have to be extremely dangerous to make these windows necessary, and particularly in the summer there was scarcely an example of the weather getting that bad.

It was eight o'clock in the evening when he said this to me, and by ten o'clock the storm was so strong that no one went to bed. Toward midnight someone knocked on our door. I inquired who was there, and to my great horror received the answer that the captain was sending the dreaded wooden windows. "It is impossible!" I exclaimed, and asked for the captain to come to us. He came right away and told us the storm had become so violent that he had been obliged to resort to this step to protect our windows from being pounded out by the waves. He assured us, however, that otherwise there was no urgent danger at hand, because the ship was so stout that it could hold out against all. The storm continued with the same intensity the whole night until sunrise, and toward morning broke one of our masts. Mrs.

Kennedy wept the whole night, especially lamenting that her sons by now had safely reached England and would survive her.

At five o'clock in the morning I went into the room where my daughters slept. I was undecided as to whether I should awaken them or to leave them sleeping in their peaceful ignorance of our dangerous situation. However, with the dreadful presentiment that we would all perish, I could not restrain myself from embracing in turn each one of them one more time. When I came to my oldest daughter, Augusta, I found her awake. She had made no sound, however, so as not to disturb me still further. "Ah, what a storm." I said. "Aren't you frightened by it?" "Oh, yes," she replied, "but my consolation is that at least we shall not have to live on without you." These few words, which so completely showed me her tender love as well as her resignation, moved me to the bottom of my heart.

Sometimes the ship took such a pounding and rocked so far on its side, that I said to myself: "One more buffet like that, and it is all over for us." At last daylight brought an end to our suffering, for although a strong wind continued, it nevertheless abated somewhat. Meanwhile it remained constantly favorable, and since it drove us with such force that we made fourteen knots, our voyage was very much shortened.

One day our captain said to us: "If the wind remains as favorable to us as it has been, we shall be in England in three days." This caused us the greatest joy, for although we had a sufficiency of almost everything—fresh bread and other foods, milk (which, moreover, is rarely had aboard ship), and even music, since the instrumentalists of my husband's regiment were with us—we were nevertheless worse off in spite of all this, than we would have been in the most miserable of huts. One night my husband, who suffered for all of us, said to me that a pigsty would have been better. He simply could not bring himself to bed, and during the whole course of our voyage I do not believe that he slept more than five or six nights in bed.

The violent buffeting which the ship received threw one of our cows from the hammock in which she was hanging, injuring her so badly that we had to slaughter her. We then presented the meat to the crew.

Toward the end of our voyage a persistent, heavy fog prevented the captain from taking his bearings, and his reckoning did not agree with that of my husband, who maintained that we had already passed the Scilly Islands (of whose rocks the captain was apprehensive) and must be very close to the English coast. In this uncertainty the captain decided toward evening of the eighteenth day of our voyage to lie to, and not run the danger of being driven onto the rocks during the night.

During this unpleasant waiting (for while a ship is lying to, gusts of wind give it a very unpleasant motion) we sat in our cabin. The gentlemen were still at the table after dinner, sad and thoughtful, and the captain had already risen and gone up on deck to make his preliminary instructions there for lying to, when my husband heard the cry, "Land! Land!" ring out above, and shortly afterwards he was called up on deck by the captain, who pointed out to him a small white speck, shimmering through the fog, which my husband would not admit was land at all. But the captain assured him, that because he had made this voyage so often, he well recognized the chalky, white shimmering coast of England.

Soon after the fog was dispelled by a gust of wind, and just as though a great curtain were raised, we saw, to our indescribable joy, the Isle of Wight and the whole English coast lying there clear and close before us. "Now," said the captain, "I must hoist all sails, for we must make it around the Isle of Wight yet this evening; otherwise I might not find anchorage and we could be driven across the Channel into the North Sea by a storm. This was no small undertaking, for it was already four in the afternoon, and the Isle of Wight is thirty leagues in length. It was also very difficult to spread sail in such a strong wind, and the captain saw a good twenty sail-yards break in this effort, all shattering like glass. But at last all was brought into order, and the ship sailed with such indescribable speed, that we arrived safely in St. Helen's Bay by eight o'clock of the same evening.

I came very near having my foot crushed that day. Like the others, I had gone up on deck to feast my eyes on the view of the nearby coast. Captain O'Connell, one of the English officers with us, leapt for joy, slipped, and in falling knocked over a pulley block, which rolled on my foot and pinned it against the side of the ship. I could not help crying out loudly in pain, and I could no longer remain standing. I was dragged into my cabin, where my foot was washed and bandaged. Sofas were fastened on either side of my cabin. I was sitting on one of them, and my seven-year-old daughter on the other, when suddenly the ship gave such a lurch, that the child flew over from the opposite sofa onto mine. It was fortunate that she landed where she did, for otherwise she might have broken an arm or leg. Although the accident to my foot was very painful at the time, there were, fortunately, no further ill consequences.

We lay the whole night in St. Helen's Bay, and thought we would be in Portsmouth the following day. However, as our ship came into harbor, it settled firmly on the sunken man-of-war, the *Royal George*,[3] or, as one says in nautical language, "rode" it. Therefore we had to spend the following night in this unpleasant position, and could only come in the next day. Because of the violent lurches which our ship took, on account of being caught on another, this night was most unpleasant. Also it was a very sad sight to see around us the wreckage of ships which were torn from their anchorage at Portsmouth and wrecked by the same terrible storm we had had at sea.

I must further point out the strange coincidence that we came to anchor in the harbor of Portsmouth exactly between the ship that took me from England to Canada and that which carried us from New York to Quebec.

Since the ebbing of the tide prevented us from landing, and since it would have taken too long to have waited for the incoming tide, my husband hired a lugger, which is a light boat, to get ashore more quickly. But even though it was no more than a half hour's trip, it cost him fifteen guineas.[4]

Thus we reached Portsmouth about the middle of September. Our hearts were very much lightened when we set foot on land, and I thanked God for the safe return of us all, and especially for having preserved my husband for me. We were driven to the best inn, and the dinner which we had there seemed to us, after all that we had experienced, one of the best of our whole lives. The white bread in

3. The *Royal George*, a hundred-gun man-of-war, the pride of the Royal Navy, "heeled too far" while a pipe below the waterline was being fixed. The ship capsized, and 900 men, women, and children were lost. Among them were Admiral Kempenfelt and Capt. Martin Waghorn. This catastrophe occurred June 28, 1782. William L. Clowes, *et al.*, *The Royal Navy, a History from the Earliest Time to the Present*, 7 vols. (London and Boston, 1897–1903), III, 540; E. Keble Chatterton, *The Story of the British Navy from the Earliest Time to the Present* (London, 1911), 266.

4. Compare Stone, trans., *General Riedesel*, II, 179. The General himself was impressed with the speedy crossing that had been made, and perhaps felt it would be a pity to spend time so near the coast. But whatever was his skill as a soldier, his knowledge of the sea and navigation left much to be desired. Stone recounts in *Mrs. General Riedesel*, 217, a tradition that on his way to America General Riedesel had inquired whether the ship had not missed Canada!

particular tasted exceptionally good; not only was it really excellent, but it actually seemed even better to us, because what we had had on the voyage was almost always badly baked, either because of the bad weather or for lack of necessities. In the evening we ate some oysters, which tasted very good. Shortly, however, we had to pay dearly, for in the night my daughter Augusta was taken with a terrible colic and incessant vomiting, which Doctor Kennedy, who fortunately still was with us, and whom I immediately summoned, pronounced as *cholera morbus*, which is supposed to be one of the most dangerous kinds of colic. He gave her medicine, which had a good effect right away. The next morning Chaplain Mylius was also very sick, yes, even sicker [than my daughter]. Finally it was discovered that the oysters had been taken in a place near Portsmouth where some copper was supposed to be, or, as a few maintain, from copper-sheathed ships lying at anchor, from which the oysters had absorbed verdigris. It is forbidden to take oysters at this spot, and if people are caught at it, they are strictly punished. However, this does not prevent some from venturing to do so, because they are taken there with less effort and cost.

On the morning of the following day my husband and his aides set out for London, and I followed in the afternoon. I had begged him to spend the night at the inn of the honest landlord, who had given me such good treatment on my first journey, but the postilions took him on another route. My postilions also had wanted to go by that road, but I insisted on my way, and I was received by the good man with sincere demonstrations of joy. He gave a family concert for me, in which a sister of his, who had been blind for seven years, played the harpsichord very nicely and also sang. She did not like having strangers know that she was blind, so she seated herself in front of the harpsichord before anyone entered with a book lying before her, and since one could not see her eyes, a person would have noticed nothing wrong. However, her brother let people know, so that if they discovered it, they would not mention it, thus grieving her. It distressed him that my husband had passed by another route. I inquired why the postilions prevented people from stopping at his place. He answered that he considered it beneath him to bribe them, but that there was an innkeeper two miles distant from him, who paid them a great deal, which he later added to the bill of his guests. "But guests who once know me," he said, "come back to me again, because they know that I go to the greatest pains to treat them well." His house was nicer than ever. The whole entrance hall and the inner court was

decorated with potted flowers and trailing vines which climbed up
the house, and amidst which were glass bowls in which goldfish were
swimming, all of which produced the most delightful effect. He again
gave me the best rooms, I had the best fare that could be had, and the
charges were ridiculously low. My husband, however, had to pay an
astonishing price at his inn.

Two days later I reached London, where we were magnificently
lodged in a large hotel named, if I remember correctly, "The King
George." Just as soon as I could, the very morning after my arrival,
I went to call upon that good family, the Russells, who during my
first stay in London, before my voyage to America, had been so good
and considerate to me. I hired a carriage, got in with my four children,
and did not let the good people know a thing in advance of my visit.
Since the husband was still dressing in his room, we went into the
shop and placed ourselves directly before Mrs. Russell, who was busy
selling sugar. As she saw me standing there before, she looked me
closely in the face and said, "Can I believe my eyes? Is this really
you?—But you had only three children, and now there are four!"
I could no longer restrain myself; my tears of joy betrayed me; I fell
upon her neck. At this moment someone grasped me from behind and
cried out: "Pardon, Milady, I must embrace you." It was the worthy,
good husband. These kind people wept very much when I left them
again, but I promised to return once more, and this time to bring my
husband to them.

Every day we were someone's guest and, among others, we dined
one day with our good New York friend, General Tryon. One day,
while we were yet at dinner, the Queen's first lady of honor, Lady
Howard,[5] sent word that we were to be received by the Queen at six
o'clock that evening. Since my court dress was not yet ready, and I
had nothing at all but a perfectly plain angloise, I directly sent my
apologies in advance, which I repeated myself when we had the honor
of being presented together to Their Majesties. But the Queen, who,
just as the King, received us most graciously, replied in the most
friendly manner, saying: "We do not look at clothes when we are
happy to see the people." They were surrounded by all their daughters,
the Princesses. The Queen, the Princesses, the first lady of honor, and
myself seated ourselves in a half-circle before the fireplace, and my

---

5. Lady Anne Howard, a daughter of the fourth Earl of Carlisle, was lady-
in-waiting. See *The Autobiography and Correspondence of Mary Granville,
Mrs. Delany*, 6 vols. (London, 1861), V, 19.

husband remained standing with the King before the fire. Tea and cakes were passed around. I sat between the Queen and one of the Princesses, and had to recount a great deal. The Queen very graciously said to me: "I have followed you everywhere, often inquiring after you, and it was always a satisfaction to hear that you were well, contented, and beloved by everyone." I had a dreadful cough at the time. Princess Sophia went herself to fetch some black currant jelly, which she recommended as a particularly good remedy, and made me accept a jar full of it.[6]

At nine o'clock in the evening the Prince of Wales also came in. His younger sisters ran up to him, and he embraced them and danced around with them. Indeed, the royal family had such a gift for removing all restraint, that one would think he were in a happy family circle of his own station. We remained there until ten o'clock, and the King talked a great deal with my husband about America, and in German, which he spoke exceedingly well. My husband was also amazed at his excellent memory. When we were taking our leave, the Queen was so gracious as to say to me, that she hoped we would not depart so soon that she would not be able to see me again, as she wished. But as we shortly received the news that the fleet was ready to carry us with our troops back to Germany, we had to hasten our departure, so that we were unable to pay our respects to the royal family again.

During our sojourn in London, I also made the acquaintance of Lord North and Mr. Fox.[7] Both paid us visits. Moreover, I made

6. Of the fifteen children of George III (among whom were nine sons), Princess Sophia (1777–1848) was the fourteenth. The Rev. William Hunt, "George III," *DNB*. The general picture given here of the royal family is idyllic. Other pictures have been presented, including those showing adverse effects of George III's treatment on the Princess Sophia. John C. Long, *George III; The Story of a Complex Man* (Boston, 1960), 306. The General also describes this meeting; Stone, trans., *General Riedesel*, II, 180. The actual closeness of the royal family to Brunswick, of course, must not be overlooked. George III's mother was a Saxe-Coburg princess, and one of her daughters, Augusta, married Karl Wilhelm Ferdinand, who had been the reigning Duke of Brunswick since 1780. *Allgemeine deutsche Biographie*, XV, 273. Also in 1795 the Prince of Wales, later George IV, married Caroline of Brunswick-Wolfenbüttel, daughter of the Duke of Brunswick and Princess Augusta. See genealogical tables in James Pope-Hennessy, *Queen Mary, 1867–1953* (London, 1959).

7. Charles James Fox (1749–1806) and Lord North, joint secretaries of state, were at this time leading the ministry in an uneasy coalition. See Sir George O. Trevelyan, *George the Third and Charles Fox, the Concluding Part of the American Revolution*, 2 vols. (London, 1921–27).

several trips into the country, partly to know London and the vicinity better, and partly to see noteworthy things. I would gladly have extended our stay, but the news that the fleet which was to carry us back to Germany was ready to sail changed all our plans, and obliged us to leave as quickly as possible.

We went to Deal, where we were supposed to embark. We were exactly at the equinox, of which we had been so fearful, and the captain would have preferred to have waited until it was past before we set off, because the storm was strong and entrance into the Elbe is said to be very difficult, particularly during contrary weather. After we had waited for a day in Deal without any improvement in the weather, my husband decided to sail, let the weather be whatever it would, for he did not want to hold up the departure of the transports any longer on his account. The wharf there is very bad, especially during a heavy storm. The ships' boats lie on the beach, where people are embarked to wait for the moment the tide comes in, when the sailors pull the boats into the water and shove off. We all became very apprehensive about this procedure, because it seemed so extraordinary and so dangerous. I had my youngest daughter, the three-year-old America, on my lap, and a crowd of people were standing around our boat. All of a sudden the frightened child began to cry out in English: "Is nobody there who will take me!" and at the same time stretched out both her little arms. A very well-dressed lady came running up at this, and was just about to snatch her from me, when the boat was shoved off. I had all I could do to keep hold of the little one, for the waves were tossing the boat back and forth. Since I had thought that we were past all dangers when we arrived in England, this unexpected new one completely disconcerted me. Finally we reached the ship safely, but new difficulties awaited us. Since the waves were very high and our boat was being tossed up and down, we did not know how we were going to get aboard ship. I declared at once that I should be the last to leave the boat, and that I wanted the others to climb up before me, in order to know first that my family was safe. My husband, therefore, went ahead, and then the sailors took my children in arm and climbed with them up the little ladder onto the ship. I was anxious and fearful during all this, for had they slipped, they would have been crushed between the ship and the boat, from which there could have been no rescue. I was drawn up on a chair. When I was on board the captain came to me and said: "I wish to congratulate you, for today you have run more danger than on your whole voyage."

The next morning we weighed anchor, and we spent three days on our passage to Stade. We had to sail back and forth, for we were not able to pass the buoys which lie there in the Elbe, marking the only place where large ships can come through with the help of the tide. At last, my husband became impatient, had himself put ashore, and continued his journey towards Stade in a calash. But I remained behind with the children, because this would have made too many difficulties.

The next day the captain, who, incidentally, and I may say fortunately, was the same one who brought us from Quebec to England, offered with his customary thoughtful courtesy to take me himself to Stade in case our ship had to remain at anchor. Accordingly, we left the ship at four in the afternoon in a large boat, after I had, at the behest of my husband, made him a present of all our provisions, which consisted of two cows, fifteen sheep, and much poultry, for we had well provided for ourselves. He expressed much gratitude for all this. We had six sailors to row us, but since we were going against the current, the poor fellows became very exhausted, and I was fearful that we would have to spend the night on the Elbe, which would have been very unpleasant. After much effort we finally reached Stade at eleven o'clock in the evening, but because of the large number of ships there, we were not able to land, especially since it was so dark. Therefore, we were forced to go ashore over the decks of three or four ships by means of boards laid from one to another.

When we finally arrived in the town, I did not know where to find my husband, since everyone was already asleep, and those whom we did meet were either drunk or unable to give us the slightest information. I had thought that everyone must know the newly arrived German general, who was so important to me, but when some said: "Ah, we do not know any such!" and others: "What is he to us!" I was mortified in front of the captain and our sailors, who were helping my faithful Rockel carry the children. Finally, we found a good soul, who took us to the inn where my husband was staying, but he led us through so many narrow streets, that I was afraid we were being led out of the way to be robbed. Therefore, we resolved not to be taken into any house that seemed suspicious to us. But when we finally reached the inn, I saw to my great joy guards from our dragoons posted before the doors, and among them an old soldier who was almost always with my husband. This good old man took me and the children by the hand and said: "How glad I am to see you safely back in Germany!"—and he said this in such a sincere tone, that we could fully see what a good and sympathetic heart he had. My husband was already in bed, and he rejoiced over our safe arrival. I wanted to serve the captain tea, but the innkeeper was peevish, and I got bad tea, bad milk, bad bread, and bad butter, and all served in such a filthy manner, that I was very much ashamed of my countrymen before the captain, and I begged him not to judge my fatherland by this example. The next day he made his departure, and we were much moved in parting from this good man, who had shown so much courtesy, kindness, and attention.

We stayed one day more in Stade. My husband was still waiting there for the rest of the troops, but I set out the following day and spent the night in Celle,[8] in the delightful expectation of being in Brunswick the next day. But in the middle of the night, I suddenly saw a soldier with a big mustache, light in hand, standing before my bed. It was a porter. I was terribly frightened, and all the more so, when he handed me a letter from my husband that had arrived by courier, because I feared that something had happened to him. But it was nothing more than a change of travel plans, by which I should first go to Wolfenbüttel.

There I found our whole house in the same order in which we had left it on our departure for America. My good friends, Madame Paasch and her daughter, had come from Brunswick for the express purpose of putting everything in order for me. They had also prepared me a fine supper and after refreshing myself with it, I retired with the most sincere and heartfelt thanks to God for having preserved me through such manifold dangers, but especially for having preserved for me all my family, and, yes, having even brought me a gift, my little daughter America.

On the very next day I had a visit from our excellent Duchess and from various of my dear old friends. About a week later I had the great satisfaction of seeing my husband with the troops in his command pass through the city. In this very same street, in which seven and a half years ago I had lost all happiness and contentment, I now saw this beautiful and stirring scene, which I cannot possibly describe —my dear and upright husband, who had lived this whole time solely for his duty, who had constantly done his utmost to support as far as

8. Madame de Riedesel spells it Zelle, but surely she meant Celle, which is directly on the route from Stade to Brunswick, from which it is about thirty miles northwest.

he could and to help (ofttimes from his own purse, which grew no fuller from it) those who were entrusted to him—standing there with tears of joy in his eyes in the midst of his soldiers, in the partly happy, partly pathetic bustle of fathers, mothers, wives, children, brothers and sisters, and friends, who all pressed about to see their loved ones again. The joy of those who were finding, or found by, their own again, and the sadness of those who had lost and looked in vain for theirs—all this cannot be described, but only felt.

The next day both of us went to Brunswick. It was Sunday, as I remember, in the autumn of 1783, when we reached there. We dined at court, where in the evening I saw again, after this long separation, most of my friends, which was a great joy, but at the same time it excited emotions in me which shook my innermost being.

Part II

Baroness von Riedesel's Correspondence

X

General Riedesel's Letters

The Trip to America
February–November
1776

❧——◀✿◗▶——☙

On January 10, 1776, Colonel Riedesel received his commission as commander of the Brunswick troops for which the British had contracted by treaty on January 9, 1776. On February 22, Riedesel and the troops left Wolfenbüttel and that night, according to instructions from Duke Karl, he was raised to the rank of major general. Along the road of march from Wolfenbüttel to the port of embarkation of Stade on the Elbe, the General kept a chain of letters moving back to Mrs. General, who was expecting her third child later in the month or early in March. His early letters are full of anxiety about his wife's safety and comfort. "May your confinement be safely passed" is his recurring theme in his early letters, and after the birth of Caroline he writes with obvious relief, "God be praised that all is happily over."

The General's letters to his wife pinpoint the route from Wolfenbüttel to Stade—Leifert, Gifhorn, Haukenbüttel, Vriestädt, Amelinghausen—where he summarizes briefly his itinerary—then on to Thomalohe, Rumelslohe, Harburg, Buxtehude, and Stade. Once aboard the transports, he wrote diary-like entries to show his wife how he spent his time on ship; he also began outlining plans for Mrs.

Riedesel's following him when she was able. After his letter of April 6, 1776, he was cut off from rapid communication, and he wrote only one long letter as he crossed the ocean, "for what is there to tell about nine weeks spent between heaven and ocean, where one day was passed exactly like another?"

After his arrival in Quebec on June 1, he sent occasional dispatches to the Baroness describing the country and army life. Not until September 23 did he receive his wife's letters written prior to her departure for England in May. But he did not receive any report after she left Wolfenbüttel until November 10, and he confessed that this lack of communication "put me in mortal dread." By then he had pretty well given up hope of her arrival before the spring of 1777. "I am," he wrote, "exceedingly worried about you, since I know not where you are."

General Riedesel
to Baroness von Riedesel

Leifert, February 22, 1776

Dearest Wife,

Never have I known greater suffering than upon my departure this morning. My heart was broken, and had I had the opportunity of going back, who knows what I might have done! However, my love, God has given me this calling, and I must follow it. I am duty and honor bound. We must comfort ourselves and not complain. Moreover, I am only concerned about your health and the child to be born, and about everything that concerns your welfare and the health of our dear daughters. Take the best care of them; I love them most tenderly.

I arrived here safely and in good health, although extremely exhausted from the suffering my soul has experienced these past days. I am looking forward to refreshing sleep, and I hope that you too will find the same.

I was appointed Major General tonight;[1] and now, my own Mrs.

1. The reference is to his Brunswick commission. *Allgemeine deutsche Biographie,* IX, 532.

General, take good care of yourself so that you can join me immediately after your confinement. I was given a fond farewell by the Duke.[2] Duke Ferdinand reviewed us in a parade and bid adieu tenderly before the troops.[3]

Your faithful husband
R.

General Riedesel
to Baroness von Riedesel

Gifhorn, February 23, 1776

Here I am at Gifhorn, which I reached without mishap, and also, thank God, without any desertions. I might have had a restful night, had not my soul been constantly with you and my beloved children. Yes, my dear wife, you did not notice, and were not supposed to notice, how I suffered these last four weeks and what it cost me to conceal my sorrow from you. My spirit has not suffered from work, for I am accustomed to that, but from sadness and sorrow. Well, it is over now! God has willed it so; His will be done!

I do not doubt that you will be able to follow me. May your confinement be safely passed. Take care of your health, and do not take too many chances with the younger children. I think that the eldest can readily stand the journey, and little Frederika as well. But you must be very careful with the baby, be it a boy or girl, and you must not let your love make you too reckless. It is far better to be separated from a beloved child for a time than to have to reproach yourself for its untimely death.

In the second place, you must not leave until you have received my first letters from America, so that you will know where I am. Thirdly and finally, you must obtain good letters of introduction for England, so that you will be comfortable there, and can take short day-trips, and not expose the children too much to the air.

2. Duke Karl I, reigning Duke of Brunswick.

3. Duke Ferdinand, brother of the reigning Duke, commander of the German troops at Minden, and close friend of General Riedesel. The last two sentences were omitted in the original edition.

General Riedesel to Baroness von Riedesel [4]

Gifhorn, February 23, 1776

Here is my second letter, my angel, which I am writing you today. If the mail will go with the same exactness from the other side of the sea, you will get more letters from America. Then you will receive more letters than you will want to pay for. I have today received two messages from the Duke. If you send letters every day to Ralgen, there will always be some chance for me to get them. I am well and I hope to sleep quietly tonight. I am rather impatient to receive your first letter to know how you and the children are. Tomorrow I will write you again and continue to do the same thing on every occasion that offers.

Your faithful,

General Riedesel to Baroness von Riedesel

Haukenbüttel, February 25, 1776

This morning, dear wife, I received your first letter, and, thanks be to God, I see that you are well and have begun to resign yourself to what duty and the will of God have demanded of me. Keep on in this spirit, and pray to God that He give you the strength needed to bear all. I have acted so sincerely in everything, that you have no grounds for doubting my sincere wish that you should follow me as soon as you have news from me and of our destinations. [5] Thanks be to God, I am well, but I cannot yet sleep, and my heart is still heavy. I miss you and my beloved children. What does little Augusta say, and what is little Frederika doing? Give my hearty greetings to Madame Paasch and her daughter, and say to the latter that she must write me a letter, which you are not to read, about your health and state of mind.

Kiss little Augusta and Frederika most tenderly for me, and be assured that I am always yours.

4. This letter has not been published previously.
5. This sentence was omitted in the original edition.

P.S.[6] I have not had a single deserter, and everyone is content. The cook is doing very well. During the march we have had six courses. Today my table is set for sixteen. Malatti sends his highest compliments.[7]

General Riedesel
to Baroness von Riedesel [8]

Haukenbüttel, February 26, 1776

My Dear Wife,

I have received your third letter. I thank Heaven that your health is so good. Your spirits will be the same in time, provided you pray a great deal to the Good Lord that he give you sufficient strength, and that all will go well, and to your satisfaction. The gracious attention of the Duke almost brought me to tears.[9] He has his faults, just as all of us do, but he remains a good man, and he becomes touched in spite of himself.

You have had a good many visits. There were two generals, one of whom saw the happiness of a good heart, while the other clearly saw jealousy. You will see that I, too, have my spies, who tell me what you do. So take care.

As you desire that I should take Rockel, and as you believe he would not be so content with you, I will write him that he should see you and you can send him to me. Then try to get a good servant, even if you have to pay him money instead of board, because in this you must not try to economize; my brother will bring you the money which you are asking for. In return, I will send you one of my servants from America.

6. This P.S. was omitted in the original edition.

7. Du Roi lists among the Hanoverian commissaries supplying the Brunswick troops on their march through that territory a "Major von Malorti"—handwriting may account for the spelling variation. Epping, trans., *Journal of Du Roi, 3.*

8. This letter has not been published previously.

9. The General is referring, in all probability, to Duke Karl I.

General Riedesel
to Baroness von Riedesel [10]

Vriestädt, February 27, 1776

My Dear Wife,

I do not understand what you have found to fear in my letter, as though I did not want you to follow me, or at least would put off your departure. Far from this idea, except for superficial trepidations, you know what I think about the whole matter. You will content yourself that I ask you to await my first letter from America before leaving. It is better that we change [our plans] about Rockel. If he wants to stay, keep him. I would like that even better than to have him follow me, for then I would be more certain that you have a servant on whom I can depend to take care of you.

General Riedesel
to Baroness von Riedesel

Amelinghausen, February 29, 1776

I want to write my diary for you in a few words. As you know, on the 22nd I was in Leifert, sad, thoughtful, and exhausted, but unable to sleep.

On the 23rd, a cold, rainy day, I was in Gifhorn, where I ate with General Bremer.[11]

On the 24th we rested in Haukenbüttel.

On the 25th and 26th we were in Vriestädt. I inspected my regiment of dragoons, which were encamped on the estate of Herr von Grote.[12]

On the 27th I went on to Ebsdorf, and on the 28th to Amelinghausen. I inspected my infantry regiment, and I did not arrive until 11 o'clock at night.

10. This letter has not been published previously.

11. This General Bremer was possibly the father of the Hanoverian minister, Friedrich Franz Dietrich, Count von Bremer. *Allgemeine deutsche Biographie,* III, 304.

12. The estate and the Herr von Grote cannot be positively identified. However, Count Otto von Grote, a Hanoverian lieutenant general and father of the Hanoverian diplomat, August Otto von Grote, may likely have been the man. *Allgemeine deutsche Biographie,* IX, 757–58.

Since yesterday my regiment of dragoons has been with me, and, moreover, I shall keep it with me until we reach Stade, which we shall reach on March 5th. Today I shall again have a large table. Our usual table is for twelve people. Days when we are on the march we have five dishes, and on rest-days six. Kitchen expense, reckoned per day, is half a louis d'or.

With this letter I enclose another to little Augusta and Frederika, whom I embrace tenderly, and with heart and soul I am forever,

Your own.

General Riedesel
to Baroness von Riedesel [13]

Thomalohe, March 2, 1776

My Dear Wife,

Now I have a chance to say to you—unfortunately in writing—that I am well, and that I love you tenderly. God willing, I may hear the same from you, and that you are beginning to become a little less upset, because this is very necessary for a successful accouchement. I am still hoping to receive the news here. I will send you a barrel of oysters from Stade. This letter is being carried by an officer of a regiment of the corps. Thus you will have a second letter today from me. I am ever completely yours.

R.

General Riedesel
to Baroness von Riedesel [14]

Rumelslohe, March 2, 1776

My Dear Wife,

The time of accouchement approaches. God grant his blessing. What company do you have? Are my sister-in-law and Za-Za still with you? Almighty God will direct all according to His holy will. . . .

Our last quarters in Amelinghausen were not the best, but these

13. This letter has not been published previously.
14. This letter has not been published previously.

here are good, and those in Harburg will be exceptionally good. General Bremer invited all of us to dine with him. Tomorrow I will write you from Buxtehude, and perhaps I shall be able to give you more definite news of our embarkation. Tell Barner [15] that the horses have arrived in good condition. The smoked geese have also fortunately arrived. Many thanks. What is Rockel doing? Are you still satisfied with him?

R.

◦———◦◦◦◦————◦

General Riedesel
to Baroness von Riedesel [16]

Harburg, March 3, 1776

My Dear Wife,

God be praised, and He will give you strength for a happy outcome of your accouchement. That is the main thing. When this is past, the rest will take care of itself. But, fi! Who would have such bad ideas as you who only speaks of dying! Rockel would have to take care to take the children away after your death. He would willingly do this. I further know that we are all mortal, and each has his time when it is necessary to leave this world, but it is never necessary to remind one's friends and those who love you of it. What is necessary is to prepare oneself so that it will come as no surprise.

Augusta's interest pleases me extremely! That she pays such great attention to everything I write to her is a mark of her spirit. The advice that she has given to Frederika has especially touched me.

My dear wife, realize that I am giving you good advice. You have the best character in the world, but often you are so unreasonable as not to hide the hate which you have for important men, and you speak in the presence of everybody. Except for your little plans for the voyage, you talk about it all the time. You know that we have many enemies, and people profit by your frankness and intrigue against you and me. My angel, be more circumspect about what you

15. Maj. Ferdinand Albrecht Barner, who died Oct. 2, 1797, as a pensioned colonel, was commander of the Jaeger Battalion, part of the second division of Brunswick troops which embarked from Stade May 30, 1776, and arrived in Quebec on Sept. 17. Stone, trans., *General Riedesel*, II, 110, 272; Epping, trans., *Journal of Du Roi*, 2, 51–53; Eelking, *German Allied Troops*, 94.

16. This letter has not been published previously.

say and the people you visit. Speak of unimportant things, and never show the hatred which you have for a certain P. H. [Hereditary Prince],[17] because he has always treated me fairly.

Yesterday at Harburg the cook got my provisions for the ship for forty-five louis, not counting the livestock, which presumably I will buy at Stade. My compliments to all your company, and many kisses for the children. Forever yours,

R.

General Riedesel
to Baroness von Riedesel [18]

Buxtehude, March 4, 1776

My Angel,

With tears of joy in my eyes I read your letter. God be praised that all is happily over.[19] I was wrong that it would be a boy. It is a child of my blood, and you and the child are getting along. I bless Heaven for this new evidence of favor, and I confess that God gives me more than I deserve. As for myself, I would like to know more about whether your health is good and that no milk-fever or the like has developed. To be sure, I am not writing this myself—I am having Wisgen write. Thank everyone who stood by you for me. As for the christening and the godparents, do whatever you please. The best to you, dear heart. God defend and protect you.

R.

General Riedesel
to Baroness von Riedesel

Stade, March 5, 1776 [20]

I am writing you this, tired indeed as I am, with a very happy heart, since the dragoon and grenadier regiments have been safely

17. Duke Karl Wilhelm Ferdinand, son of Duke Karl I, was the Hereditary Prince, and became the reigning Duke in 1780.

18. This letter has not been published previously.

19. The birth of the Riedesel's daughter Caroline.

20. Stone erroneously dates this letter as Mar. 3, 1776.

embarked. At seven o'clock all were aboard ship, and in less than three hours not a man was left in the city; all were on the Elbe, an hour and a half journey from here. The departure of the small boats from the city was the most beautiful spectacle one could see! All were content and happy, and the people in the city could not praise highly enough the quiet way in which the troops boarded ship and their good conduct during their stay here. Tomorrow Prince Frederick's regiment and my own will arrive, but I do not yet know when they will embark, because half of our ships are still missing. It is not known when they will come, since they were not ready to sail when those which are here sailed from England.

I believe, therefore, that I shall remain in the city for at least another week. I shall have a good officer on my ship, Captain Foy, whom you will remember having seen in Minden. He was an English artillery officer, and a very tall man. He wants his wife to come to America as soon as things become a bit quieter, and he would like it if she could accompany you, but not before he and I know where we shall be.

This Foy will remain with me until we have safely arrived in America, and he tells me our crossing will be a mere trifle. The ship on which I shall sail from here is the *Pallas*,[21] a very good ship, but with a rather small cabin for seven officers, whom I shall be obliged to keep with me. But Foy assures me that from Portsmouth I shall be on a warship, and a large one at that. Today I inspected all the ships that are here.

But enough of myself, my dearest wife, and now let me speak of you, in whom I am much more interested than in myself. I hope that you are completely recovered from your confinement, and that toward April you will be ready to march.

General Riedesel
to Baroness von Riedesel

Stade, March 18, 1776

Dear Wife,

Here I am on the point of embarking, submitting myself fully to God's mercy, which will guide me as lovingly as heretofore. Do not

21. The *Pallas*, Captain Bell, was a fifth-rate, 36-gun warship. *Royal Kalendar* (1778), p. 145.

be frightened, and be assured that life aboard ship is good. I have very good company, and when I reach the coast of England and have been transferred to a man-of-war, I shall be in a still better situation.

It is decided, then, that you will come to Plymouth as soon as your health, and that of our newborn daughter Caroline, will permit, and that you will wait there for my further reports from America. Do not be impatient. God's love for us is too great not to unite us again as soon as possible.

My brother will dine with me once more tomorrow, and then all this will be past. This is still another sad moment for me. Embrace our dear children! Yes, our dear children, for me! The ship is waiting. I must go. Goodbye! Love me always. Take care of your precious health for my sake, and be assured that I am forever completely yours.

General Riedesel
to Baroness von Riedesel [22]

Aboard the *Pallas,* March 20, 1776

Today you get three letters from me, evidence that one can write in comfort aboard ship. I have just received two letters from you, which have brought me much satisfaction. The only thing that distresses me is your own distress over the distance between us, which, I fear, may do you harm. Good heavens, what distress you have! I am quite well and lack nothing. I am in the hands of God, who is able to take all your cares from you and to have compassion for you, to console you and make you understand that you have nothing to fear for me, and to tell you the truth, I do not foresee the slightest danger for myself. I must admit our departure at Wolfenbüttel upset you a bit. We shall scarcely be at Spithead, near Portsmouth, by the end of the month, and we shall hardly reach our destination by the end of May. Even with all imaginable luck, you will not be able to have instructions from America before June or July. . . . I am glad that the first shipment of H. [oysters] has arrived, and I hope that your condition allows you to eat them. I hope that Dachenhausen sends a second shipment as soon as they have more of them. Dearest wife, do not grieve your-

22. This letter has not been published previously.

self, and you will not be sad. Be assured that I will not become an American, and I shall take care of my health. Kiss our good Augusta, and little Frederika and Caroline.

Your own.

◦━━◂◖❂❧◗▸━━◦

General Riedesel
to Baroness von Riedesel

Aboard the *Pallas,* March 21, 1776

Here we still lie before Stade on account of unfavorable winds, and so we have to have patience. However, we shall sail at midday for Fryburg, near Glückstadt, to wait there for more favorable winds to carry us out into the sea, bound for England. In the meantime, we are comfortable, and only your presence is needed to complete my happiness, for I confess that I have a great longing to see you again.

For your amusement I am sending you a diary so you can see how we spend our time.

To begin with, we have a stateroom that is about as large as your room. On either side is a small cabin, in one of which is my bed, and in the other that of Captain Foy. On the sides of the cabin itself are four beds, in which Captains Hensch, Gerlach, Cleve, and the Cavalry Captain Fricke sleep.[23] The paymaster and his sergeant, as well as the secretary, are in the space where the troops are quartered, in a cabin especially partitioned for them.

I rise in the morning at about seven o'clock, after having said my prayers while yet in bed. We get dressed right away and have breakfast English-style, with tea and bread and butter. Then I go up on

23. Captain Hensch (or Heusch) was a Brunswick aide-de-camp, according to the General's letter, May 24, 1776, and Capt. Heinrich Gerlach, a quartermaster. The latter died in 1798 as a pensioned lieutenant colonel in Brunswick. He was a field officer under Riedesel, and he had particular difficulties during the march from Virginia to New York. Stone, trans., *General Riedesel,* II, 100, 265. The Cleve of whom Riedesel spoke was undoubtedly Friedrich Christian. *Ibid.,* I and II, *passim.* Captain Fricke is probably Heinrich Christian Fricke, a member of the Dragoon Regiment. *Ibid.,* II, 265.

deck to smoke my pipe, and after this I write or read, drink coffee, walk up and down with both the Englishmen, and thus with a pipe or two of tobacco I spend my time until dinner, which we have at two o'clock. There are nine persons at our table, we have three courses, and the meal lasts about an hour. Then the tablecloth is removed, and for half or three-quarters of an hour we drink the following toasts: 1) to the King, 2) to the Duke, 3) to you and the children, 4) to Captain Foy's wife, 5) to a good voyage, and 6) to a good expedition in America. At four o'clock we are finished. Our daily consumption amounts to four bottles of wine and half a bottle of arrack for punch. After this I drink coffee with the Englishmen. The other gentlemen take care of themselves. After coffee I visit other ships, and in the evening I play a game of whist. At 8:30 cold meat is served, wine, if anyone wants it, and beer, and at ten o'clock everyone goes to bed. Thus one day passes after another. Very shortly you will receive the eighteen louis d'or which I gave General Kilmansegg and also the two louis from my brother.[24]

Captain Foy is going from Dover to London to make his report to the King, and will rejoin me at Portsmouth. After his arrival there I shall be transferred to a man-of-war, where all will be arranged more to my comfort.

General Gage returned from America on this ship,[25] and at that time it had eight small cabins, quarters for the General, and a dining room, and it is supposed to be again so arranged. In my report from Portsmouth you will hear of all this, of the way things stand in America, and of how we can again see each other in the speediest and safest manner. Until then remain altogether quiet. Moreover, and most particularly, do not talk to others about what I will write to you about American affairs. I embrace you.[26]

R.

24. This sentence was omitted from the original edition. This was probably Count George Ludwig von Kielmansegg, a Brunswick general, whose sister, Sophie Charlotte Marie, was the mother of Admiral Lord Howe and General Howe.

25. Gen. Thomas Gage (1721–87), who had turned over his command in Boston to Howe, embarked at Boston for England on the *Pallas*, Oct. 11, 1775. John R. Alden, *General Gage in America . . .* (Baton Rouge, 1948), 283.

26. The last three sentences were omitted in the original edition.

General Riedesel
to Baroness von Riedesel

Aboard the *Pallas* on open sea, at the Red Buoy,
where pilots leave their ships, March 22, 1776

Here we are on open sea. The pilots are leaving, and through them I am writing you this last letter from the farthest borders of Germany. Fear not, we are all feeling very well, and I hope that we shall continue to do so during the crossing to Spithead, and that once accustomed to the broad sea we will reach America in perfect health. All goes so well that you will be glad to thank God for the fortune we have had, and I wish you the same fortune. You see that people speak far too much about the terrors of the sea. Courage, my angel. God guides us, and not only will we be fortunate, but also He will soon reunite us. Embrace the children, and tell little Augusta that the sea is fascinating.[27]

Foy promises me that we shall be at Spithead by Wednesday at the latest, and my first thought will be to report to you our arrival and the state of my health.

General Riedesel
to Baroness von Riedesel

Aboard the *Pallas,* off Dover, March 26, 1776

I am writing to you at the very minute we are catching our first glimpse of the English coast. Captain Foy, who is going to London, will post this letter there. I can tell you with satisfaction that I was not ill one moment, still less was I seasick. Quite the contrary, my appetite was always good, and I slept well. The soldiers, however, and my servants as well, were all sick, and, for the most part, still are. The poor cook is so sick, that he not only cannot work at all, he cannot even raise his head. This is very inconvenient for us, since Captain Foy and I are obliged to do our own cooking, which would amuse you, if you could see us.

I will give you a brief account of our voyage. Thursday we sailed from Stade to Fryburg. It was a magnificent sight to see all the charming villages along both banks. Glückstadt, a fine Danish fortress, we

27. The last five sentences were omitted in the original edition.

passed by at our right. We were in fine spirits, ate and drank well, and played whist in the evening.

On Friday we sailed to Ritzebüttel, or Cuxhaven, which we reached by evening; we went ashore, saw the city, and played whist in the evening.

Saturday we went to sea with a very gentle wind. We almost felt as though we were not at sea. Everyone was well and ate with a good appetite. From the Red Buoy, where the Hanoverian pilots left us, I wrote you the last letter. In the afternoon, fishermen from Helgoland came aboard, and I bought a large codfish, twenty haddocks, and four flounders for two reichsthalers, which in Brunswick could not be had for ten. Then rainy weather began.

Sunday morning we had a heavy fog and the sea became stormy. Two guns were fired from our ship to indicate to the others what course to follow. The fog rose, the wind and waves grew stronger, but there was no storm. Now everyone got sick. The cook could not cook, Müller could not help me dress, Valentin could find nothing—in short, great lamentations and confusion all over. I was hungry, but had nothing to eat. Before long Captain Foy and I cooked ourselves some pea soup in the sailors' kitchen and ate some cold roast beef. This was our entire dinner. The soldiers ate nothing at all.

Monday the weather was somewhat milder, and some of the people got better, but most of them remained sick. Again Captain Foy cooked, this time bouillon, haddock with anchovy sauce, ragout of roast beef, and some roast veal with potatoes.

Tuesday we had the most beautiful weather, and some of the men were well again. The soldiers cooked for themselves, but the cook was still unable to do anything, so I cooked again with Foy. We had rice soup, carrots and beef, codfish with anchovy sauce, veal stew. At a distance land could be seen.

Today, Wednesday, we are off Dover. Captain Foy is going ashore and will post this letter. Dearest angel, remember that everyone gets sick at sea and that your servants cannot do a thing for you. You must, therefore, take the shortest crossing, and I consider the best way is from Calais. Take only one servant with you—Rockel. All will be better for you if you get an English servant in England, especially one who has already been on the seas. So I advise you to let the coachman go. In the inns you will always find somebody to help Rockel put up the bed for you and the children.[28]

28. The last three sentences were omitted in the original edition.

Captain Foy says that so long as Quebec is still ours and there is no American army this side of Montreal, not only he, but General Carleton as well, will have his wife come. Before this you absolutely must not come, but you could travel with them, and you would be safer if you had their company and attendance on the way, and you would want for nothing.[29] Only for Heaven's sake do not undertake this trip alone. It is very hard, and you will have no help on the way. Your servants will all be sick. If you come to Plymouth you can write to Mrs. Foy, who will not only answer but give you reports as to whether it is time to depart. When you reach England, write Lord Germain for me, who will arrange things for you. I do not know whether I wrote you that the Brunswickers will not go to the Carolinas, but to Quebec in Canada under General Carleton, so we will not have very much to do.

I am sure that this letter will give you much satisfaction, to hear that the voyage was a good one, and that I was not sick at all. Adieu, my angel. Keep loving me. Nearby is the wife of a soldier on the ship, who has a nursing child. The child is well, but the mother is sick. She has not lost her milk, however.

General Riedesel to Baroness von Riedesel

Aboard the *Pallas* in Portsmouth harbor,
March 28, 1776

You see, dear wife, that I let slip no opportunity of giving you news of myself. Here we are, safely arrived in the harbor of Portsmouth, and I am on the point of making a visit in the city to Admiral Douglas[30] and the other generals, who, like myself, are here for embarkation to America. Our servants are well again, and the cook has again returned to my service, to the great benefit of my stomach. You cannot imagine the beautiful spectacle we had yesterday morning at six o'clock when we were so near to Calais that we could distinguish every house, while at the same time and from the same spot we could see the city of Dover on the English coast.

29. The remainder of this letter was omitted in the original edition.
30. The Baroness visited Admiral Douglas during her stay in Portsmouth. See above, p. 17.

At nine o'clock Foy left us to go to London, and the whole day we sailed along the English coast, and at every moment a new town came into view. People plowing in the fields and travelers gazed curiously at our little fleet. So time passed until evening. Then I slept peacefully, and at five o'clock this morning we came in sight of Portsmouth. At nine o'clock we anchored here, and we are about ready to go ashore.

Captain Foy has been gone for two days to deliver a report to the King. I will be able to tell you a good deal about your projected trip to America and your stay in England, and the best recommendations will be gotten for you. Captain Foy's wife is an American. She has property and relatives in America. She hates England and wishes to return as soon as possible and be reunited with her husband, whom, as one can see from letters, she loves very much.[31]

General Riedesel
to Baroness von Riedesel [32]

Aboard the *Pallas*, Portsmouth harbor,
March 29, 1776

Dearest Wife,

I am often longing for you, and I am suffering from real homesickness. Captain Foy has not yet returned from London. I think that he will have many positive things to say about our plans and voyage. He is not to be contradicted, and is completely sure that the maneuver of the rebels before Quebec is defeated, that they are dispersed, and that Quebec is saved. He also says that the Canadians want to be on our side, and that our position will be much more advantageous that that of the Hessians. I dine this noon at Admiral Douglas', and tomorrow with Intendant Gambier.[33] It is not known when we will depart. In the meantime you will have news as often as possible. The post is leaving, so I should close. I kiss you. I shall always love you. God guide you.

31. This paragraph was omitted in the original edition.

32. This letter has not been published previously.

33. James Gambier (1723–89) was the resident commissioner of the navy at Portsmouth. J. K. Laughton, "Gambier, James," *DNB*.

General Riedesel
to Baroness von Riedesel [34]

Aboard the *Pallas,* Portsmouth Harbor,
March 31, 1776

My dear wife,

I hope that you have received the three letters I have already written you from England. I have not yet received any of yours here. Surely it is not your fault. It is the fault of the distance and the passage overseas. I am sure that mine have the same fate, and that you will pass many unquiet hours before receiving my news, but that such long delays will not upset you. Only believe that we are ever in the hands of the Almighty God, and that He will take care of us. Deliver yourself entirely to His Holy Will, and be assured that neither will one jot of my love for you suffer by our separation nor still less will my fidelity to you be branded with dishonor. . . . Give me some report on these charming children and of yourself, and whether you still love me.

Captain Foy is not yet back from London. I understand that things are going well in Canada, and that Quebec is ours again and will remain this time; the rebels have almost no troops in Canada, and as soon as our army is assembled there, they will go. All this will be clear as soon as we arrive at Quebec. Then Captain Foy will write his wife to come, and at the same time I will ask you to undertake this long voyage. You will have Mrs. Foy with you. I will in no way be disturbed about you, and you will have double accommodations and even servants with you in case of need. It is therefore up to you to go to Plymouth in the meantime, or if you prefer to the other city Foy has named. I believe that you will do better to establish yourself in the city where Mrs. Foy herself has gone, Bristol, because then you would always have the most recent news, and you would both be more able to join each other in case of need. Foy believes that you would be able to live comfortably, but on a small scale, in all three places for 15 to 20 pounds sterling, that is 90 to 120 écus, with a servant and two maids. Do not forget an English dictionary and grammar. It is only necessary to take enough money for your trip to England, but get an open bill of exchange and letter of recommendation made out by Hertz Samson in London so that you can draw as

34. This letter has not been published previously.

much money as you need in any case, for it is never necessary to be without resources in foreign countries, and when you have enough money, you will be able to reside where you wish.

When you have arrived in England it will be necessary to address all your letters to me to Mylord Suffolk, Minister of the King in London.[35] He has promised to send all, and I will do the same. His address is:

> To
> The Earl of Suffolk
> One of His Majesty's Principal Secretaries
> of State
>> at St. James
>> London.

It is necessary to inform Mylord Suffolk where you will live and when you will arrive in England.

Now I will send you my journal about my stay beginning with our arrival at the pier until today. The day before yesterday we arrived at 9 o'clock at the pier; we anchored and at 10 o'clock I went down to the city. I called on Admiral Douglas and the Commissioner General of the navy, Mr. Gambier. The former invited me for dinner tomorrow and the latter for Sunday; everybody was extremely polite and all the officers called on me. I saw the fortress, the city, and all the men-of-war. I dined in the city and returned to my ship in the evening.

Yesterday I visited all the transport vessels and found the troops in good health and very happy. The officers are enthusiastic about the beauty of the city and the agreeable way in which one lives here. At 10 o'clock I went down to the town and called on all the gentlemen who had called on me. I wrote a letter to you, and at 3 o'clock I went to dine with the Admiral in company of 6 ladies and 9 gentlemen, all of them captains of the men-of-war. By the way, there was one lady whose name I don't know, but she looked exactly like Madame Bianconi. After dinner at half past six I went home, where I met Captain Edmondstone, my English aide-de-camp, who had arrived from London. He is a charming fellow and speaks German. This morning I went to see the men-of-war and later I will have my Lieutenant

35. Henry Howard, 12th Earl of Suffolk (1739–79), served in Lord North's ministry as Secretary of State for the Northern Department from 1771 until his death in 1779 and thus was head of the department in charge of the arrangements with the German troops.

Colonels and several English officers for dinner. I will not finish the letter today as the first mail will not leave until tomorrow.

Tentative budget on your expenses in England

		Pounds	Sh.
1)	Lodging 4£ with Goltz [?]	4	
2)	Food for children and female servants, daily 6 shillings, for thirty days	9	
3)	Beverages [?], daily 1½ shillings	2	5
4)	Tea and sugar		10
5)	Wage and food for man servant daily 1 shilling	1	10
6)	Maids		10
		17	15

General Burgoyne who arrived today and on whom I called was extremely polite to me. He assured me that everything will go well and that I should be glad about our expedition. Otherwise nothing remarkable has happened since yesterday.

I embrace you tenderly and I am forever yours
This March 31, 1776.

Foy has not arrived yet and I don't know when we are going to leave. If Barner is still in Wolfenbüttel, tell him that his sorrel horse perished at sea. If you travel by The Hague get some good recommendations from Chevalier Yorke.[36] Also in my opinion I certainly think you will do well to stay in Bristol where Madame Foy lives, because in her company you will do well and she will help you with everything.

General Riedesel
to Baroness von Riedesel

Portsmouth, April 4, 1776

Don't complain, dear angel, that I am too lazy to write to you. I think this is the sixth letter I am sending you from Portsmouth, and I don't imagine that it will travel very fast. After our departure there

36. Sir Joseph Yorke (1724–92), British ambassador to The Hague, had been involved in the negotiations for German troops. Thomas Seccombe, "Yorke, Joseph," *DNB*.

will be a short stay at the coast of Ireland. But patience, after you have received the first letter from America you will have one regularly the next week or the second week thereafter.

Do not get excited about all the wild ideas people will give you about the savages of Canada; and besides you will have nothing to do with these people. You must wait patiently for the directions Captain Foy will give you and you will have nothing to risk. I think it will be best if you wait in Bristol and arrange everything with Madame Foy; rest calm and content. I have made arrangements with the doctor of the regiment that I will give him a special signal, if we should need him in a hurry. . . . I attended a court martial dealing with an officer who had deserted; Captain Milbanke [37] also entertained me for dinner on board ship. Today I returned to the *Pallas*.

I wish you could see all the conveniences I have, indeed everything possible. I embrace all of you a million times, that is, the three children and my worthy, good wife. Follow my advice and be convinced that for all my life I will be yours.

R.

◀━━━●◆✦◗●▶━━◗

General Riedesel
to Baroness von Riedesel

Aboard the *Pallas,* between Plymouth
and Portsmouth, April 6, 1776

Our departure from Portsmouth came sooner than I had expected. Since the wind became favorable, we weighed anchor in order not to let the opportunity slip, and at eleven o'clock day before yesterday we were off, thirty sail strong, in the best possible weather, amid the salutes of all our cannon and those of the fleet that was still lying off the harbor at Spithead. On the fifth the wind became unfavorable and remained this way until this morning. But now we are again sailing under a good wind straight for Plymouth, where, to be sure, we shall not stop, but I hope nevertheless to be able to post this letter to you. God be praised that he has kept your husband well! Various officers are already sick, among them my English aide, but I am quite well, I have a good appetite, and I am sleeping well, and I hope, therefore, to remain well right up to our arrival in America.

37. Admiral Mark Milbanke (1725?–1805) commanded the *Barfleur,* guardship at Portsmouth, in 1775–76. J. K. Laughton, "Milbanke, Mark," *DNB*.

I believe this will be the last letter you will receive from me before our arrival in America, unless we should meet some ships on the way, to which I could entrust letters, an opportunity for which I shall ever be on the watch.

Do not be alarmed or intimidated by the talk of men who have neither experience nor good sense. There are no Indians in Quebec or on the banks of the St. Lawrence. These inhabitants, once upon a time savage, live in the interior, where we are not going. . . . I love you too much—just as Captain Foy loves his wife. We shall know when you will be able to arrive without risk, and Foy will certainly indicate the means by which you will be able to obtain passage on a man-of-war.[38]

There are yet several points upon which I must give you advice. Before you leave Brunswick you must get letters of introduction in order that when in London you may get lodging in a private house rather than in a hotel. That way you will be able to make a definite arrangement for those days you will remain there for dinner and supper, as well as for rooms and breakfast. If the people have a carriage, you can make a far better arrangement with them than you might in a hotel, where everything is three times as expensive. For example, for seven days' lodging for myself, my two aides, and our servants, one dinner and seven suppers, the dinner for twelve persons, the suppers for four each time, I had to pay twenty-two pounds sterling, or in our money, 132 reichsthalers.

You must make this sort of arrangement wherever you want to stay for a few days. If you go to Exeter, to Plymouth, or to Bristol, where Mrs. Foy is staying, you must make inquiry as to private lodgings you can find. In England there are plenty of such private places, where for a definite sum of money you may have board and lodging. Further, I would advise you that while in London or elsewhere, you should look over the ships that are in passenger service in order to make your plans in accordance with the sleeping accommodations you will need. For you cannot let more than one child sleep with you. The nursemaid must take one of them, and the baby will have to sleep in a hammock.

You must buy bouillon cubes in London, so that you and the children can at least have some good soup, should fresh meat become unavailable.

38. This paragraph was omitted in the original edition.

General Riedesel
to Baroness von Riedesel

Aboard the *Pallas*, April 24, 1776

Dearest Wife,

It is sad that this magnificent sea cuts off every connection with my dearest possession in the world, even depriving me of the consolation of having news of you, the sole resource which had remained for me till now. Neither my heart nor my thoughts are separated from you in our sad solitude. The thought of you and the children consoles me and makes me able to bear this boredom. I write this letter in uncertainty as to whether it will reach you, and I do not even know whether I will have the opportunity to send it before our arrival at Quebec. I always write on the chance that I will be able to send it by the first vessel which comes by. Up until now we have not sighted a single vessel which is going to England, or anywhere else.[39]

Since the 4th, the day of our departure from Portsmouth, we have been sailing on the wide ocean, sometimes with a good wind, sometimes with a bad wind, and three times we had such strong winds that they came near to being a storm. Everyone was sick, but, thanks be to God, all went well with me, and I came through in the best of health.

We have now sailed fully 507 German miles since we left Stade, and we have yet 300 miles to make before we reach Quebec. In five or six days we will see, I hope, the coast of Newfoundland, and shortly thereafter we will enter the St. Lawrence, where the voyage will become more pleasant, and the widespread seasickness will be ended.

Dearest and best of wives, in spite of my love for you and my burning desire to see you again as soon as possible, had I not promised to let you follow me, and had I known of all the hardships of such a long voyage, I would never have suggested that you make such a trip, especially with your children. I must confess that I tremble at this great an undertaking, but my word has been given, so I must submit and trust that God will bestow His blessing upon it.

But, for Heaven's sake, do not travel alone, and wait for Mrs. Foy or some other lady of quality who may embark on the same ship with you. It must be a lady who has already made the trip to America, one who knows what has to be done, and who can advise and help

39. This paragraph was omitted in the original edition.

you in case you or the children should be sick. You must realize, dearest wife, that you and the children, and all the servants might very easily become ill on the way, and if not all the time, at least at the first strong wind. For on my ship there were not five people who were well all the while, and everyone recognizes that it is extraordinary that I was an exception. In such a situation you and the children would be in your beds without the least help, you would not have a thing to eat or drink, and there would not be a soul to offer you the most necessary aid. The crew of the ship are, for the most part, swine, rogues, and the crudest sort of people. They cook nothing but salted meat, half-done, which is in no way fit to be eaten. And one thing more, the water will eventually become so bad and odoriferous, that you will not be able to drink it. You will have to get a filter, through which you can strain the water, and the children will have to become accustomed to drinking beer, or you will have to boil the water in the morning for the rest of the day.

My poor cook is sick almost all the time, which is most inconvenient for me. There are many days when we know neither what nor how we are going to eat. Besides, our fresh meat is exhausted, and there remain only the salted meat and poultry. Soon we shall begin to slaughter the sheep. The worst of it is that, because of the sickness of the cook, no one looks after the provisions, part of which spoil, and part of which are stolen.

Enough—I would not be telling the truth if I were to say that this life is pleasant. The best that I can say is that, the Lord be praised, I am well, and, as a result, able to bear with patience all these discomforts.

<hr>

General Riedesel
to Baroness von Riedesel's Mother [40]

Commenced May 24, 1776, on the St. Lawrence River
. . . after having journeyed from Stade 889 leagues
Most gracious mother

Madame, you will pardon me that I have not written earlier and asked about your health, nor have I told you about mine. However,

40. This letter has not been published previously. From the contents of this

the tremendous business of our march and of the embarkation, as well as the impossibility of writing during the constant movement of our ship, have prevented me against my will from paying you my regards. Nevertheless, my thoughts have gone to you frequently. Nothing hurts me more than that duty forced me to leave you when I could have been of greatest help to you. How are you, Madame; have the matters of the inheritance been settled? Does Beyer look after you; do your revenues arrive promptly from Lartzenburg [?]? Have you been able to make money out of the furniture, pictures, and the rest of the jewels and other precious objects? These are matters of interest to me and I wish you would let me know if you succeeded in everything, as this would relieve me of all my embarrassment.

Concerning myself, it is true that my situation looks rather brilliant from the outside, but regarded more closely my affairs are rather risky, and I am in no way in a well-established position, which I had rather expected. True, my yearly revenues amount to 12,000 thalers, but against this you must hold the exorbitant prices charged in the country where this war is being fought, the lot of servants I am obliged to keep, as well as the dinner table which is always set for eight or ten guests. Also I have to maintain two households, as my wife is absent, so I believe there will not be much left at the end of the year. But I certainly will beware of making debts. The greatest inconvenience, however, is that my present title as general bars me from entering the service of the King [King Frederick II of Prussia], which always was my idea, though I [never] spoke about it. My own family affairs I have to neglect, e.g., the prebend . . . , indeed, all such matters I must neglect, and instead I have to take care of the interests of those I serve, to whom in fact I am quite alien. I am surrounded only by Englishmen who are drunk with haughtiness. With these people I have to get along; if something disadvantageous happens, it will be all my fault. When peace comes, everything will have come to an end and will be recorded only in the great Book of Oblivion, as indeed in the past it has happened to greater people than me. So this is a sketch of my circumstances. All this I reveal only to you,

---

letter it would appear that the Baroness' father, General von Massow, had recently died. His widow, née von Crausee, was named head lady-in-waiting to Princess Louise Amalie of Prussia, whose son Frederick William II, was heir to Frederick the Great.

Madame, and I beg you to keep it a secret. In spite of this I do not lose my course, for I rely on God, who turns everything to the best, and await everything with the greatest patience. Nor do I miss any opportunity to do my duty with zeal and courage.

God knows what my wife and children are doing at this time. She had planned to set forth for England on May 13. On April 4 I wrote her my last letter to Plymouth and begged her not to travel to America all by herself; rather she should wait in England till some other lady of rank leaves to follow her husband. The voyage is most cumbersome, though not perilous, and there are many diseases one might get. I tremble when I think about her undertaking and all the things that might happen to her and the children. God will be her Saviour.

Now I will begin to tell you briefly about our travel: It took us from February 22 until March 5 to march to Stade. Here we had to wait until the 20th of March for boats, embarkation, and all the rest of this troublesome business. On March 27 we arrived in England at Portsmouth. While at sea there were stormy winds. Everybody, two or three soldiers excepted, was seasick. In Portsmouth we stayed for six days and everyone was most polite to us. On April 4 we set sail and did not see land again until May 13; this was our first view of the American coast. From then on we went down the St. Lawrence River to Quebec. While we were on the ocean, we had a storm one day and a quiet sea the next, frost and rain alternating with snow. Among the troops some became sick, others stayed in good health. As for myself, I always stayed well, but one day was like the other and I must say I had a tedious time. Our daily occupation is as follows. We breakfast at 8 in the morning in English style; thereafter everybody goes along with his business. We dine again at 3 o'clock; at my table I have 1) Captain Foy, commissary of the Brunswick troops, 2) Captain Hensch, Brunswick aide-de-camp, 3) Captain Bell, the ship's captain, 4) Captain Edmondstone, my English aide-de-camp, 5) Gerlach, my quartermaster general, 6) Lieutenant Cleve, my German aide-de-camp, 7) Gödecke, my paymaster, and 8) Langmeier, my secretary. After dinner we take a promenade on the deck, then we play Tarock [a card game], at 10 we eat supper and we go to bed at half past eleven. Every day is like the next.

June 1. Today we arrived at Quebec. Everybody debarks here; from now on we will march on foot.

I must conclude this letter as I have to go to meet General Carleton in town.

I recommend myself to you, Madame, and remain as ever in deepest respect

Your most obedient and faithful son,
Riedesel

On the boat *Pallas* in the
face of Quebec
June 1, 1776

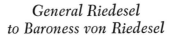

General Riedesel
to Baroness von Riedesel

Aboard the *Pallas,* two leagues this side
of Quebec, June 1, 1776

I have had at least as much anxiety as you have had since the time you have been without my letters. I not only share this anxiety, I assure you that I have suffered as much as you from our separation.[41]

I cannot give you a detailed description of our voyage, for what is there to tell about nine weeks spent between heaven and ocean, where one day was passed exactly like another? Here we are, after much hardship, two miles from Quebec, where we shall arrive this evening, but without tarrying, since General Carleton has driven the rebels from the vicinity of Quebec and is pursuing them. For this reason we shall sail farther up the river in order to join the General. Therefore, it is still too soon to give you any instructions about your departure. Captain Foy thinks we should wait and see where the expedition leads us. All I can say is, do not travel alone and without the company of a lady of quality, be she General Carleton's wife, Mrs. Foy, or some other lady. I must close, because I will have to send this letter on the man-of-war which will carry it. As soon as I have joined General Carleton I will write you in detail about all that has happened, how I am, and about your trip.

41. This paragraph was omitted in the original edition.

General Riedesel
to Baroness von Riedesel

Between Quebec and Montreal, June 8, 1776
I hope that you have received my two letters, one of the 24th of
April and the second the 1st of June, the day we arrived at Quebec.
Thank God the sea voyage is over, I feel well, and I lack nothing for
complete happiness, except to have you and the children here.[42]
Here, in a few words, is everything that has happened since our
arrival in Quebec the first of June. We arrived off Quebec at six
o'clock in the evening. I went ashore right away to visit General
Carleton, who received me in the most courteous and friendly manner,
and invited me to dinner the next day. In order to form a picture of
his personal appearance, imagine Abbot Jerusalem [43]—the very same
figure, face, gait, and tone of voice, and if he wore a black gown and
wig, one would not be able to tell the slightest difference.
On the second of June, after dining with General Carleton, I saw
the captured rebels. These poor rascals were a pity to see. You would
lose all fear of your husband falling before this poor race of humans.[44]
In the evening I paid a visit to Commodore Douglas, who commands
the fleet, and who saluted me at my departure with thirteen cannon.[45]
The third, my birthday, I spent aboard my ship. It did not seem
quite right to me to receive an order from General Carleton to leave
my dragoons and the Prince Frederick Regiment in garrison at
Quebec. Captain Foy was appointed adjutant-general and secretary
to General Carleton.
On the fourth, since it was the birthday of the King of England,
I paid a courtesy visit on the General, together with my whole corps

42. This paragraph was omitted in the original edition.
43. The Abbé Jerusalem played an important role in the cultural development of Brunswick. He was the person who drew the plan for the Carolinum,
an institute halfway between a school and a university, which included various
kinds of practical training. *Allgemeine deutsche Biographie*, XV, 269. Moreover, he had been the tutor of the Hereditary Prince, Karl Wilhelm Ferdinand.
Stone, *Letters of Brunswick and Hessian Officers*, 21.
44. These two sentences were omitted in the original edition.
45. Sir Charles Douglas (d. 1789), rear admiral, relieved the blockade of
Quebec on May 6, 1776, and was awarded a baronetcy for this action, which
enabled the British to repulse the enemy. He later played an important role
in the battle of Dominica in 1782. J. K. Laughton, "Douglas, Sir Charles,"
DNB.

of officers, to offer our congratulations. Cannon were fired from the fortress and all the ships, and afterwards there was a great ball.

On the fifth General Carleton gave me command of a special corps, which I did not expect, and which has caused a great sensation.[46]

On the sixth, as there was a favorable wind, I was sent off by General Carleton and sailed with my assigned corps. So here I am now on Lake Champlain; but rest easy with regard to the enemy. They have completely disappeared, and we have not seen a single one of them this side of Lake Champlain.

Dear soul, no place would be more comfortable for you than Quebec. You can even conveniently go as far as Montreal, and await word there where you can follow us. In Montreal there is a very well-organized post, so that you can very easily go by land from one place to another, and I shall make arrangements, so that you will find every comfort in Montreal. You will like this country; everything you see is beautiful.[47]

This winter you will have all the comforts to be had, for there is every indication that I will be in command of this province. This is the good news; and now for the bad. I have lost the English horse my brother gave me and the brown mare as well. I now have only one saddle horse left and the carriage horses. I have left all the horses behind, and I march on foot, as do General Carleton and all the English. I have sent this letter to England and a copy through Germany, so that you will not fail to receive one, and I wish you from the bottom of my heart a good journey. God guide you in all your undertakings. I swear to you from the bottom of my heart that I am thinking of you.

R.

P.S. My Dearest Little Augusta,

What is my dear child doing? I hope you are as well as your father. I hope I have the satisfaction of seeing you soon. May God be with you. Keep loving me. Honor and obey your mother. I am ever

Your devoted father

46. On June 4 Carleton appointed the General head of a corps consisting of an English battalion, the Brunswick battalion of grenadiers, the Riedesel Regiment, 150 Canadians, and 300 Indians. Stone, trans., *General Riedesel*, I, 42.

47. The remainder of this letter was omitted in the original edition.

General Riedesel
to Baroness von Riedesel

La Prairie, June 28, 1776

I have recently given you a detailed account of our arrival in Quebec. From there we went to Trois Rivières, where I, together with all the generals, arrived too late for the affair which took place there. From there we went farther by ship and landed at Vergère. Our march here was very tiring, but now we are resting. All of my things have arrived, and we are living very well, but it is expensive. My table is usually set for ten or twelve persons, and we have six dishes. But I am not able to manage such for less than two guineas a day. One bottle of wine costs a thaler in our money though I am paid amply.[48] However, one can spend a lot of money here. All that I could save in four months was 100 guineas, and I suppose if I lived properly my savings could go up to 3,000 écus per year. But this is just between us. . . .

Here I am alone with all the German troops. I seem to have found favor with General Carleton. He always treats me with special kindness, and if this continues I shall have every reason to be satisfied. I hope this business will not last long. We have conquered all of Canada already, and as soon as the boats are ready we will cross over Lake Champlain and press into New England, where all the rebels are, and where General Howe is also, who, it is said, already has gained some advantages over them. This by itself will place our contingent under the protection of the King.[49]

In my last letter, I have pointed out to you that even though Captain Foy has not written his wife that she must follow him, he has however assured me verbally that he would be pleased if she would accompany him on his campaign. Give my respects to her, to whom I would be eternally grateful if she would remain your traveling companion.[50] When once you get here, I will endeavor to take you back comfortably in my ship, where you will fare better, as I am now

48. The rest of this paragraph was omitted in the original edition.
49. This sentence was omitted in the original edition.
50. These first two sentences were omitted in the original edition.

somewhat more accustomed to seafaring and can therefore do much to avoid the discomforts that beset one aboard ship.

If you undertake the voyage, you will find Lieutenant Colonel Baum [51] with the dragoons in Quebec, who has already taken care to find good quarters for you. You will then write me immediately and take a few days rest in Quebec. You will then proceed to Trois Rivières, a very pretty town, where you will find good quarters, in which General Carleton formerly resided. This town is thirty leagues from Quebec, and from there you will yet have thirty leagues to Montreal, where you will either find me or my further instructions.

I have not once been sick. I became exceedingly tired on a three-day march, but it did me no harm. I have a great deal to do, and I have many complaints. Soon I must be with the troops, and, as a matter of policy, with the English; but everything will go well with a bit of good will and a bit of work. [52]

You will find the country here magnificent. It is only a pity that the colonies are still in their infancy, so that vegetables, fruit, and other food are scarce, but there is an abundance of meat, poultry, and milk. The houses are all of only one story, but they have many rooms and are very clean. An ordinary peasant's house would afford accommodations for our entire family. The inhabitants are exceedingly courteous and helpful, and I do not believe that our peasants would match them under similar circumstances.

You appear to have a good deal of pity for some of these rebels, you and those who are of the same mind. There are only a few dozen ambitious people who direct this whole affair and who make the whole land unhappy. These people enrich themselves as a result. As for the others, they do not even know why they fight. They are unpaid, they lack everything, and they will never have the boldness to face us. You will see them soon asking clemency of the King. Tell me what you think the Duke holds against me. Since we embarked he has not written me one letter, although I always kept in close touch with him.

---

51. Lt. Col. Frederick Baum, head of the Brunswick Dragoon Regiment, was wounded in the battle near Bennington on Aug. 17, 1777, and died two days later. Stone, trans., *General Riedesel*, II, 265; Eelking, *German Allied Troops*, 130-32.

52. This paragraph was omitted in the original edition.

Only Feronce has written a few hasty lines, sending me the Duke's very best compliments. But I did not receive the attention I thought I would after having such a close relationship with him and after the sacrifice I made in my career solely out of my regard for him. The hundred guineas which I saved in the beginning are a present for Augusta in order to put her on par in a small way with Frederika. However, so that nothing should get out about this in Germany, I will send it to Berlin to Madame Woklen so that she gets it and deposits it somewhere safely. If the King of Prussia does not give his permission to sell my prebend, I consider that as divine intervention. However, if God leads me back to Europe and Germany, I will turn heaven and earth to sell it in order to put my poor daughters at ease. I am much pleased that the King of Prussia has come to his own again, as my brother points out to me, and I hope that the good man does not die before I get back.[53]

I have no news whatever to send you. Everything here is very quiet. General Carleton is at Chambly with part of the army, General Fraser is in St. Johns, and I am here, traveling about the countryside to become acquainted with it. I have my dinner every day at three o'clock, generally go to bed a bit tired, and at three or four o'clock in the morning I am again on the highway.

Before sending off this letter I had a conversation with General Carleton. It was about you and his wife. He told me that his wife had already been told to come here. Thus, if God has so ordained that you have been long enough in England, you may have departed with her. Good Lord, what a blessing for me if you have had the good fortune to go with the wife of this worthy man, and that I should have the pleasure of seeing you here! Four weeks will probably pass before we cross Lake Champlain.[54]

Adieu, my angel, I am completely yours.[55]

R.

53. This paragraph was omitted in the original edition.

54. All of this paragraph except the last sentence was omitted in the original edition.

55. This sentence was omitted in the original edition.

General Riedesel
to Baroness von Riedesel

La Savanne, September 12, 1776

The army is encamped for the purpose of keeping more closely together. I have a very good post at a place called La Savanne, and since I command a special corps, I have a great deal to do, and I do not lack for exercise, which is very beneficial for my health. The nights are already a bit cold, and we are already thinking and speaking of winter quarters, into which I think we shall withdraw during the month of October. What a satisfaction it would be for me to enjoy in peace then the company of you and my children! Truly I would value this above all else. But where can you now be? Perhaps in the middle of the ocean, perhaps even in danger? How many of my nights have been filled with such anxiety for you! May God soon take this fear from me and bless me with the happiness of holding you in my arms again! The fourth of this month, after exercising the troops, I gave a great dinner for General Carleton and the principal officers of the army. There were thirty-six people and twenty-six courses, each served twice. Everyone seemed satisfied. I gave it in honor of my sovereign and for the benefit of his troops, and I have certainly succeeded, for everyone is my friend, and I am on good terms with everybody.

General Riedesel
to Baroness von Riedesel

In camp at La Savanne, September 23, 1776

At last, dearest wife, I have received your letters of the 9th, 13th, 20th, and 30th of April and of the 12th of May. All of these letters have given me great satisfaction, and I have thanked God from the bottom of my heart that you and the children are so well. I embrace you warmly, and the children as well. Other letters about you I have received from people in England have given me a similar satisfaction, and I thank Providence for blessing you on your journey. I know, dear wife, that you arrived in London about the twelfth, and around the eighteenth you departed for Bristol, that you are well, and so are the children. O'Connell, whom Colonel Specht had sent to London, has talked personally with the landlord of the inn where you stayed in London, and you had left for Bristol just three hours before his arrival. I am not addressing this letter for England, but instead I am giving it to the first ship leaving for England so that the captain, if he should meet you, can give it to you, so that you can both be quieted and given cause for rejoicing over my completely good health. When you arrive at Mrs. Murray's[56] in Quebec you will find all necessary further instructions from me. I will have my winter quarters at Trois Rivières, where you can quietly await my return.[57]

I have had several letters from my brother, and I am well informed as to the knavish trick the Hereditary Prince has tried to play on me. Rest at ease. I have a good conscience, and you do not have to be concerned about these unscrupulous things. I know him well. He cannot exist without intrigue. But then he changes his course and becomes the most assiduous protector of those whose reputations he had sought to ruin. I have had thorough proof of this trait, and I can speak from experience. I am more distressed about the Duke, my dear master, who has been paralyzed completely on his right side. He cannot speak intelligibly, and we will have to wait for some great change. I am only disquieted over the subject on which my brother and my sister-in-law spoke there perhaps a bit indiscreetly, the affections of the Prince and his ties with me. I will serve him as best I can. If he does not eventually show his gratitude in such a way as to reward my efforts, I intend to retire with my income of sixteen hundred [reichsthalers], which will enable me to live happily at Lauterbach, without any need of *grands seigneurs* and their benefactions.

I believe this campaign will be over in four weeks. Then we will quietly go into winter quarters on the other side of the lake. Next year we will proceed into New England, and I am almost certain that by then the whole affair will be finished, and that in 1778 we will return to our fatherland.

56. For some speculation about Madame de Riedesel's attitude toward Mrs. Murray, whom she does not mention in her journal, see Tharp, *The Baroness and the General*, 366–67.

57. The remainder of this letter was omitted in the original edition.

General Riedesel
to Baroness von Riedesel

Crown Point, on board the *Washington,*
a prize taken from the rebels,
October 26, 1776

Dearest Wife,

Heaven only knows where you are! I have had no reports since your departure from Wolfenbüttel. I know from a letter Mrs. Foy wrote from Portsmouth asking about your baggage that you had arrived at Bristol, but I have received nothing from you yourself, and I confess that you put me in mortal dread.[58]

We have destroyed the fleet of the rebels and have taken Crown Point. We shall now go into winter quarters. Our campaign is finished, and I shall return to Trois Rivières, where I shall have my winter quarters, awaiting you with the greatest impatience. Good Lord, how happy I would be if you were to come this winter, and how I would be able to enjoy your pleasant company! The winter quarters will be very quiet, and I will be able to live for you alone.

General Carleton fought with the fleet like a hero, having left the whole army behind. He spared the married men as much as possible, and if this war is waged in the same manner next year, I shall be safer here in the midst of it than on the drill fields in Wolfenbüttel and Brunswick. If you are already at sea, General Burgoyne, who is the bearer of this letter, will do his utmost to see that it is delivered to you while still at sea; if you are still in England, he will make every effort to obtain passage for you on a good ship early next spring, and in this case you need only write him. I have been here six days as a volunteer. We have seen the rebel camp at Fort Carillon[59] at very close quarters, and we took a few prisoners.

General Riedesel
to Baroness von Riedesel

Trois Rivières, November 10, 1776

My Dearest Wife,

How thankful I am in having just received the first letter from your hands from Bristol, England! I confess, I was in mortal distress about

58. This paragraph was omitted in the original edition.
59. Fort Ticonderoga. Stone, trans., *General Riedesel,* I, 111, 293.

you and our dear children. Your good letter has consoled me. Lord knows where you are now, whether you are at sea, or whether you have remained in England. I have already read in the London papers of the arrival of *Monsieur le Maître*. It was on this ship that I had sent my first letters from America. I cannot imagine why in the world you have remained in England. I cannot understand why you have not come, because large numbers of ships have since arrived. Good Lord, I would despair if I had to stay here all alone this winter. I am badly lodged here, but I am having all steps taken to make the house habitable for you and our children. All these cares will be in vain [if you do not come]. You write nice things, but nothing about the trip to France, or of the crossing from Calais to Dover. You say nothing about whether you have seen the Queen, or whether you are coming. I am living like a miserable hermit.[60] I have very little hope of your coming here this winter. Therefore I am sending this letter so that, if you are still in England, you will not be without news from me.

I am well, thank the Lord, but I am exceedingly worried about you since I do not know where you are. Meanwhile, much as I would have enjoyed having you here, I shall not complain if you do not come. God, who in His infinite wisdom controls everything, may have thereby saved you from some disaster. The uncertainty of your whereabouts, especially at this late time of the year, is my chief anxiety. I must close, as the post is about to leave for Quebec. May God help and protect you. I embrace you and our dear children, and I cajole myself with the thought that you will at least be coming next spring.

60. This first portion of the letter was omitted in the original edition.

XI

Baroness von Riedesel's Letters

Preparations and Delay
March–September
1776

Although Mrs. Riedesel and her husband had perfected their plans for a reunion in America after the Baroness had given birth to her baby, they reckoned without consulting Mrs. von Massow, Frederika's mother. As soon as she heard that her daughter planned to hazard the trip to America with her small children, she begged her daughter —indeed, commanded her—not to go. With charming firmness, Mrs. Riedesel informed her mother that she would "have to disobey you deliberately for the first time in my life." Mrs. von Massow finally reconciled herself to her daughter's trip, and on May 3 the Baroness wrote to say she would leave in a fortnight. She promised to write regularly.[1]

In her journal Mrs. Riedesel describes her frustrating experience in trying to persuade Mrs. Foy to embark for America.[2] But she does not really reveal the inner depths of her anguish, which she bared to her husband in her previously unpublished letter of September 19, 1776.

1. For Madame de Riedesel's letters to her mother from America, see Chap. 14 below.

2. See above, pp. 15–17.

Baroness von Riedesel
to her mother

Wolfenbüttel, March 8, 1776

Dearest and best of Mothers,

I was almost beside myself over your last letter. Some parts in it would seem to indicate that you were annoyed with me, while in other places you showed so much concern and love for me, that it pained me to have to disobey you deliberately for the first time in my life. Believe me, if anything could have made me hesitate, it would have been the bliss of seeing you with me. But I understood my own nature and how hard it would have been for me to leave you or to refuse you anything, and in my last letter I refrained from asking you to come to me. I could not bear the thought of separating myself from you, especially for so long a time, but the thought that you had begged me, even commanded me, to remain here made me shudder. To remain here when the best, the tenderest of husbands gave me permission to follow him would have been impossible for me. Duty, love, and conscience forbade me. It is the duty of a wife to forsake all and follow her husband. You know my love for him, as well as his love for me and the children. . . .

You may be sure that my husband never begged for his position. When he was asked to accept his command, he regarded it as sent by Providence. I would never have thought of persuading him to take leave. I also cannot imagine who else might have been proposed for the post. The others were either too old or were not fit.[3]

Baroness von Riedesel
to General Riedesel[4]

Wolfenbüttel, March 18, 1776

I should have been delighted to see you depart, so that I would learn that much sooner the place of our reunion. And I confess that on receiving your letter number 22 I was overwhelmed with trembling. The Duke was good enough to send it to me yesterday . . . at eight o'clock in the evening. Your number 21 is missing, and therefore I

3. This paragraph was omitted from the original edition.
4. This letter has not been published previously.

did not know the second transport had arrived. God help you and be the faithful guide of the most beloved of men! I am beginning to believe that you honestly think you will want to let me follow you, even though . . . you had insisted that I remain behind in Brunswick. But what are you thinking of when you urgently repeat that I must not be in too great a hurry? Is it hurrying to stay until the end of April? In short, my health and the season of the year will be best then, and, God willing, Caroline will also be strong enough. If you knew how I languish to see you, you would hasten our reunion.

Madame Hundertmarken has changed her mind and told me today that she could not resolve to join in my service, that she had believed that I was not serious, but in case I stay she will be at my service. That idea could well tempt me; however, I believe that you will remain my first choice. It is therefore resolved that Mrs. Curssingen will take care of the children according to your first idea; she is happy about it and has told me, if I ever should take her on as a servant, she will not abandon me, and will be happy to be with me and to follow you. In short I would be grateful all my life for her attachment. I will therefore try to have a good and skilled *femme de chambre,* and I think that I shall indeed find one. If you do not send the coachman back, do you think it necessary that I should engage another? This will depend entirely on you. Meanwhile, I fear that you will not receive this letter at Stade.

I will be delighted if Mrs. Foy will be my traveling companion. I will be much relieved. Tell me where she lives. Oh my dear, one more time, do not deceive me, let me follow, and make it at the beginning of the month of June or the end of May. I know I can follow, or I will tell you if I cannot. I will be at Plymouth, where I will await your orders. Believe me, to delay my happiness is to tax my life, because I love you so much, and it is certain that never have I loved you so much as at present.

Little Louisa is still waiting for an answer from you and I am waiting for a letter from Mr. [Cleve]. Why does he not write? After all, he had promised to give me news about your good health. This upsets me and gives me many vexing thoughts. Pass this on to him from me.

The seas separate us, but my heart is always with you, you may be sure. How soon can I have letters from England, and when will I know my fate? The children embrace you. They are well and talk all the time of you and of the voyage. In short, you would be the meanest and the most unjust and cruel of men if you are deceiving me. You are not capable of it. Do I doubt your promise? But people here give me anxiety. I do not forget your avowal: "Riedesel is and remains an honorable fellow and surely will never be able to forget his wife." I always carry that letter with me. However, do tell me that again, before something happens to you; a word like that lifts me up completely. Farewell, best of all men, don't forget your children and your poor wife; be careful with yourself for our sakes, we all love you so dearly. Once more farewell. I embrace you and kiss you a thousand times and remain your faithful, sincere wife and friend,

Yours,
[Frederika] de Riedesel

Baroness von Riedesel
to her mother

Wolfenbüttel, May 3, 1776

If you only knew how happy I am to see from your letter that you are beginning to be reconciled with my journey! I have this satisfaction now from all sides, and everyone agrees that it is my duty to go. Yes, I am setting forth with the certain confidence that God, who knows my innermost thoughts, and therefore my purpose, will protect me and preserve the children for me. The only thing that troubles me, dear gracious mother, is leaving you behind, but I hope this is not for long, for perhaps God will grant peace, and then we will be able to spend our days more quietly. May God grant his blessing to everyone. Meanwhile pray for us and for our children, so that all will always be well with us. For my part, my warmest wishes and my most fervent prayers will be made daily to God, worthiest of mothers, to preserve you and to let you spend your days in happiness. Love us always, just as we will always honor and love you. I beg of you, write me yet once again, and assure me of your love. If you write immediately, I shall get the letter before I leave, which, if we all remain well, will be around the thirteenth of this month. Thereafter please address your letters to Bristol, where I shall be awaiting the instructions of my husband.[5]

I will write you about everything that happens to me, and every

5. The remainder of this letter was omitted from the original edition.

two, or at the most three, weeks you will have a letter from me, and I hope I will have the same good fortune about letters from you.

I am going to take the antiques with me to England, where the arts are important, where I hope to sell them at a good price. Perhaps also in France. I am traveling by Calais, since I would be on the sea only around four hours. The jewels are still in Leipzig. The two portraits I still have with me; no one will have them. The 84 ells of linen will be ready in a week, not yet being bleached. Tell me when I should send it to you. Have the goodness not to part with the land for less than 7500 [reichsthalers]. Moreover, I will not happily see it sold, and [only] if the children and I have the misfortune to lose the best of fathers and husbands, it would not then be the greatest loss. Since the capital must yet remain in Prussian [investments], we are seeking considerably less revenue. Since my husband so desires, I will do my best. If I too remain quiet about the income, nothing will get out. In this case do us the favor of making use of the revenue as you will. Are we not your children, and are not children who love their parents their best friends?

Baroness von Riedesel
to General Riedesel [6]

Portsmouth, September 19, 1776

If you have received my letter of the 14th or 15th of this month, you will believe that I have gone mad to have followed so far as this a woman who, ready to do everything at first, changes [her mind] just like the wind. God knows what I suffer from all this! I believe that I already mentioned in my last letter that Mrs. Foy had received a letter from her husband telling her to come and that she had written to Lord George Germain begging him for a vessel. We received the word that a good and large vessel, the *London*, Captain Hall, had orders to receive us. We are leaving, and we are spending all our cash to come here and to buy for ourselves what we expect to need; upon arriving here a gentleman of her acquaintance tells her it is too late to leave, and she changes her mind in an instant; this morning another gentleman comes to say that it is a very fine ship, and that she is begged to

6. This letter has not been published previously.

take note that the vessel has not yet arrived here; she resolves again to depart; this afternoon another gentleman comes to say that it is too late; that, besides, you have all marched to New York; that in any case you will be staying there, and that we can join you anytime there; that, on the other hand, if we are at Quebec and you at New York, all communication, even by letter, is forbidden us. We are assured that it would be a miracle if we should arrive at Quebec before the river is frozen. . . . If Mrs. Foy would have gone I would not have resisted one moment, but you have forbidden me to go away alone. Unfortunately, I had to follow you when I was able to do so. I am not, therefore, setting out with the dangers of the hurricane season. If you but knew how I suffer! When I think of the six or seven months when I shall not be able to have your precious news, I wish I were dead. I have no money. I will be your ruin in spite of myself. There has been, with all the traveling and my sojourn at Bristol, with all my things coming here, 1500 écus of expenditure, and I am more miserable than ever. Up to now the hope, yes, the possibility, of joining you sustained me. Now it is not only the sea but the ice which separates us. God knows what I suffer. In the name of God, and of our love, do your best to keep writing me as long as possible. Do not send any money either, if it makes it necessary to have your letters come through the other country. They are the only thing which sustains me. Oh, God, eight or nine months without you, and with what suffering! Do not be anxious about me. I am able to obtain enough money, but also do not be angry about my expenditures. Be assured that I will not make any unnecessary ones. I can have as much [money] as I wish at Bristol, and rest assured that I will in no way abuse [the privilege]. I will try to make twelve guineas a month suffice, I will deny myself everything, I will deny everything to the children. Augusta has the best heart that exists! This morning we were passing in front of a shop. She saw a little windmill and came to me saying, "Mama, I would be so happy if I had that!" I asked the price of it and was told two and a half shillings. I said that was too expensive. She looked at me and smiled and said, "No, no, I do not want it. You have other expenses more needful, and Papa is not here." I kissed her and promised her that if God restores you to me, she shall have it twelve-fold. The children are well, and all the servants, just as I am, are longing to join you. This morning I prayed to God on my knees with all my heart to do all that would be best for us. He will give me grace not to complain. Here are some letters which I found, and others which people have given me for America. I beg you to take charge of them. Here I am in front of a fireplace, your portrait on my bracelet, which I always wear, in front of me, the children asleep in a bed beside me, and my heart, oh, that is with you. Oh, do not forget me, pity me, love me always, as I love you.

Your faithful wife

XII

General Riedesel to Baroness von Riedesel

The Family Reunion Delayed
Spring, 1777

❦————◄◖✕◗►————❧

Vacillating between impatience and resignation, General Riedesel awaited the arrival of his family, trying, as he said, "to divert my thoughts from my sorrow" of not seeing them as soon as he had hoped. In letters from Trois Rivières, he outlined alternative courses for his wife to follow upon her arrival, since he had to move south with his troops. But at least he knew that she would soon arrive, for General Burgoyne, who had just returned from England to lead the invasion of New York, had told him on May 6 that plans for the Baroness' departure had been made before he sailed. And finally, on June 13, he could send a letter welcoming his "beloved angel" to the "Canadian continent." On the 15th the Riedesel family was reunited for the first time in nearly sixteen months.

❦————◄◖✕◗►————❧

General Riedesel
to Baroness von Riedesel

Trois Rivières, April 16, 1777

What a sad exchange of happiness for unhappiness! At Isle aux Noix at the end of the last campaign I received the good news that you and the children had safely arrived at Quebec. I was beside myself with joy over the prospect of spending the most pleasant and quiet winter in your company and with my dear family. But how my expectations were deceived when I arrived here, and, instead of finding you, received your last letter, which came on the ship, the *London,* in which I saw that your trip had been postponed until next spring! That was a thunderbolt for me, and the only consolation remaining for me was that I could thank Heaven that you and my dear children at least were all well.

The *London,* by which you were scheduled to make the passage, arrived at Quebec December 8 without the slightest mishap. The rooms for you and our small family were furnished and arranged for you comfortably enough. Perhaps we could have spent together one of the happiest winters of our married life! All that has come to naught. But it was God's will. We must not complain, but submit to His holy decision. I have tried to divert my thoughts from my sorrow, but in vain. I was in Quebec from December 30 until January 16, in order to pay my respects to General Carleton, and I was overwhelmed with courtesy and distinction. After my return I celebrated the Queen's birthday with a big dinner, ball, and supper. Thereafter, following the example of the other generals, I gave a ball and supper every week, partly in order to gain favor with the inhabitants here, and partly also to give the officers the opportunity for innocent amusement, and thereby to keep them from visiting the taverns and getting into bad company. General Phillips visited me for the month of February. At various times I have inspected our regiments in their winter quarters, and at the beginning of March General Carleton visited me here and reviewed all our troops. He was very satisfied with everything. I accompanied him to Montreal, where we spent a week together with General Phillips. On the way back he stayed yet another two days with me. Since that time I have been traveling about, inspecting our regiments. The week after Easter I spent alone in the country, in order to meditate in peace; and now that the time of year has come when we have already begun to have good weather and can look forward to seeing ships from Europe and can send them over, I immediately seize my pen to get in touch with you, since I still do not know whether or when you are coming, and in any event I do not want you to be without news from me. I hope, however, that this letter is unnecessary, and that I will have the joy of seeing you arrive on the next ship.

In this letter you have a brief report of everything I have done this winter, and I would only like to add now (in order to give you an idea of the speed with which people travel here in sleighs), that between February 20 and April 10 I traveled 580 leagues, that is a good 435 German miles, partly on the snow, but for the most part on the frozen St. Lawrence. I still do not know when the army will break camp and head for New England. If you yet come, as I am ever fondly hoping, rest a few days in Quebec, where you can stay with my good friend Mr. Murray, whose wife, a worthy woman, you will like. If we should have broken camp, stay at Trois Rivières, where you will find my quarters emptied, and readied for you. For this purpose I shall leave the rest of my things in this house. The grand vicar, M. Saint-Onge,[1] will give you the keys upon your arrival, and he and the Tonnaucourt family will lend you anything you need for furniture.

I received a letter from my mother-in-law telling me that she had sold my prebend for 7500 reichsthalers, and that Herr Blumenthal[2] had invested the capital well. To convince you that I am no prodigal, although I do not make such economies as would offend the honor of my master, I am happy to tell you that I have already sent 7750 thalers to Europe and placed them in security, in order that our future resources might be increased for the benefit of our children, and I believe that if God permits me to live through the campaign, I may be able to double this sum before we go back to Germany.[3]

You will find the garden a pleasant place in which to stroll, as well as adequate for the needs of the kitchen, and you can stay here until we have fixed quarters on the other side of the lake in New England. I will endeavor to get a large ship to carry you across the lake, and I will send a reliable officer to fetch you. I believe that when you reach Quebec you will not like it. General Carleton's wife will not be to your liking either; she is too proud. Mrs. Murray is a worthy woman; all the officers think she looks like you, and that for that reason I liked her better than all the other ladies. Here in Trois Rivières you will find three houses in which you will be overwhelmed with courtesy, and where all that you could wish will be done for you. The first is the home of the grand vicar, who has a cousin by the name of Cabenac, a girl of intelligence, whom I feel certain you will like.

1. For the grand vicar, see above, pp. 37, 40.

2. Joachim Christian, Count von Blumenthal (1720–92), was a minister in the Prussian regime and a special confidant of Frederick II. *Allgemeine deutsche Biographie*, II, 751–52.

3. This paragraph was omitted in the original edition.

Then there is the home of Monsieur Tonnaucourt, a colonel in the militia and a widower,[4] who has three daughters who have had a good upbringing and will be good company for you. And finally there is the convent, where our two older girls will find pleasant companionship. I believe you will prefer Trois Rivières to Quebec for reasons of economy, since a person can live here at half the expense Quebec or Montreal would be.

I am writing this letter in duplicate and am sending one copy to England, in case you have not yet started your journey, and the other to Quebec, where you will find it at Mrs. Murray's when you arrive.

Now as for the children, I am burning with impatience to see them. Little Augusta will be a big girl. I hope they speak a little English and have a good opportunity to learn it here this winter.[5]

Your tender and faithful husband

General Riedesel
to Baroness von Riedesel

Trois Rivières, June 5, 1777

Dearest Wife,

General Burgoyne arrived here on the 6th from England and brought me the good news that you were about to sail on Mr. Watson's ship. For the past four weeks I have awaited you with the greatest of impatience, and now that your ship is so long in coming, I have to leave without the joy of seeing you, which grieves me inexpressably. However, as it cannot be helped, I will not complain, for it is God's will, and He arranges everything in the wisest way, and more often for our own good than often we realize.

At the moment, my dear, I am about to leave for St. Johns in order to cross Lake Champlain and to come from there into New England. I leave it entirely up to you whether to stay in Quebec, Trois Rivières, or Montreal. I believe Trois Rivières would suit you the best because

4. Tonnaucourt (Tonneucourt, Tonnaucour) was also a fabulous merchant, who engaged in great wholesale operations and also the pettiest kind of exchange. Although Jewish, he acquired the ridiculous popular designation, "Pope of Canada." See Stone, *Letters of Brunswick and Hessian Officers*, 45–46.

5. This paragraph was omitted in the original edition.

it is cheaper, and you will have for yourself a fully furnished house and a garden, and you will be among compatriots, for Lieutenant Colonel Ehrenkrock has command here.[6] Furthermore, you will be near the paymaster, so you will not want for money.[7] Moreover, you will find a supply of wine here and all sorts of other things. I shall also leave Captain-at-Arms Buhring, of my company, to aid you in everything, and to show you where you can get food. Your servants can get food from the canteen. Since I flatter myself that the inhabitants here like me, I am certain they will be courteous to you.

If you want to go riding with the children, you need only take the post. It costs only a shilling a league. Moreover, be at ease, my dear, I will not leave you waiting long for me, and as soon as our situation becomes a bit quieter, I shall send for you right away.

Everything was so expensive during the winter that I was not able to have new coats made for the domestics. In case some material arrives with your boat, I beg you to consult Mrs. Murray and to buy what is indicated in this note and to send it to me by one of General Burgoyne's orderlies. Buy enough material and thread to make four uniforms. Thank you very much for the pretty [drawing] you sent me. The idea of the three children surrounding the urn of love worked out very nicely. I carry it with me day and night, and I love it like our engagement ring. I beg you not to believe all the tales people are telling concerning our army. I will write you often and tell you all my news, whether it be good or bad. Do not become sad, for that will do no good.[8]

Goodbye, dearest wife. My heart is heavy, because I must leave without seeing you, but I hope it will not be for long.

General Riedesel
to Baroness von Riedesel

Chambly, June 10, 1777

Although I am far from you, dearest wife, I am constantly with you in spirit, and I seek seclusion from others so that I may converse

6. Lt. Col. Johann Gustavus Ehrenkrock was commander of the Rhetz Regiment. He died in Trois Rivières, Mar. 22, 1783. Stone, trans., *General Riedesel*, II, 268.

7. For the Baroness' problems with the paymaster, see above, pp. 41–42.

8. This paragraph was omitted in the original edition.

with you and to recall to memory the happy hours we have spent together in the past.

A few days before my departure from Trois Rivières I was so careless as to leave open my bedroom window, from which I took a fever. To be sure, I recovered by the 6th, the day of our departure, but this left me very weak during the first days of our march. Now, thank goodness, I am completely recovered. I shall go to St. Johns tomorrow in order to have our boats repaired. I hope that by this time you will have safely arrived at Quebec, and I am awaiting your first letter with the greatest impatience. I shall scarcely have the courage to open it for fear that it might contain the bad news that something happened to you or to one of the children on the voyage. But if I find in it that you and the children are well, I shall give thanks to God and be inexpressibly happy. And then we shall not be separated much longer, for I shall send for you just as soon as things have become a little quieter with us.

I do not have any more time to write you a longer letter. Goodbye, and do not worry. God will be your protector and mine wherever we may go.

General Riedesel
to Baroness von Riedesel

St. Johns, June 13, 1777

Welcome to the Canadian continent, my beloved angel!

According to news from others you arrived with the three children in good health. I trust I will be getting this same good news from yourself soon. When you have the time, give me an account of your voyage. Had you but come a week sooner, I would have had the satisfaction of seeing you. But who knows but what a rendezvous of only a few hours would not have increased the pain of immediate separation instead of giving pleasure from the brief reunion. Be patient, our separation will not last very much longer. In case you are planning to go to Trois Rivières, I advise you to do so by boat. Any small amount of wind will take you there in a day, saving you bad roads and also much expense.[9]

9. This paragraph was omitted in the original edition.

I was just having dinner at General Phillips' with the other generals when the messenger came and brought me the joyful news that the fleet from Portsmouth had already been sighted off the Island of Bic in full sight of Quebec,[10] that the news had been received that you and the children were aboard, and that you were all well. Undoubtedly, therefore, you arrived that same evening.

The whole company showed general joy and drank a good toast to your safe arrival. It makes me very happy to see how everyone shares my joy. I could only have wished you had come a week earlier, for then I would have had the good fortune to have seen you. I had made up my mind, that if you were to arrive before I had crossed the St. Lawrence, to return and take you in my arms. But now it was too late and could not be done. Let us be patient, dear wife; our separation cannot last much longer, only until you can come here with some measure of safety, quiet, and comfort. Now that we can correspond more regularly, please make some kind of a diary for yourself and the children. So both of us may know all about the other, I am now beginning to keep my own.

On June 5 at eight o'clock in the morning I left Trois Rivières, had dinner at Rivière du Loup with the pastor, and slept at Maskinonge, where I arrived very tired. On the 6th I went to Berthier, where I had dinner. In the afternoon I crossed the St. Lawrence in a *canot d'écorce* (a boat made here from the bark of a tree according to the local custom), and spent the night in Sorel with the pastor.

On the 7th I left at six in the morning, had dinner at St. Denis with Lieutenant Colonel Specht of our troops, and arrived in Chambly in the evening.

On the 8th the Barner and Breymann Battalions marched for St. Johns, and two others replaced them. Since my things were not able to follow me so rapidly, all looked rather badly, since I had neither food nor drink. But finally everything came in the evening. I exhausted myself in getting the troops across the St. Lawrence, but all went very well.

General Phillips dined with me on the 10th and on the 11th General Burgoyne had breakfast with me. At noon that day I left Chambly

10. The Isle of Bic, which the General spelled "Bie," is named for the town of Bic, which is about ten miles south of Rimouski. It is, of course, the Province of Quebec which is in sight here, since this is very near the mouth of the St. Lawrence.

for St. Johns and stopped at Ste. Thérèse to have dinner with Colonel MacKenzie.[11]

On the 12th, in company with General Carleton and General Burgoyne, I had dinner with General Phillips, and it was there that I was so lucky as to receive word of your arrival. I am now hopeful of receiving a letter from you soon, telling me how all of you were on the voyage. Either today or tomorrow I shall leave for Crown Point. You shall have a report from me whenever I have a minute to spare.

Goodbye, and embrace our three dear children heartily for me. I hope you are not short of money. In Quebec you will be able to borrow as much money in my name as you want, and in Trois Rivières you will find our paymaster Gödecke, who will give you as much money as you may need. Once more goodbye, my dear. May God continue to guide us as heretofore. Write me soon, and be assured that I am forever completely yours.

11. Lt. Col. Alexander MacKenzie of the 31st English Infantry, which was stationed in Canada and came to be known as the "Huntingdonshire Regiment." Colonel MacKenzie had long served in America. Ford, *British Officers,* 6, 118.

XIII

General Riedesel to Baroness von Riedesel

An Interlude Before Saratoga
Summer, 1777

The family reunion at Chambly lasted a brief two days before General Riedesel joined the British march south and Mrs. Riedesel returned to Trois Rivières to await instructions about joining her husband. After two weeks of campaigning, the General took time out to write his wife on his "first day of rest" since leaving Chambly. Four weeks later he wrote from Castleton, promising to send Captain Willoe for her and the girls as soon as he could do so "without risk to your life, your children, or your honor." Neither of his letters has been published previously.

General Riedesel
to Baroness von Riedesel

[Between Crown Point and Ticonderoga]
June 29, 1777

This is the first day of rest, which gives me time to reflect on my good fortune of being able to have you here in America. You are so near that just a line that I might write you would enable me to enjoy your charming presence, as well as that of the children. The children are lovely and, thanks to your care, they are healthy and well-trained, and I owe you my most sincere thanks. I vow that my health was somewhat upset by a fever which I had sometime ago. I vow that my blood has never felt that way since our first meeting. The news of the good luck [of your arrival] was too great for my system to take without great emotions. To sum up, I was a lucky mortal at Chambly, and all this catastrophe is still like a dream when I think of it. You must have made a real sacrifice, and it has been blessed by God. I love and adore you for all you have done. Do not worry or be concerned about your expenses. Even had they been double I would not have cared. Now that we are together we can arrange economies to put things in order. I would be glad if we could put aside 50 livres a month, for otherwise someone might have to suffer when the war is over in case the big men wish to give trouble. In case of my death there would be some money for our poor daughters. If you think you could manage with 90 livres a month, I believe we may be able to follow this plan, but for Heaven's sake do not stint yourself of anything you need.

General Riedesel
to Baroness von Riedesel

In camp at Castleton, July 22, 1777

My more than dear wife,

When I wrote you yesterday, I was sure I was going to be able to send an officer to get you as soon as I had definite news from Captain Willoe, whom I had sent to headquarters expressly for that purpose, about the movement of the army. The letter from Brigadier Hamilton,[1] which I sent to you yesterday, has not discouraged me, since I know your eagerness to join me and the way you content yourself with few comforts. However, when Captain Willoe returned, he brought me the order of General Burgoyne that I would have to move on to Skenesborough tomorrow, that I would have to remain there the 24th, and then go on to Fort Anne the 25th. From Fort Anne I am to proceed to Fort Edward, which the rebels are holding with the remainder of their army, but probably they will withdraw at our

1. Brig. Gen. James Hamilton (?–1803) was appointed a brigadier in 1776 and in July 1777 was head of the 1st English Brigade. After Gen. Phillips' parole in 1779, Hamilton became the commanding officer of the British Convention troops in Virginia. Hadden, *Journal*, 468–71.

approach, for they have neither the cannon nor the troops to hold it against our whole army. When we have reached Fort Edward and are masters of the Hudson River, we will make a real halt to wait for our boats and supplies, which will arrive by Lake George, and there I hope to see you again and to embrace you and our dear children, and immediately upon your arrival I will send Captain Willoe or some other officer to get you. Be patient, dearest wife, and do not allow time to weigh too heavily upon you. Be assured that I will not hesitate a moment to let you come when I can do so without risk to your life, your children, and your honor.

As commander of a corps, I have been extremely busy. Either I am on horseback reconnoitering or I am bound to my desk, drafting orders and settling affairs. That is why my letters are so short.

At last I have received the case you sent me, with part of the papers and the Mourray wine. It came in very handy, as we have been dry, and nothing is more disagreeable than to lack wine when you are tired.

Your ball at the convent amused me greatly, and I am much pleased that everyone is treating you with due respect at Trois Rivières. Accept anything offered you from the stores, for these things are not paid for by General Carleton, but by the King, and the King is richer than we are. Hug the children for me, and thank little Augusta for the nice letter she wrote me. I am always delighted when this dear child thinks of me and shows courtesies towards me. Say the same thing to little Frederika also.

Adieu, my angel. A few days more of patience, and you will see how I am a man of my word.

I embrace you, best of women, dearest angel. I am ever completely yours.

> Your faithful husband,
> **Riedesel**

XIV

Baroness Von Riedesel to Her Mother
Cambridge to Canada
1778–1782

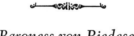

After their capture at Saratoga, the Riedesels joined the Convention troops interned at Cambridge, Massachusetts, and later at Charlottesville, Virginia. Redeeming her promise to write her mother, the Baroness dispatched letters periodically. Nine of these have been preserved, along with a fascinating letter from Augusta to her grandmother. Fortunately, there is at least one letter from each of the Riedesels' major locations—one from Cambridge in 1778, one from Colle in 1779, four from New York in 1780–81, one en route from New York to Canada in 1781, and two from Canada in 1782. None of these have been published previously.

Baroness von Riedesel
to her mother

Cambridge, May 12, 1778

My dearest mother,

I hope you have safely received all my letters. When shall we ever be so happy as to welcome you again? Just now it does not seem as though that would be very soon. The Americans either like us too much or are too afraid of us. What good would it be for us if it were true that there will be a general war in Europe? This would only make things worse for us. I entrust myself to God and wish for nothing more than to see you and my family again. To this hope I cling with all my heart.

We are getting along quite well, living in a nice house with a garden, and are able to get everything we need if we are willing to spend the money. We cannot, to be sure, build up our capital. I beg you once again not to arrange a marriage for Lisette before we return. Captain Edmonstone, who I believe is now a major, is a young Scot who will be very wealthy after the death of his father.[1] He has been my husband's aide for two years and has always been most devoted to him. He is twenty-three years of age, well-built, and a fine gentleman. I am sure that you and Lisette will like him. He will be a member of Parliament after his father's death, and will then bear the title of Baronet or Earl. Give my respects to my gracious aunts and my compliments to all my good friends. My husband sends his respects to you, and so do the children. Today little Frederika is four years old. Soon it will be four [two] years since we left Germany.

I commend myself to your kindness, and as long as I live I am your most obedient daughter,

de Riedesel (née Massow)

Baroness von Riedesel
to her mother

Colle in Virginia, near Charlottesville, July 4, 1779

Captain Edmonstone, my husband's aide has gotten aboard ship. He has been called home by his father. He is carrying this letter with him, and I hope it reaches you safely. If only we could all go too. But this seems more and more impossible, since the Americans reject everything proposed to them to this end. We must be patient. If only the summer were soon over. The heat is terrific, and everyone is much bothered by it. My husband has not been at all well. The heat causes blood to go to his head, and now his arms are swelling, a trouble which, I hope, the doctors will be able to check. In ten days we are going to a spa 130 miles away, where it is said to be cool.[2] It has been more than 103 degrees, and they say that it may be still hotter in August. The children are well. Little Frederika often asks about her Grandmama. She is always eager to set off to see you. I am beginning

1. For Capt. Edmonstone, see above, pp. 74, 88, and below, 204.
2. See above, p. 84, for Frederick Springs, or Berkeley Springs.

to get homesick, and I wish I would receive some letters. It has been two years since I knew where you were and what you were doing. This distresses me. I wonder what my sisters are doing. I cannot believe that they have not written, but no [letters] have arrived.

Baroness von Riedesel
to her mother

New York, March 24, 1780

My dearest mother,

How happy I am to tell you about my successful confinement! I was not sick for a single day, but you will scold me: It is another daughter. However, it is the most darling child you can imagine, with dark blue eyes and long brown hair. She is as strong as my dear Herman [3] was and seems to be very healthy. At first Riedesel was a bit sad, but gradually he is becoming very fond of her. For my part, I am fully satisfied if God but protects my four daughters. The children have all been well, except for Caroline, who had a fever for a week, but she is better now. Riedesel is also better, and I hope that a prolonged stay here will cure him completely. It seems that we shall not be leaving soon. At least we shall remain as long as the Americans allow us to do so. They have again refused to exchange our troops, for which we had been hoping a week ago. Who knows what good may come of it? We must leave all to God's will. I will send this letter by one of our aides and hope that you may receive it. He will not stay very long, so please do not fail to give him a letter. Your last letter is thirteen months old, and I am very eager to have news. Many ships have arrived, but no letters from Europe.

Baroness von Riedesel
to her mother

New York, September 9, 1780

My dearest mother,

It was with the greatest joy that I received a letter today, which Captain Cleve brought from you. He landed safely a week ago. I

3. One of the names of her first son, Christian. See above, p. xxv.

wish someone would arrive from the fatherland every week, so that we might learn how everyone is and what they are doing. Two weeks ago I was very worried, because my husband had a dreadful fever, and even the doctor thought it was dangerous. Augusta also had a bad fever for two weeks, and both recovered only slowly and are very weak. God knows what I endured.

So many people are dying of this fever, that I am dreadfully alarmed. Both are taking quinine and have to be very careful of themselves. The worst of it was that during their sickness the heat was terrific. In the city fifty to sixty people are dying every day. One day alone seventy-two were buried. We expect to remain here until November, for it is quite pleasant in the countryside. My eye is once more inflamed, and I shall have to take special care of it.

Our good Captain Edmonstone has passed away. He caught a cold on his voyage and died of consumption. He remained our friend to the last. I regret his passing all the more, since I am certain he would have made such a fine brother-in-law. I had to conceal it from little Augusta, who was so attached to him. Day before yesterday she heard about it and almost fainted. She is forever looking at little portraits he painted and weeping. She is a sensitive child, and I am very much touched by this. We have all bewailed his loss, and we shall never forget him. His father is quite beside himself and wrote Riedesel a letter.

Once again something is going on concerning our exchange. In case this should take place within the next three weeks, I suppose we would go to Canada this year. I hope such will not be the case, since it would be a long and dangerous journey, and we would be cut off from all our friends for six months, as ice will cover the St. Lawrence from the beginning of December to the end of May. People are talking again of peace, but I fear there will be none yet.

America is the most charming child.[4] She is pretty and really clever. We would not exchange her for twenty boys. The Generals Knyphausen and Phillips and our old friend Wurmb were godfathers. She has also been vaccinated, and was left with only two little scars. You are right. The Almighty, who never withholds due reward, will take care both of those left behind and of my husband.

4. Of the child's given names, the Baroness chose "Wilhelmina," rather than the somewhat unconventional "America," when writing to her mother.

Baroness von Riedesel
to her mother

New York, October 29, 1780

Most gracious mother dear,

Again it has been a long time since I have been so fortunate as to have a letter from you, although many ships have arrived. I have received many letters from Brunswick. Some say you were in Berlin, while others report you were in R_____ or in Breslau. I hope the latter.

At last my husband and his aides have been exchanged. If only we could have peace! We shall be making a voyage again early in the year to Canada, and this takes just as long as to go to Germany. My husband's health is not the best, which distresses me. He cannot drink anything sweet, and confines himself to dry wine.

The children are growing like shoats. They are obedient, good children, and give me no trouble. They know I think they are good. The baby is a strong, healthy child, very pretty and smart. God preserve them all for me, that I may bring them all home again from America. When this may happen there is not yet an indication, but the time will come, and then for the first time we shall understand what it means to be united. We still live in the country, and probably shall not go into the city before next month. The weather is too nice for this, and here we can live more independently.

Augusta Riedesel
to her grandmother [von Massow]

New York, December 15, 1780

Gracious Grandmama,

The satisfaction of being able to communicate with you by letter is to me most delightful. I should like nothing so much as for you to find yourself quite well again. God preserve you, so that my ardent wish to see you healthy and well again may be fulfilled. I left our fatherland too young a child fully to realize the love of my grandparents. Now I know better how to treasure this blessing when I think of the tenderness which they have for us, and I shall feel all this to an even greater degree when I see you, and when I shall be able to assure you with my own lips in what high esteem I hold you and with what tender child's love towards you my heart is filled. Already I find extraordinary joy in assuring you that I am, my gracious Grandmama, with childlike respect, your most obedient

Augusta

━━━━◄◌◄╳◌►━━━━

Baroness von Riedesel
to her mother

New York, January 23, 1781

Dearest mother,

As the fleet is leaving here after all the unrest there has been, I seize the opportunity for sending you a letter. If I could only receive more news! My husband is no better yet, but I do hope that he will yet recover. He has now been ill nearly two years. He is certainly a sensitive person, and gladly would help anyone, but he cannot do much. These five years in America have made him twenty years older. I wish he were home again. If he could only find real rest, he would recover.

I am sure that it will be a long time before we have peace. Moreover, it seems as though affairs are becoming ever more complicated. It is a sad war, and it is costing England more than it is worth.

This year we are having a mild winter. Today is our first real winter day. We can still take our daily walk. I wonder how my good friends in Berlin are: Minister Blumenthal, the Schwerins,[5] the Geuders, and the Wedels. Probably they have completely forgotten us, forsaken in America. Sometime ago I heard the King [Frederick II] was dead. Although this was later denied, this made me think. In event of his death, the Prince [Frederick William II] will be entitled to fill the first vacancy in every foundation in Prussia. Since I have four daughters, and will have less to spend the longer we stay here, it might be well to get one of those prebends. The Prince has always been gracious toward me. Perhaps I can do something for these poor girls. Please think about this.

I commend myself to you. I hope you love me as I love you.

5. Of the members of this prominent Prussian military family, she probably particularly had in mind Count Wilhelm Friedrich Karl von Schwerin, who became a lt. general, and who had served in the Seven Years' War. *Allgemeine deutsche Biographie,* XXXIII, 427–28.

Baroness von Riedesel
to her mother

July 27, 1781

I write you this letter on the ship en route to Canada. We are on a small but very comfortable ship. No one is seasick. Only America is rather miserable, as she is cutting teeth. She is very uncomfortable and has screamed more in these last three weeks than ever before in her life. I do not like having to leave New York, as I have many good friends there, though we have lost our dear and worthy friend, General Phillips, the best of them all. He died on a military expedition [after first] having taken cold. May God protect us and help us bring this awkward journey to a happy end.

***

Baroness von Riedesel
to her mother

Sorel, July 21, 1782

I am writing for the first time in a week, because in a couple of days the ship sails, and I seize with joy this opportunity. I intend to write you by every ship that leaves, which, however, we can only do for another three months, after which no answers can be expected before next year. That is why I hate this country so much. For eight months of the year a person is imprisoned, although this is the most pleasant time of the year for those who like the cold. This must be a good land in time of peace. All sorts of foods are to be had, and for the most part there are lots of good fish and many doves. Some people shoot them with a kind of gun that brings down fifty or sixty at a single shot. Although there are at times great flocks of wild ducks and pheasants, at other times in the winter nothing is to be seen. There is an abundance of venison, and everyone prepares his meat in November. First it is put into the ground or in the snow, and when one is ready to eat it, it is placed in warm water if it is to be eaten the next day. It tastes as good as fresh meat. The coldness is so uninterrupted, that the meat keeps until April or May.

Clothing and all beverages are very expensive, because procurement of them is so uncertain. The Governor is our friend, and wants no more than to make us forget the despair we have felt up to now.

Moreover, we have no enemies and many friends among the English and Germans. However, I long very much to return to Europe, and to be away is dreadful.

I hope I receive some letters soon.

Baroness von Riedesel
to her mother

Sorel, October 14, 1782

Dearest mother,

At last I am so lucky as to receive two letters from you, although they are very old, dating from June and July of last year. I was amazed when you told me you had remarried. I confess, it touched me at a sensitive point, to have another father, for where could you find another husband as worthy as our dear father? I thought how very much difference you must notice if the new one did not turn out so well. How pleased I was, and how I laughed, when I saw the name! I hope this new papa will permit me to protest and to check this marriage business, because it is ever necessary for me to flatter myself that I may spend my days with you.

There was indeed hope for peace, but all hope has again vanished.

Although my husband still is not completely well, he is nevertheless out of danger. I have had much anxiety over him. There is nothing to be gained by saying it, but I assure you that everyone who knows Riedesel likes him more and more. He has suffered so much, that he is able to understand the suffering of others. He is God-fearing, most just, and not irritable. And although we have been married twenty years, we love each other more than ever, and he is still so full of attention towards me that everyone is amazed.

You have told me that you write every month. In two years I have received no more than three letters. I do not know what happens to the mail. The Germans all complain about this situation. I have just received the first letter from Lieutenant —— [?]. Our captured officers are all in Quebec, where my husband has been for several days.

XV

General Riedesel to Baroness von Riedesel

Canadian Postscript

1782–1783

Mrs. Riedesel and her daughters lived with the General at his new post in Canada, residing first in a private home in Sorel before moving into their new home on Christmas Day, 1781. During the General's trips from headquarters in 1782, she remained at home, being pregnant once again. From Isle aux Noix he wrote that "there is no greater pleasure for me, when away, than to write to you," and he urged his wife to "take care of your health as much as is possible."

Little Canada was born on November 1, 1782, but lived only five months, and General Haldimand invited the Riedesels to visit him in Quebec in order to change the scene of sorrow. While there they received word that they would soon sail for Germany, and the General returned to Sorel to make arrangements for the withdrawal of the troops. Mrs. Riedesel and the children remained in Quebec where the Baroness attended a gala celebration of the King's birthday. In a letter from Sorel, the General reported on the windup of his command in Canada and speculated on his military future in Brunswick. Neither of his letters has been published previously.

General Riedesel
to Baroness von Riedesel

Isle aux Noix, September 14, 1782

My more than dear wife,

I promised you in my short letter of yesterday that I would write to you today, and I am fulfilling my promise with pleasure. There is no greater pleasure for me, when away, than to write to you, as this brings me into contact with the dearest thing to me on earth. You wrote me you were calmer. This will help you recover from all your anxieties, and will be good for you and the child you are bearing. My dear, remember that your husband is a soldier, and that Providence has placed him in such situation as the commanding general has had to employ him. Much depends on my zeal and my ardor, and as we are approaching peace, my destiny, as certainly that of my family, my reputation, my future, and my tranquillity depend on the fashion in which I will be able to return to Europe. I will only feel satisfied with myself if people in England, my master [the Duke of Brunswick], and even my family receive me with satisfaction, gratitude, and attention. Could one reasonably say that he has neglected his duty, his wife, his family, then one would have contempt for himself. . . . Every man playing a role in human society should adore and love the great God who gave us our existence, and our first duty is to be of public service and to contribute to human society. The second duty is to think of one's own welfare, to love one's wife, and to take care in the education of one's children. The third is to make their existence happy, and the fourth is to be a good neighbor. These four duties we must observe, for herein lies true religion. It is a sin to think too much of ourselves and to neglect all else. This will be punished sooner or later.

Take care of your health as much as is possible, and address your most ardent and sincere prayers to our Lord for the protection of your husband and children, the duty of a true mother. And now I beg you to send me a boatload of food. It is beef which we need the most. Give directions to the petty officer who is in charge of the boat. Some melons would be very acceptable, and send me two or three sheep and some potatoes. I have a lot to do. I dine at three and go through the camp in the afternoon. In the evening I play a game of cards, and at ten o'clock I go to bed.

Canadian Postscript, 1782-1783

General Riedesel
to Baroness von Riedesel

Sorel, June 9, 1783

My most beloved wife,

I trust that Captain Pauttel has given you my last letter and that you rested from the fatigues of the King's birthday celebration. Your health is better, and I am pleased to tell you that I am doing rather well though the skimmed milk *(petit lait)* I am taking weakens me somewhat. But I have high hopes that when the blood will be refreshed and consequently circulation will be regular, my head will also be more relieved. On orders of Bause [1] I also let my head work as little as possible, all the more so as I get some exercise in the morning usually by marching in company of my dragoons and my infantry regiment. At eight o'clock I rest for two hours; we dine as usual.

The big commission for auditing all the accounts of the regiments, of which Brigadier Spät is president,[2] was formed last Saturday, and is expected to have finished in two weeks. I spend my time exercising the troops. When I shall have received the report of the commission and approved it, I shall return to Quebec, although I cannot make a definite promise. I flatter myself that I can leave this Sunday or in two weeks, and that consequently I will be able to be with you in two weeks. Be convinced that my desire to embrace you will be as great as perhaps yours. As our future well being depends on my career, you will be aware that my conscience demands to bring it to an end in correct fashion. When I think of my father this gives me great elation, the piety of this worthy man, his ardent prayers to the Lord have laid the foundation for our strikingly good luck and the fact that so far we have been protected so miraculously.[3] We must keep this up by

1. Chaplain Johann Carl Bause of the Specht Regiment was also a surgeon. Stone, trans., *General Riedesel*, II, 292.

2. The transcript reads Spät, but this may have been Johann Friedrich Specht, whom the General had left in command at Charlottesville. He returned to Canada after his exchange in Oct. 1780 and led the second division of Brunswick troops home in Oct. 1783. Baxter, ed., *Digby's Journal*, 197–99; Hadden, *Journal*, 45; Stone, trans., *General Riedesel*, II, 184. See above, chap. 6, n. 30.

3. General Riedesel had just recently received the news of his father's death. See above, p. 127.

our own devotion, our faith and our actions, without this we would soon experience adversity. It is a great satisfaction to see that my circumstances have been improved so much through the good service of my brother. . . . We can live honorably without my serving [in the army], but by continuing to serve we could live well indeed (*largement*). You may be assured that we will be perfectly at ease in the future concerning my military standing. The Duke has sent me word that he is so well satisfied with me that he is going to promote me and will give me such an advantageous salary that I may have whatever regiment I choose and live where it pleases me. You know my predilection for Wolfenbüttel; this would be my choice. However, if you prefer Brunswick, I would do as you wish in order to be with you and my children and to make them as happy as possible.[4] The two gardens are in good order; although 120 [plants] have failed, everything else is thriving. By the time we come back there will be an abundance of strawberries and vegetables.

Your faithful husband

4. The Riedesels settled in Brunswick.

Index

Index

Church, John Barker (Mr. Carter), 69*n*, 70, 71
Civil war, Baroness comments on, 70–71
Cleve, Capt. Friedrich Christian, 158, 172, 185, 203
Clinton, Gen. Henry, death of, xv, 110; and supplies for Convention troops, xxxiii; and British surrender at Saratoga, 62*n*; friendship with General Phillips, 92; visits Riedesels, 96; country home of, 97, 104–5; friendship with Baroness, 104, 105; gives Gen. Riedesel active duty, 107; transfers Gen. Riedesel to Canada, 110–11
Colle, Va., xxxiii, 80–84, 86, 202–3
Congregation (Sun) Inn, Bethlehem, Pa., 93
Continental Congress, xxxi–iv, xxxvi, 62*n*, 72*n*
Convention, xxxi, 62–63, 72*n*
Convention army, in Massachusetts, xxxi–iii, 68, 72; in Charlottesville, Va., xxxiv–vi, 80, 81, 82, 87; crosses Hudson River, 78; not exchanged, 107; Riedesels join, 201
Cornwallis, Gen. Charles, xxxvii, 92, 95, 96, 99, 100–101
Crown Point, N. Y., xxx, 181, 197
Cumberland Head, xxx
Curssingen, Mrs., 185
Cuxhaven, Ger., 161

D

Dachenhausen, Herr, 157
Deal, Eng., xxxviii, 141
Deutschland, Baroness' consciousness of, xxiii
Diamond Point, xlvi–vii; vignette of, xliii
Doughoregan, Carroll plantation in Md., 88–89
Douglas, Commodore Sir Charles, 174
Douglas, Adm. Sir James, 17, 19, 162, 163
Dover, Eng., 6, 7, 160, 161, 162

Dress, English, xxviii, xxxviii, 10–11, 12–13, 18, 139; Canadian, 33–34, 38; in New York, 107
Dusky Bay, 113

E

Ebsdorf, Ger., 152
Edmonstone, Captain, 88, 165, 172, 202, 204; travels with Baroness to Va., 74, 79–80
Eelking, Max von, xv
Ehrenkrock, Lt. Col. Johann Gustavus, 194
Elbe River, 141–42
Elizabeth, N. J., xxxvi, 92, 95
Elliot, Andrew, 99*n*
England. *See* Great Britain
Exeter, Eng., 168

F

Faucit, Col. William, xxvi, 8*n*, 10*n*
Favart, Charles, composer of *Ninette à la Cour,* 17
Fenton, Captain, 13, 70
Ferdinand, Duke of Brunswick, xv, xxiv–v, 47–48, 149, 184; Gen. Riedesel writes to, 103*n*, 105*n*, 108*n*, 127*n*
Feronce von Notenkruez, Jean Baptiste, 8, 178
Fitzgerald, Adj. George Tobias, 59
Flags, Brunswick, 72–73, 114*n*
Fonblanque, Edward de, xviii
Fort Anne, 199
Fort Carillon. *See* Fort Ticonderoga
Fort Edward, xxx, 44, 199–200
Fort George, 44
Fort John [?], 43
Fort St. Johns, 178, 193, 195
Fort Ticonderoga, xxx, 43–44, 181
Fox, Charles James, xxxviii, 140
Foy, Capt. Edward, 11*n*, 156–63 *passim,* 168, 172, 174, 187
Foy, Mrs. Hannah Van Horne, with Baroness in Eng., xxviii, 11, 13, 15–17, 183, 187–88; sails with Baroness, 25, 30, 33; and Gen. John

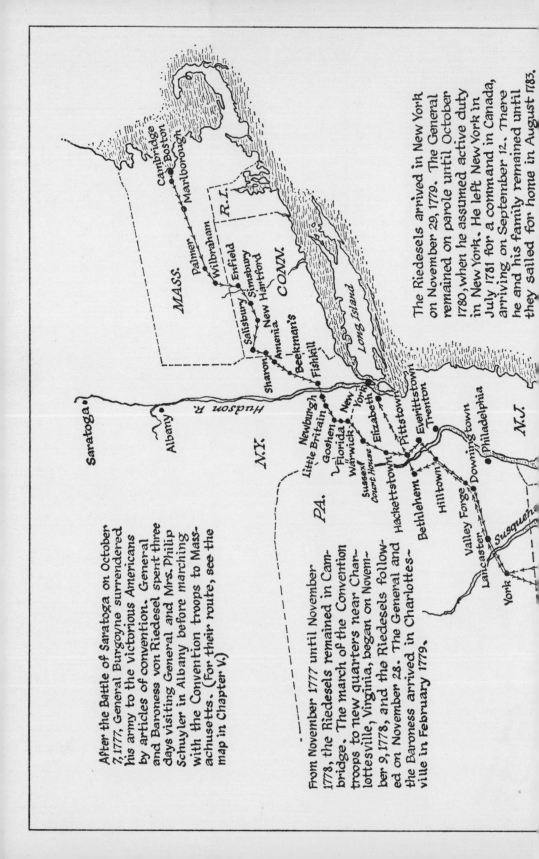

After the Battle of Saratoga on October 7, 1777, General Burgoyne surrendered his army to the victorious Americans by articles of convention. General and Baroness von Riedesel spent three days visiting General and Mrs. Philip Schuyler in Albany before marching with the Convention troops to Massachusetts. (For their route, see the map in Chapter V.)

From November 1777 until November 1778, the Riedesels remained in Cambridge. The march of the Convention troops to new quarters near Charlottesville, Virginia, began on November 9, 1778, and the Riedesels followed on November 28. The General and the Baroness arrived in Charlottesville in February 1779.

The Riedesels arrived in New York on November 29, 1779. The General remained on parole until October 1780, when he assumed active duty in New York. He left New York in July 1781 for a command in Canada, arriving on September 12. There he and his family remained until they sailed for home in August 1783.

Saratoga •

Albany •

Hudson R.

MASS.

Boston
Cambridge
Marlborough

Palmer
Wilbraham
Enfield
Simsbury
New Hartford
CONN.

Salisbury
Amenia
Sharon
Beekman's
Fishkill

R.I.

Long Island

N.Y.

Little Britain
Newburgh
Goshen
Florida
New Warwick
York
Sussex Court House
Elizabeth
Pittstown
Everittstown
Trenton

PA.

Hackettstown
Bethlehem
Hilltown

Valley Forge
Downingtown
Philadelphia

Lancaster
Susqueh —

York

N.J.